Q&A
Questions & Answers

Financial
Accounting-
Company Accounts

Questions & Answers

Financial Accounting-
Company Accounts

Dr. J. A. Roche
G. Pitchford &
M. J. Irvin

Financial Training

First published in Great Britain by Financial Training Publications Limited,
Avenue House, 131 Holland Park Avenue, London W11 4UT

© Financial Training Publications Limited, 1984

ISBN: 0 906322 37 5

Typeset by Formset Ltd, Crowborough and printed by The Pitman Press, Bath

Contents

Introduction   vii

Acknowledgements   ix

Abbreviations   xi

1   SSAP 8   1

2   SSAP 15   *OUT* *New SSAP is a* SEE NOTE   23

3   SSAP 6   41

4   SSAP 9   57

5   SSAP 12 and SSAP 19   81

6   SSAP 13   97

7   SSAP 3   105

8   SSAPs 2, 4, 17 and 18   119

9   Issue and redemption of securities   *OUT*   129

10 Preparation of financial statements for publication   149

11 Transfer of a business to a limited company, amalgamations
    and absorptions   *OUT*   189

12 Reorganisations, reconstructions and capital reductions   *OUT*   215

13 Income, capital and value measurement   247

14 SSAP 16   255

15 Stock Exchange requirements and the City Code   297

16 Users and objectives of accounts   307

17 Accounting Standards Committee and other regulatory influences   315

18 Transfer pricing   *OUT*   327

    Index   335

v

FINANCIAL ACCOUNTING – ADVANCED TECHNIQUES

Contents

1 Goodwill, acquisition accounting and merger accounting

2 SSAP 1: associated companies

3 SSAP 14: consolidated balance sheets

4 SSAP 14: consolidated profit and loss accounts

5 SSAP 14: combined group balance sheet and operating statements, including associated companies

6 Advanced consolidation

7 SSAP 10: funds flow statements

8 Interpretation of accounts

9 Branch accounts (excluding foreign branches)

10 SSAP 20: Translation of foreign currencies

11 Leasing and hire purchase

12 Joint ventures and partnerships

13 Incomplete records, including SSAP 5

14 Cost behaviour

15 Miscellaneous topics

16 Estate and executor accounts

17 Value added statements

18 Valuation of businesses

Introduction

This book contains 100 questions and answers on Financial Accounting topics which give excellent coverage of the legal and professional requirements in the preparation of accounts.

Most professional students using this book will find it best used in conjunction with the complementary title in this series, *Financial Accounting – Advanced Techniques* which deals with the advanced accounting techniques required in the preparation of accounts. The contents of this companion volume have been listed on page vi.

These two books are an invaluable aid for all students studying Financial Accounting at an advanced level either for professional examinations or for degree courses. They are especially suitable for students sitting the following examinations:

Association of Certified Accountants:

Level 2, Paper 2.8, The Regulatory Framework of Accounting;
Level 2, Paper 2.9, Advanced Accounting Practice.

Students are recommended to take these two papers, for which these two books provide excellent coverage, at the same sitting.

Level 3, Paper 3.1, Advanced Financial Accounting.

Candidates will find much in these books that will provide ideal practice and revision but will be catered for more precisely by a further title to be published in 1984 entitled – appropriately – *Advanced Financial Accounting*.

Institute of Cost and Management Accountants:

Paper 7, Financial Acounting 2;
Paper 13, Financial Accounting 3.

Students preparing for these two papers are again recommended to purchase both books referred to above. A student studying for Financial Accounting 2 will find that certain of the chapters in this book and the companion volume on advanced techniques are inappropriate for the level 2 examination. In particular, the last 4 chapters of this book and the chapters on group accounts and foreign currency in the advanced techniques title are examined only at Financial

Accounting 3 level. However, a student studying for Financial Accounting 2 may purchase both books confident that he will be able to take them through to his Financial Accounting 3 studies with equal benefit.

Institute of Chartered Accountants in England and Wales:

Students preparing for Accounting Techinques and Financial Accounting in the PEI examination will find that this book together with its companion volume provide an invaluable selection of questions particularly suited to these examinations.

Acknowledgements

The authors and publishers wish to thank the following professional bodies for their kind permission to include selected past examination questions in this publication:

The Association of Certified Accountants
The Institute of Chartered Accountants in England and Wales
The Institute of Cost and Management Accountants

ABOUT THE AUTHORS

Tony Roche holds the degrees of Bachelor of Science, Master of Science in Chemical Engineering and a Doctorate in Business and Administration from the University of Strathclyde. He became a Chartered Engineer in 1971. During his career, he moved from Chemical Engineering into internal audit and began to specialise in accountancy. He has written articles for accounting journals and is the author of: *Accountancy Control Systems*, Longman; and *The Analysis of the Interaction of Business Control Systems with Human Behaviour*, University Microfilms International, London.

He is currently Examiner for an accountancy body and Senior Lecturer in Accounting at the Huddersfield Polytechnic specialising in Financial Accounting and Financial Management.

Geoffrey Pitchford qualified as an Associate Member of the Institute of Chartered Accountants in England and Wales in 1964 and obtained a Fellowship in 1974. In 1969 he was admitted as an Associate Member of the Institute of Taxation and in 1980 became a Fellow of the Association of Certified Accountants.

He has twelve years experience in professional accountancy firms. Four of these years were spent as Training Manager for Price Waterhouse & Co. Chartered Accountants. Whilst with Price Waterhouse he was located for three years in Johannesburg, South Africa, with special responsibility for the inplementation of a professional development programme for all levels of staff in the Southern African firm.

He has twelve years experience as a polytechnic lecturer and is currently Senior Lecturer in Accountancy at the Huddersfield Polytechnic. He has lectured on many degree, professional and non-professional courses, specialising in particular in Financial Accounting and Auditing. He is a former examiner in Auditing and Investigations and Assessor in Advanced Accounting Practice for the Association of Certified Accountants.

Michael Irvin qualified as a Chartered Accountant in 1970 and became a Certified Accountant in 1981. He is a Fellow of both.

After seven years in the accountancy profession he worked in industry for eight years and then undertook an MBA course at the University of Bradford Management Centre before entering further education in 1979.

He is currently a Senior Lecturer at Huddersfield Polytechnic, specialising in Advanced Financial Accounting and Auditing, and a part-time tutor for the Open University. He has been connected with the examination system of a major accountancy body since 1980.

Abbreviations

ACT   advance corporation tax

ASC   Accounting Standards Committee

b/d   brought down

b/f   brought forward

BEPS   basic earnings per share

CCA   current cost accounting

CCAB   Consultative Committee of Accountancy Bodies

c/d   carried down

c/f   carried forward

COSA   cost of sales adjustment

EPS   earnings per share

FDEPS   fully diluted earnings per share

FII   franked investment income

HCA   historical cost accounting

ICAEW   Institute of Chartered Accountants in England and Wales

MCT   mainstream corporation tax

MWCA   monetary working capital adjustment

NBV   net book value

NRV   net realisable value

P & L   profit and loss

PAYE   Pay As You Earn

plc   plublic limited company

SORP   Statement of Recommended Practice

SSAP   Statement of Standard Accounting Practice

UFII   unfranked investment income

VAT	value added tax
W	working
WIP	work in progress

1   SSAP 8

INTRODUCTION

This chapter contains questions relating to the treatment of taxation under the imputation system in the accounts of companies.

In order to appreciate fully the implications of the solutions to the questions in this chapter, the reader will necessarily have to study SSAP 8. However, the rules for payment, recovery and set-off of ACT are briefly summarised here so that the statement may be understood more readily.

A company's due date for paying corporation tax depends upon the date when the business was first incorporated. If the company was incorporated before 4 April 1965, then the Inland Revenue start with the company's year end, proceed to the following April and then proceed to the following 1 January which is then the due date for payment.

For example, if the company's year end is 31 May 1982 and the company was incorporated prior to 1965, then its due date for payment of corporation tax on the profits for the year ended 31 May 1982, will be 1 January 1984.

For a company which was incorporated after 1965, the due date for payment of corporation tax is nine months after the period of account, or 30 days after the issue of the assessment, whichever is the later.

Whenever a company pays a dividend, the dividend is paid without deduction of tax. In other words, whatever a company declares as a dividend, is what it pays out. However, the dividend carries a tax credit of 30% of the grossed-up amount of the actual dividend payment. Thus the shareholder receiving the dividend is deemed to have paid income tax at the basic rate of 30% on the dividend he receives. As a result of a dividend payment, the company is required to make a payment of advance corporation tax (ACT) equal to the tax credit previously mentioned. The due date for payment of ACT is 14 days after the end of the quarter in which the dividend was paid. Quarterly periods end on 31 March, 30 June, 30 September and 31 December. The ACT payments can be set off against the corporation tax on the profits of the year in which the dividend was paid. The resulting reduced corporation tax bill is known as mainstream corporation tax (MCT).

If a company receives dividends, then the tax credit on the dividends received can be set off against any ACT that the company is liable to pay as a result of paying dividends out.

If a company receives dividends, the dividends are known as franked investment income (FII), 'franked' referring to the fact that the income has been derived from earnings which have already been subject to corporation tax. FII is not subject to corporation tax by the recipient company. Contrast this type of income to a company receiving debenture interest. The debenture interest is classified as Schedule F income and is subject to basic-rate income tax which is deducted at source by the paying company.

Because debenture interest is an expense in the paying company's profit and loss account, this interest received by the payee company has not been subject to corporation tax. The receiving company therefore grosses up the unfranked investment income (UFII), i.e., income which has not yet suffered corporation tax, and this grossed-up unfranked investment income will be subject to corporation tax in the receiving company's accounts. The income tax deducted at source from debenture interest is available for offset against any income tax deducted by the company from its own charges.

If the income tax on unfranked investment income exceeds the income tax on unfranked payments, then the excess can be set off against the company's liability to mainstream corporation tax.

There are six questions in this chapter which cover most aspects you are likely to be confronted with in examinations. You are, however, advised to study SSAP 8 after reading this introduction.

QUESTIONS

1   Preston Ltd made trading profits of £255,000 in year 1 and paid a dividend of £63,000 whilst in year 2, a trading profit of £300,000 was made and a dividend of £252,000 was paid.

In both years, interest was paid on £120,000 of 6% debentures.

The following amounts were received from investments in other companies:

	Year 1 £	Year 2 £
Franked investment income (net)	4,200	6,300
Unfranked income (net)	1,680	2,100

Assume corporation tax to be at a rate of 50% and income tax to be at a basic rate of 30%.

From the above information, you are required to write up the necessary accounts making it clear what is:

(a)   Mainstream corporation tax for years 1 and 2.
(b)   Advance corporation tax for years 1 and 2.
(c)   Income tax liability for years 1 and 2.

15 marks

2   The following summarised trial balance has been extracted from the books of Disken Ltd for the year ended 30 September 1983:

	£	£
10% debentures		320,000
Debenture interest paid (gross)	32,000	
Deferred taxation		272,000
Franked investment income received net		56,000
Reserves at 30 September 1982		440,000
Sales		2,400,000
Ordinary share capital		800,000
Sundry assets	2,368,000	
Sundry costs	2,048,000	
Sundry creditors		160,000
	4,448,000	4,448,000

Adjustments have to be made for the following items:

(a)   Corporation tax has been calculated on income which includes franked investment income for the year ended 30 September 1983.

(b)   A cash payment of £84,000 is to be made to shareholders on 1 February 1984 in respect of a proposed dividend.

3

Disken Ltd commenced trading in 1974.

Assume a basic rate of income tax of 30% and corporation tax at 50%.

You are required to prepare an operating statement for the reference period ended 30 September 1983 and a balance sheet as at that date. Show all your workings.

20 marks

3 The accounts of Lynch Ltd as at 30 November 1982 included the following balances:

	£	£
Interim dividend	19,200	
Advance corporation tax	8,229	
Corporation tax payable 1 January 1983		64,000
Deferred taxation		105,440

The following information is available:

(a) Corporation tax payable on the adjusted profits for the year is estimated at £34,000 and the liability for the previous year has recently been agreed at £63,504.

(b) The balance of the deferred taxation account comprises transfers in respect of relief for increases in stock values of £117,804 less recoverable ACT on the previous year's dividend amounting to £12,364 (no interim dividend being paid in the previous year).

A further £101,200 is to be transferred to the deferred taxation account in respect of originating timing differences resulting from accelerated capital allowances.

(c) A proposed final dividend of £14,400 is to be provided for.

(d) The ACT rate is 30% and the corporation tax rate is 50%.

You are required to prepare the extracts from the published operating statement and balance sheet in respect of all matters of taxation. Workings must be shown.

20 marks

4 Bradley Ltd has been trading for 10 years. The trial balance at 31 October 1983 was as follows:

	£	£
Share capital (ordinary shares of 20p)		100,000
Revenue reserves		40,000
Deferred taxation		10,000
Trading profit for year		30,000
carried forward		180,000

	£	£
brought forward		180,000
5% debentures 1987		50,000
Debenture interest (net)	1,750	
Fixed assets (net)	125,000	
Investments: quoted shares	20,000	
Investments: 10% quoted debentures	50,000	
Dividends received (net)		10,500
Interest received (net)		3,500
Interim dividend paid	14,000	
Corporation tax: year to 31 October 1982 b/f		
(agreed with the Inspector at £15,500)		15,000
ACT	1,500	
Debtors	30,000	
Stock	20,000	
Balance at bank	34,616	
Creditors		37,866
	296,866	296,866

Corporation tax on the year's profit has been estimated at £12,250 (at 52%), and the transfer to deferred taxation at £4,000. The directors have declared a final dividend of 7%. No dividends were paid in the previous year.

You are required to prepare:

(a) Corporation tax account.   *7 marks*
(b) Deferred taxation account.   *3 marks*
(c) Income tax account.   *2 marks*
(d) The taxation extracts from the profit and loss account and balance sheet at 31 October 1983.   *9 marks*

Assume that the relevant rates of ACT and income tax for the above transactions were 30/70 and 30% respectively.

Total 21 marks

5   As the accountant of Taxtiles plc you are responsible for the preparation of its accounts for publication. You have been presented with an agreed trial balance for the year ended 30 September 1982 including the following accounts, which, whilst balanced, are incomplete because of the omission of the entries reflecting taxation.

DIVIDENDS RECEIVED

Dr		£			Cr £
1982 30 Sep Balance c/f		476	1982 4 Mar Bank		476
			1982 30 Sep Balance b/f		476

ROYALTIES RECEIVABLE

Dr			£					Cr £
1982 30 Sep	Balance c/f		871	1981	30 Nov	Bank		403
				1982	31 Aug	Bank		468
			871					871
				1982	30 Sep	Balance b/f		871

DEBENTURE INTEREST PAYABLE

Dr							Cr
1982 31 Jan	Bank	2,100	1981	1 Oct	Balance b/f		1,000
1982 31 Jul	Bank	2,100	1982	30 Sep	Balance c/f		3,200
		4,200					4,200
1982 30 Sep	Balance b/f	3,200					

TAXATION ACCOUNT

Dr							Cr
1981 1 Oct	Balance b/f	3,058	1981	1 Oct	Balance b/f		35,547
1981 31 Dec	Bank	3,058					
1982 1 Jan	Bank	15,489					
1982 31 Mar	Bank	833					
1982 30 Sep	Bank	798					
1982 30 Sep	Balance c/f	12,311					
		35,547					35,547
			1982	30 Sep	Balance b/f		12,311

The following information is relevant:

1 Dividends received. These arise from a 5% equity shareholding in a UK registered company quoted on the Stock Exchange. The associated tax credit amounts to £204.

2 Royalties receivable. These were received under deduction of tax.

3 Debenture interest payable. The payments made are the half-yearly instalments in respect of £80,000 7½% mortgage debentures, made on the due dates under deduction of tax.

4 Taxation account. Only payments to the Inland Revenue have been dealt with. The opening debit balance represents advance corporation tax recoverable. The opening credit balance comprises the agreed corporation tax liability of £15,489, based on the accounting year ended 30 September 1980; £17,000, the estimated liability for corporation tax based on the accounting year ended 30 September 1981, and advance corporation tax liability of £3,058.

5 The basic rate of income tax is to be taken as 30%.

6 You need to deal with a proposal to provide for a dividend of £6,500 for 1982. The 1981 dividend was paid on 20 December 1981, and associated ACT of £3,058 on 31 December 1981.

7 The corporation tax liability based on the accounting year ended 30 September 1982 is estimated to be £18,000, while the corporation tax liability based on the year ended 30 September 1981 had been agreed at £15,844.

You are required, using the information available:

(a) To continue and to complete the accounts by making the necessary entries.
20 marks

(b) To show, by way of extracts from the accounts, how the resultant figures would be revealed in the published profit and loss account and balance sheet conforming with contemporary legal and accounting standards. *15 marks*
Total 35 marks

6 K.P. Jones Ltd has an issued share capital of £500,000 in fully paid £1 ordinary shares. At 31 December 1983 the following balances were included in the company's balance sheet:

	£
Agreed corporation tax liability on 1982 profits	33,000
Estimated corporation tax liability on 1983 profits	10,000
Deferred taxation account	40,000
Profit and loss account (credit)	60,000

No dividends have been paid or proposed in respect of 1983.

The following information relates to the year ended 31 December 1984:

1 Corporation tax liability for 1982 was settled in January 1984.
2 An interim dividend of 5p per share was paid in August.
3 Advance corporation tax on the interim dividend was paid in October.
4 Corporation tax liability for 1983 was agreed at £6,000 in December.
5 Net profit for 1984 before taxation was calculated at £160,000.
6 Corporation tax based on the 1984 profits was estimated to be £60,000.
7 The directors propose a final dividend of 9p per share.
8 A transfer to the deferred taxation account of £14,000 for 1984 is to be made in respect of accelerated capital allowances.

You are required to make all the entries in the ledger accounts and complete the profit and loss account for 1984. Show how the final balances would appear in the balance sheet as at 31 December 1984.

Assume that the basic rate of income tax is 30%.

25 marks

ANSWERS

1

<h2 align="center">Corporation tax</h2>

	£		£
Yr 1 ACT recoverable	25,200	Yr 1 P & L	125,100
Yr 1 MCT c/d	99,900		
	125,100		125,100
Yr 2 Cash Book	99,900	Yr 2 MCT b/d	99,900
Yr 2 ACT recoverable	93,060	Yr 2 P & L	155,100
Yr 2 MCT c/d	62,040		
	255,000		255,000

<h2 align="center">ACT payable</h2>

	£		£
Yr 1 ACT recoverable (£4,200 × 0.3/0.7)	1,800	Yr 1 ACT recoverable	27,000
Yr 1 Cash book	25,200		
	27,000		27,000
Yr 2 ACT recoverable (£6,300 × 0.3/0.7)	2,700	Yr 2 ACT recoverable	108,000
Yr 2 Cash book	105,300		
	108,000		108,000

<h2 align="center">ACT recoverable</h2>

	£		£
Yr 1 ACT payable	27,000	Yr 1 ACT payable	1,800
		Yr 1 Corporation tax (set off)	25,200
	27,000		27,000
Yr 2 ACT payable	108,000	Yr 2 ACT payable	2,700
		Yr 2 Corporation tax (set off) restricted to 30% × £147,900	44,370
		Yr 2 Balance c/d unrelieved (£63,630 − £2,700)	60,930
	108,000		108,000

Schedule F tax

	£		£
Yr 1 UFII (30% × £2,400)	720	Yr 1 Debenture interest paid	
Yr 1 Cash book	1,440	(30% × £7,200)	2,160
	2,160		2,160
Yr 2 UFII (30% × £3,000)	900	Yr 2 Debenture interest paid	
Yr 2 Cash book	1,260	(30% × £7,200)	2,160
	2,160		2,160

Workings

Year 1

	£	
Trading profits	255,000	
Add: Unfranked investment income, gross	2,400	(£1,680 × 100/70)
	257,400	
Less: Debenture interest, gross	7,200	£120,000 × 0.06)
	250,200	
Gross corporation tax liability	125,100	(50% × £250,200)
	125,100	
Dividend paid (net)	63,000	(Gross: £90,000)

Year 2

	£	
Trading profits	300,000	
Add: Unfranked investment income, gross	3,000	(£2,100 × 100/70)
	303,000	
Less: Debenture interest, gross	7,200	(£120,000 × 0.06)
	295,800	
Gross corporation tax liability	147,900	(50% × £295,800)
	147,900	
Dividend paid (net)	252,000	(Gross: £360,000)

Note for Year 2

Maximum ACT available for relief (statutory) is 30% × £147,900	44,370
ACT arising on dividend paid is £252,000 × 30/70	108,000
Unrelieved ACT	63,630

This amount will be reduced by the FII tax credit to (£63,630 − £2,700) = £60,930.

2

Operating statement for year ended 30 September 1983

	£	£
Turnover		2,400,000
Sundry costs	2,048,000	
Debenture interest	32,000	2,080,000
		320,000
Franked investment income		80,000
		400,000
Corporation tax on profits of year	160,000	
Tax credit on franked investment income	24,000	184,000
		216,000
Proposed dividend		84,000
		132,000
Reserves brought forward		440,000
Retained profits carried forward		572,000

Balance sheet as at 30 September 1983

	£	£
Assets employed		
Sundry assets		2,368,000
Creditors: amounts falling due within one year		
Corporation tax	160,000	
ACT payable	12,000	
Sundry creditors	160,000	
Proposed dividends	84,000	(416,000)
Total assets less current liabilities		1,952,000
Creditors: amounts falling due after more than one year		
10% debentures		(320,000)
		1,632,000
Capital and reserves		
Ordinary share capital		800,000
Reserves		572,000
Deferred taxation		260,000
		1,632,000

Summary P & L

	£		£
Sundry costs	2,048,000	Sales	2,400,000
Gross debenture interest	32,000		
Net profit c/d	320,000		
	2,400,000		2,400,000
Corporation tax	160,000	Net profit b/d	320,000
Proposed dividend	84,000	FII gross (£56,000/0.7)	80,000
Tax credit on FII	24,000		
Retained profits c/d	572,000	Retained profits b/fwd	440,000
	840,000		840,000

Corporation tax

	£		£
Balance c/d	160,000	P & L	160,000

ACT payable

	£		£
ACT recoverable (£80,000 × 0.3)	24,000	ACT recoverable (£84,000 × 0.3/0.7)	36,000
Balance c/d	12,000		
	36,000		36,000

ACT recoverable

	£		£
ACT payable	36,000	ACT payable	24,000
		Deferred taxation	12,000
	36,000		36,000

Deferred taxation

	£		£
ACT recoverable	12,000	Balance b/d	272,000
Balance c/d	260,000		
	272,000		272,000

Schedule F income tax

	£		£
Balance c/d	9,600	Debenture interest (30% × £32,000)	9,600

3

Deferred tax

	£		£
Balance b/d	12,364	Balance b/d	117,804
ACT recoverable	6,171	ACT recoverable	12,364
Balance c/d	212,833	P & L	101,200
	231,368		231,368

ACT recoverable

	£		£
Deferred tax	12,364	Corporation tax	12,364
ACT payable	8,229	Corporation tax	8,229
ACT payable	6,171	Balance c/d	6,171
	26,764		26,764
Balance b/d	6,171	Deferred tax	6,171

ACT payable

	£		£
Cash book	8,229	ACT recoverable (interim dividend)	8,229
Balance c/d	6,171	ACT recoverable (proposed dividend)	6,171
	14,400		14,400
		Balance b/d	6,171

Corporation tax

	£		£
P & L (overprovision)	496	Balance b/d (due 1 January 1983)	64,000
ACT recoverable	12,364	P & L (for year ended	
ACT recoverable	8,229	30 November 1982)	34,000

	£		£
brought forward	21,089		98,000
Balance c/d			
(£64,000 − £496)	63,504		
current liability			
Balance c/d			
(£34,000 − £12,364 −			
£8,229)	13,407		
Long-term liability			
	98,000		98,000

Dividends payable

	£		£
CB	19,200	P & L (interim)	19,200
Balance c/d	14,400	P & L (proposed final)	14,400
	33,600		33,600
		Balance b/d	14,400

P & L appropriation

	£		£
Corporation tax	34,000	Balance b/d	X
Deferred tax	101,200	Net profit for year b/d	X
Corporation tax			
(overprovision)	(496)		
Dividend payable (interim)	19,200		
Dividend payable (final)	14,400		

Extracts from published accounts

Operating statement for year ended 30 November 1982

	£	£
Net operating profit for year before taxation		X
Corporation tax on profits of year	34,000	
Less overprovision on previous year	(496)	
	33,504	
Deferred tax transfer	101,200	134,704
Net operating profit after taxation		X
Less: Interim dividend paid	19,200	
Final proposed dividend	14,400	
Retained profit carried forward		33,600
		X

13

Balance sheet extracts

	£
Creditors: amounts falling due within one year	
Corporation tax	63,504
ACT payable	6,171
Proposed dividend	14,400
Creditors: amounts falling due after more than one year	
Corporation tax	13,407
Deferred taxation	212,833

4

Corporation tax

	£		£
31 Oct 1983		31 Oct 1982	
ACT recoverable	1,500	Balance b/d	15,000
31 Oct 1983		31 Oct 1983	
Schedule F tax	750	P & L (underprovision)	500
31 Oct 1983 MCT c/d		31 Oct 1983 P & L	12,250
(£12,250 − £2,250)	10,000		
31 Oct 1983 Balance c/d	15,500		
	27,750		27,750

ACT payable

	£		£
To 31 Oct 1983		To 31 Oct 1983	
ACT payable		ACT recoverable	
(£10,500 × 30/70)	4,500	(£14,000 × 30/70)	6,000
To 31 Oct 1983		To 31 Oct 1983	
Cash book		ACT recoverable	
(£6,000 − £4,500)	1,500	(£7,000 × 30/70)	3,000
31 Oct 1983 Balance b/d	3,000		
	9,000		9,000

ACT recoverable

	£		£
To 31 Oct 1983		To 31 Oct 1983	
ACT payable	6,000	ACT payable	4,500
To 31 Oct 1983		To 31 Oct 1983	
ACT payable	3,000	Corporation tax	1,500
		To 31 Oct 1983	
		Deferred tax	3,000
	9,000		9,000

Deferred taxation

	£		£
31 Oct 1983		31 Oct 1983	
ACT recoverable	3,000	Balance b/d	10,000
31 Oct 1983		31 October 1983	
Balance c/d	11,000	P & L	4,000
	14,000		14,000

Schedule F tax

	£		£
31 Oct 1983		31 Oct 1983	
Debenture interest		Debenture interest	
received (30% X £5,000)	1,500	(30% X £2,500)	750
		31 Oct 1983	
		Corporation tax	750
	1,500		1,500

Operating statement extracts for year ended 31 October 1983

	£	£
Trading profit before tax		30,000
Franked investment income: quoted (gross)		15,000
Unfranked income (gross)		5,000
		50,000
Debenture interest paid (gross)		(2,500)
Net profits before taxation		47,500
Appropriations:		
Corporation tax on profits of year	12,250	
Tax credit on FII	4,500	
Underprovision for corporation tax on		
previous year's profits	500	
Transfer to deferred tax	4,000	(21,250)
Net profit after taxation		26,250
Revenue reserves brought forward		40,000
		66,250
Interim dividend paid	14,000	
Proposed final dividend	7,000	(21,000)
Revenue reserves carried forward		45,250

Balance sheet as at 31 October 1983

	£	£	£
Fixed assets			
Tangible assets			125,000
Investments			
Other investments			
Quoted shares		20,000	
10% quoted debentures		50,000	70,000
			195,000
Current assets			
Stocks		20,000	
Debtors		30,000	
		50,000	
Cash at bank		34,616	
		84,616	
Creditors: amounts falling due within one year			
Corporation tax	15,500		
ACT payable	3,000		
Creditors	37,866		
Proposed dividend	7,000	(63,366)	
Net current assets			21,250
Total assets less current liabilities			216,250
Creditors: amounts falling due after more than one year			
5% Debentures 1987		50,000	
Deferred tax		11,000	
Corporation tax provision		10,000	71,000
			145,250
Capital and reserves			
Ordinary share capital of 20p fully paid			100,000
Revenue reserves			45,250
			145,250

5

Dividends received

	£		£

30 Sep 1982
  P & L
	680	4 Mar 1982
		  Cash book
			476 Note 1

		30 Sep 1982 P & L (tax credit on FII)	204 Note 1

ACT recoverable

	£		£

1 Oct 1981
  ACT payable
	3,058	31 Dec 1981
		  Corporation tax
			3,058 Note 6

30 Sep 1982
  ACT payable
	2,786	4 Mar 1982
		  ACT payable
			204 Note 1

30 Sep 1982
  Balance c/d
	204	30 Sep 1982
		  Balance c/d
			2,786

	2,990		2,990
Balance b/d	2,786	Balance b/d	204

ACT payable

	£		£

31 Dec 1981
  Cash Book
	3,058	1 Oct 1981
		  ACT receivable
			3,058 Note 4

4 Mar 1982
  ACT receivable
	204	30 Sep 1982
		  ACT receivable
			2,786 Note 6

30 Sep 1982
  Balance c/d
	2,786	30 Sep 1982
		  Balance c/d
			204

	2,990		2,990
Balance b/d	204	Balance b/d	2,786

17

Corporation tax

	£		£
31 Dec 1981		1 Oct 1981	
ACT receivable	3,058	Balance b/d	
1 Jan 1982		(corporation tax	
Cash book	15,489	agreed on 1980	
1981/82 P & L		profits)	15,489 Note 4
(overprovision)		1 Oct 1981	
on 1981 profits	1,156	Balance b/d	
30 Sep 1982		(estimated	
Balance c/d (MCT on		corporation tax	
1982 profits)		on 1981 profits	17,000 Note 4
(£18,000 − £3,058)	14,942	30 Sep 1982 P & L	
30 Sep 1982		(estimated	
Balance c/d (MCT on		corporation tax	
1981 profits)		on 1982 profits)	18,000
(£17,000 − £1,156)	15,844		
	——		——
	50,489		50,489
	═══		═══
		Balance b/d (MCT on	
		1982 profits)	14,942
		Balance b/d	
		(corporation tax	
		on 1981 profits)	15,844

Schedule F income tax

	£		£
30 Nov 1981		31 Jan 1982	
Royalties receivable		Debenture interest	
(£403 × 30/70)	173	payable	900
31 Aug 1982		31 Jul 1982	
Royalties receivable		Debenture interest	
(£468 × 30/70)	201	payable	900
1 Mar 1982 Cash book			
((£900 − £173)	727		
30 Sep 1982 P & L			
(£900 − £201)	699		
	——		——
	1,800		1,800
	═══		═══

Royalties receivable

	£		£
30 Sep 1982 P & L		30 Nov 1981	
(£871 × 100/70)	1,245	Cash book	403
		31 Aug 1982	
		Cash book	468
		30 Nov 1981 Schedule F	
		income tax	173
		31 Aug 1982 Schedule F	
		income tax	201
	1,245		1,245

Proposed dividend

		£
	30 Sep 1982 P & L	6,500

Debenture interest payable

	£		£
31 Jan 1982		1 Oct 1981	
Cash book (6 months)	2,100	Balance b/d	
31 Jul 1982		(2 months)	1,000
Cash book (6 months)	2,100	30 Sep 1982 P & L	
31 Jan 1982 Schedule F		(7½% × £80,000)	
(6 months)	900	(12 months)	6,000
31 Jul 1982 Schedule F			
(6 months)	900		
30 Sep 1982 Balance c/d			
(2 months)	1,000		
	7,000		7,000
		Balance b/d	1,000

Analysis of debenture interest payable

7½% × £80,000	£6,000	
Basic-rate tax: 30% × £6,000	£1,800	(half is £900)
Net payable	£4,200	(half is £2,100)

Extracts from operating statement for year ended 30 September 1982

	£	£
Trading profit for the year		
(including £1,245 gross royalties)		X
After charging debenture interest (gross)	6,000	

19

	£	£
brought forward	6,000	X
After crediting FII (gross)	680	
Profits before taxation		X
Corporation tax on profits for year	18,000	
Tax credit on dividends received	204	
	18,204	
Corporation tax overprovided	1,156	17,048
Profits after tax		X
Proposed dividends		6,500
Undistributed profits of year carried forward		X
Retained profits at beginning of year		X
Retained profits at year end		X

Extracts from balance sheet

	£
Creditors: amounts falling due within one year	
Corporation tax (payable 1 Jan 1983)	15,844
ACT payable (£2,786 − £204)	2,582
Debenture interest	1,000
Proposed dividends	6,500
Creditors: amounts falling due after more than one year	
Mainstream corporation tax on 1982 profits	14,942

6

ACT payable

	£		£
Oct 1984 Cash book	10,714	Aug 1984 ACT received (tax credit on interim dividend)	10,714
31 Dec 1984 Balance c/d	19,286	Dec 1984 ACT received (tax credit on final dividend)	19,286
	30,000		30,000
		Balance b/d	19,286

ACT recoverable

	£		£
Aug 1984 ACT payable	10,714	Oct 1984 Corporation tax	
Dec 1984 ACT payable	19,286	(set-off)	10,714
		31 Dec 1984 Balance c/d	19,286
	30,000		30,000
Balance b/d	19,286	To deferred tax	19,286

Corporation tax

	£		£
Jan 1984 Cash book	33,000	1 Jan 1984 Balance b/d	
1984 P & L (overprovision		(on 1982 profits)	33,000
on 1983 profits)	4,000	1 Jan 1984 Balance b/d	
31 Dec 1984 Balance c/d		(on 1983 profits)	10,000
(1983 profits)	6,000	31 Dec 1984 P & L	
Oct 1984 ACT recoverable	10,714	(on 1984 profits)	60,000
31 Dec Balance c/d (MCT)	49,286		
	103,000		103,000
		Balance b/d (short-term)	6,000
		Balance b/d (long-term)	49,286

Deferred tax

	£		£
31 Dec 1984		1 Jan 1984	
ACT recoverable	19,286	Balance b/d	40,000
31 Dec 1984 Balance c/d	34,714	31 Dec 1984 P & L	14,000
	54,000		54,000
		Balance b/d	34,714

Dividends payable

	£		£
Aug 1984 Cash book	25,000	Aug 1984 P & L	
31 Dec 1984 Balance c/d	45,000	(interim dividend)	25,000
		Dec 1984 P & L (proposed	
		final dividend)	45,000
	70,000		70,000
		Balance b/d	45,000

Profit and loss account

	£		£
Aug 1984 Interim dividend	25,000	1 Jan 1984 Balance b/d	60,000
31 Dec 1984 Corporation		31 Dec 1984 Net profit	
tax (on 1984 profits)	60,000	for 1984	160,000
31 Dec 1984		1984 Corporation tax	
To deferred tax	14,000	(overprovision no longer	
31 Dec 1984		required)	4,000
Proposed dividend	45,000		
31 Dec 1984 Balance c/d	80,000		
	224,000		224,000

Extracts from operating statement for year ending 31 December 1984

	£	£
Net operating profits before taxation		160,000
Corporation tax on profits of year	60,000	
Transfer to deferred tax	14,000	
Overprovision for tax	(4,000)	(70,000)
Profits after taxation		90,000
Interim dividend paid	25,000	
Final proposed dividend	45,000	(70,000)
		20,000
Retained profits brought forward		60,000
Retained profits carried forward		80,000

Extracts from balance sheet as at 31 December 1984

	£	£
Creditors: amounts falling due within one year		
Corporation tax	6,000	
ACT payable	19,286	
Proposed dividends	45,000	(70,286)
Creditors: amounts falling due after more than one year		
Corporation tax	60,000	
Deferred taxation	34,714	(94,714)
		X

	£
Capital and reserves	
Ordinary shares of £1 each fully paid	500,000
Profit and loss	80,000
	X

2 SSAP 15

INTRODUCTION

Timing differences arise as a result of the different computation of profits for tax purposes compared with profits computed from a financial accounting point of view.

The simplest example of originating timing differences is where a company procures machinery which is depreciated in the accounts over its expected useful life of, say, five years. From a tax point of view, the machinery can be wholly written off in the accounting period in which it was acquired. This means that the profits from a financial accounting viewpoint will be more than the profits which are taxable because of the 100% capital allowance claimed on the machinery compared with a depreciation policy which writes off the cost over say a five-year period. In the following year, however, notwithstanding other acquisitions the profits subject to tax will be greater than the profits in the financial accounts. This arises because the depreciation charge in the second year will not be allowable from a tax point of view.

A deferred taxation account is therefore set up so that the reversing timing differences of subsequent years can be provided for out of the deferred taxation account.

There are other varieties of timing differences and the reader is referred to SSAP 15 for other examples.

SSAP 15 does permit the postponement of a provision for liability where:

(a) The company is a going concern.
(b) There is reasonable evidence that no liability is likely to arise as a result of reversal of timing differences for at least three years ahead.
(c) Crystallisation of liabilities is unlikely beyond three years.

Two methods are available for accounting for deferred taxation: the liability method and the deferral method.

Under the liability method, taxation resulting from timing differences is regarded as a liability or as an asset representing recoverable taxes. The computation is always made by reference to the most recent tax rates. Further, opening balances are always revised to current tax rates.

Under the deferral method, the tax on timing differences is regarded as deferrals of taxation (payable or recoverable) to be allocated to future periods when the differences reverse. The balances on the deferred taxation account are thus regarded as deferred charges or credits and not as amounts payable or recoverable.

Two techniques of accounting are available under the deferral method:

(a) Accounting for each reversing timing difference in a year by the rate of tax applying in the year the originating timing difference occurred.

(b) Accounting for the 'net change' whereby the net amount of all the originating and reversing timing differences is calculated.

If the net timing differences are originating, then the current tax rate is applied. If the net timing differences are net reversing, then:

(a) FIFO: where rates applying to the earlier timing differences making up the deferred tax account, are used.

(b) AVERAGE BASIS: where the rate applying is arrived at by: balance on deferred tax at beginning of period ÷ Total of related timing differences.

Questions 4 and 5 should assist you in understanding the average basis technique.

QUESTIONS

1

(a) You are required to define timing differences, distinguishing between originating and reversing timing differences and giving two examples of short-term and two examples of long-term differences. *8 marks*

(b) You are required to state the conditions under which it is permissible to postpone the need for making provisions to deferred tax. *7 marks*
Total 15 marks

2 The auditors of Foley Ltd have advised you, the chief accountant of Foley Ltd, that it is now necessary to implement a deferred tax system as required by SSAP 15.

You are required to identify and to explain fully the two main methods of accounting for timing differences and to identify and explain two techniques which sometimes need to be applied under one of the above methods.
20 marks

3 Cloth Ltd is a medium-sized company in the textile trade. The profit and loss accounts for the three years ended 30 June 1982 are summarised as follows:

	1980 £	1981 £	Draft 1982 £
Profit before taxation	31,000	34,500	64,000
Less: Corporation tax	—	—	—
Deferred tax	12,000	12,500	21,000
Profit after taxation	19,000	22,000	43,000
Proposed dividend	4,800	10,500	21,000
Unappropriated profit for the year	14,200	11,500	22,000
Balance bought forward	64,800	79,000	90,500
Profit retained	79,000	90,500	112,500

Until recently, 100% of the shares in Cloth Ltd were held by Fabrik Inc., a US company, and hence Cloth Ltd has provided for deferred tax on all originating timing differences in accordance with Generally Accepted US Accounting Principles.

During 1982 Fabrik Inc. disposed of its holding to Leather Ltd, a UK company, and now Cloth Ltd wishes to apply SSAP 15 in order to make its accounting policies consistent with those of other companies in the group.

The balance on deferred tax at 30 June 1982 is made up as follows:

	1980 £	1981 £	1982 £
Excess capital allowances	215,000	267,000	316,000
Short-term timing difference	5,200	5,200	5,200
Losses carried forward	(212,500)	(252,000)	(280,000)
Corporation tax on chargeable gain on revaluation surplus	15,000	15,000	15,000
Advance corporation tax unrelieved	(4,250)	(8,750)	(17,750)
	18,450	26,450	38,450

Capital expenditure, which has been at the rate of £250,000 p.a., is expected to continue at that rate for at least the next three years while the depreciation charge for the same period is not expected to amount to more than £150,000 in any year.

The short-term timing differences arise from accrued interest receivable.

The revaluation surplus relates to the company's freehold factory premises and there are no plans to dispose of this property.

On the basis of the profit forecast for the year ending 30 June 1983, together with the anticipated capital expenditure, it is expected that further tax losses will arise in that year.

You are required:

(a)   To state, with reasons, the adjustments you would make to the draft accounts in order to reflect the decision to comply with SSAP 15.   *11 marks*

(b)   To draft the notes, including comparative figures, to be included in the final statutory accounts.   *9 marks*
        Total 20 marks

Note. The statutory profit and loss account and balance sheet are not required. Assume a rate of corporation tax of 52% and a rate of ACT of 30/70ths.

4   The managing director of SPL Ltd has called you into his office and shows you an illustration of the computation of deferred tax on timing differences which he received from the company's auditors in this morning's post.

The illustration appears as follows:

	Tax rate	Timing differences originating (reversing) £	Transfers to (from) deferred tax — Liability method £	Deferral method: net change — Average £	Deferral method: net change — FIFO £
Year 1	50%				
Capital allowances		8,000			
Depreciation		2,500			
		5,500	2,750	2,750	2,750
Year 2	52%				
Tax rate adjustment			110	–	–
Capital allowances		12,500			
Depreciation		5,500			
		7,000	3,640	3,640	3,640
		12,500	6,500	6,390	6,390
Year 3	53%				
Tax rate adjustment			125	–	–
Capital allowances		4,375			
Depreciation		6,500	(2,125)	(1,126)	(1,086)	(1,062)
		10,375	5,499	5,304	5,328
Year 4	51%				
Tax rate adjustment			(207)	–	–
Capital allowances		14,281			
Depreciation		10,000			
		4,281	2,183	2,183	2,183
		14,656	7,475	7,487	7,511

You are required to analyse this illustration making it clear how the figures have been arrived at, particularly showing how the balances have been arrived at in year 3 and what rates of tax have been applied.

20 marks

5   Potts Ltd, a machine tool manufacturing company, commenced trading on 1 April 1982; at present, 31 March 1983, the management are undecided about which of the two main methods to use in accounting for deferred taxation arising from timing differences; that is, the liability or deferral method.

The actual and estimated capital expenditure for the five years to 31 March 1987 is given below.

Year ended 31 March	Capital expenditure Machine type	Cost	Actual or anticipated rate of corporation tax
1983	X	9,000	52%
1984	Y	12,000	55%
1985	Z	4,500	50%
1986	A	15,000	50%
1987		Nil	45%

All capital expenditure qualifies for 100% first-year allowance which the company intends claiming. The machines all have an estimated useful life of four years and have no residual values.

You are required, using both the liability and deferral method, to calculate the charges to the profit and loss account in respect of deferred taxation for each year together with the balance on the deferred taxation account which would appear on each balance sheet.

25 marks

6 PJ Ltd has, for the last three years, followed SSAP 15 and has provided for deferred taxation on all short-term timing differences and on other originating timing differences that are expected to reverse in the future. The balance on its deferred taxation account at 30 June 1983 was made up as follows:

	£000
Short-term timing differences	(2.6)
Accelerated capital allowances	26.0
	23.4

This provision was made after taking into account the following forecasts which were made at 30 June 1983:

Year ended 30 June	1984 £000	1985 £000	1986 £000
Capital allowances	80	70	150
Depreciation	100	100	100

The short-term timing differences relate to interest paid. The accumulated timing differences at 30 June 1983 relating to accelerated capital allowances amounted to £750,000 and the company had to date received a total of £250,000 of stock relief.

During the year ended 30 June 1984, the figures were as follows:

	£000
Capital allowances	70
Depreciation	100
Interest paid	22
Interest charged to P & L	20

28

The company also received £15,000 of stock relief under the Finance Act 1981 rules.

The forecasts of future capital allowances and depreciation as at 30 June 1984 are:

Year ended 30 June	1985	1986	1987
	£000	£000	£000
Capital allowances	70	150	120
Depreciation	100	100	100

There is no indication that further timing differences will reverse, after 30 June 1987.

You are required to show how deferred taxation would be disclosed in the accounts for the year ended 30 June 1984 including all of the requirements of SSAP 15.

Assume corporation tax at 52%.

25 marks

ANSWERS

1

(a) The amount of taxation payable on the profits of a particular period often bears little relationship to the amounts of income and expenditure appearing in the profit and loss account. This results from the different basis on which profits are arrived at for the purpose of computing taxation as opposed to the amounts at which profits are stated in the accounts. The differences are known as timing differences.

Originating timing differences occur when the profits assessable to tax are less than the profits reported in the accounts in any given year.

Reversing timing differences occur in subsequent years when the profits assessable to tax are greater than the profits reported for that year in the accounts.

Originating timing differences can broadly be classified into short-term and long-term timing differences.

Short-term timing differences are expected to reverse in the next accounting period. For example, interest receivable accrued in the accounting period but taxed when received or dividends from foreign subsidiaries accrued in a period prior to that in which they arise for tax purposes.

Long-term timing differences are expected to reverse over a period exceeding one year. For example, accelerated capital allowances claimed in excess of the depreciation charge or a claim for roll-over relief.

(b) It is permissible not to make a provision for a deferred tax liability if all the following conditions are met:

   (i)   The company is a going concern.

   (ii) There is reasonable evidence to indicate that a reversal of timing differences will not occur within a period of at least three years, because of a stable and growing investment policy in relation to the procurement of capital assets. The assessment of reasonable evidence should be made in the light of current intentions of the directors and of the company's expectations and plans for the future viewed in relation to the historical pattern of capital expenditure.

   (iii) There is no indication that after this period of at least three years the situation is likely to change so as to crystallise the liabilities.

2 The two main methods of accounting for timing differences are the 'deferral' method and the 'liability' method. Whichever method is employed, the amounts taken to the deferred taxation account represent tax on the originating timing differences at the rate in force for the year in which those differences arose. The deferral method, however, requires that those amounts remain unchanged, despite subsequent changes in the tax rate, and that reversals take place at the same, original rate.

Thus, the balance, at any time, on the deferred taxation account will represent the sum of the tax savings which have been obtained on those originating timing differences which have not been wholly reversed.

In many businesses there will occur, within the same year, both originating and reversing timing differences, which on a strict application of the deferral method, would require treatment at different rates dependent upon when the originating timing differences occurred. However, it is a matter of expendience that regard be given only to the net position, that is, the excess of originating over reversing timing differences, or vice versa, transfers being made to or from deferred taxation account accordingly. This procedure is referred to as the 'net change method'. Under this method, any net originating timing difference should be calculated at the current rate of taxation. The tax on a net reversing timing difference may be calculated either on a 'first-in-first-out' basis or on an 'average' basis, the latter being arrived at by dividing the balance on the deferred tax account at the beginning of the current period by the total of the related timing differences. Alternatively, the same result would be achieved if originating timing differences are individually divided by the cumulative related timing differences to the beginning of the current period and multiplied by the rate of corporation tax applicable at the time the originating timing difference occurred.

Under the deferral method, balances on the deferred tax account are thus regarded as deferred charges (if debit balances) or deferred credits (if credit balances), and not as amounts recoverable or payable.

In contrast, the liability method views timing differences as liabilities, or assets, representing recoverable taxes, which are ultimately owed by or due to the company. The tax charge in the account is computed on the profit shown by those accounts (after adjusting for permanent timing differences) and the difference between the tax charge and the amount of tax assessable for the year is treated as either a future liability for, or prepayment of, tax, as the case may be. Thus deferred taxation balances, on this approach, are maintained at the current rate of tax, since the latest known rate is regarded as the best indication of the position which will obtain when the liability falls due or the benefit of the prepayment is received. All balances are always revised to the current tax rate under the liability method.

3

(a)   Under SSAP 15, part of the provision for deferred taxation may not be required where certain criteria are met. In establishing the provision required it is necessary to consider each component of the deferred taxation account in turn.

Firstly, under SSAP 15, deferred taxation should be accounted for on all short-term timing differences and thus the provision of £5,200 should remain.

Deferred taxation in respect of the tax effects arising from other timing differences need not be provided for if it can be demonstrated with reasonable probability that the tax effects will continue in the future. It is assumed that Cloth Ltd is a going concern.

Deferred taxation in respect of excess capital allowances may be written back since capital allowances are forecast to exceed the depreciation charge for the foreseeable future and there is no indication that the situation is likely to change beyond the forecast period.

Since there are no plans to dispose of the freehold factory, the deferred taxation provided in respect of the revaluation surplus on the factory is no longer required.

With regard to losses carried forward, SSAP 15 states that the tax effects of a trading loss should only be recognised to the extent that there is a credit balance on the deferred taxation account in respect of tax on income which can properly be offset against the loss for tax purposes. In the preceding paragraphs, it has been established that under SSAP 15 no provision for deferred taxation is required in respect of capital allowances or chargeable gains on the revaluation surplus. The only provision required is in respect of short-term timing differences which arise from accrued interest receivable. Since trading losses carried forward can only be offset against future profits of the same trade they would not be offsetable against the future interest receivable and therefore the tax effects of the losses carried forward should not be recognised in the deferred taxation account under SSAP 15.

A debit balance in respect of unrelieved ACT should only be recognised in two circumstances. The first circumstance is where its recoverability is foreseen in the immediate future which should normally not extend beyond the next accounting period. Since Cloth Ltd forecasts further tax losses in the next accounting period it would be imprudent to treat the unrelieved ACT as recoverable on this basis. The second circumstance is where there is a credit balance on the deferred taxation account in respect of timing differences that will reverse in the future and therefore give rise to corporation tax payable. In this situation, unrelieved ACT may be deducted from the balance on the deferred taxation account to the extent that it will be properly offsetable. The offset of ACT is restricted to 30% of taxable income and therefore the deduction from the deferred taxation account will be restricted to 30/52 of the tax provided. In the case of Cloth Ltd the maximum deduction will therefore be £3,000 (£5,200 × 30/52). The remainder of the unrelieved ACT should be written off as irrecoverable.

(b) A summary of the adjustments to the draft accounts for 1982 would therefore be as follows:

Provision for deferred taxation under SSAP 15

	At 30 June 1981 £	At 30 June 1982 £
Short-term timing differences	5,200	5,200
ACT unrelieved	(3,000)	(3,000)
	2,200	2,200

The revised provision above indicates that there would be no charge in the profit and loss account for the year ended 30 June 1982 in respect of deferred taxation (adjustment of £21,000). However, there should be a charge in the profit and loss account in respect of irrecoverable ACT arising during the year. This would amount to £9,000 being 30/70ths of the dividend (£21,000). In addition, there would be a prior-year adjustment to reserves brought forward at 1 July 1981 of £24,250 being the release of the deferred tax provision no longer required under SSAP 15 (£26,450 − £2,200).

The revised draft profit and loss account for the year ending 30 June 1982 would be as follows:

	£	£
Profit before taxation		64,000
Taxation: irrecoverable ACT		9,000
Profit after taxation		55,000
Proposed dividend		21,000
Retained profit for the year		34,000
Reserves brought forward	90,500	
Prior-year adjustment	24,250	
Reserves brought forward as restated		114,750
Reserves carried forward		148,750

4

Liability method:

Year		£	
1	£5,500 × 50% =	2,750	originating
2	£5,500 × 2% =	110	originating
3	£5,500 × 1% =	55	originating
4	£5,500 × 2% =	(110)	reversing
2	£7,000 × 52% =	3,640	
3	£7,000 × 1% =	70	
4	£7,000 × 2% =	(140)	
3	(£2,125) × 53% =	(1,126)	
4	£2,125 × 2% =	42.5	
4	£4,281 × 51% =	2,183	

Summary

	£
Year 1	2,750
Year 2 £110 + £3,640	3,750
Year 3 £55 + £70 − £1,126	(1,001)
Year 4 − £110 − £140 + £42.5 + £2,183	1,977.5

Cumulative deferred tax balances

	£
Year 1	2,750
Year 2 £2,750 + £3,750	6,500
Year 3 £6,500 − £1,001	5,499
Year 4 £5,499 + £1,977.5	7,476.5

Deferral method

Net change: FIFO basis

Year					Cumulative deferred tax balance £
1	50%	× £5,500	=	£2,750	2,750
2	52%	× £7,000	=	£3,640	6,390
3	50%	× (£2,125)	=	(£1,062)	5,328
4	51%	× £4,281	=	£2,183	7,511

Net change: average basis

Year					Cumulative deferred tax balance £
1	50%	× £5,500	=	£2,750	2,750
2	52%	× £7,000	=	£3,640	6,390
3*	51.12%	× (£2,125)	=	(£1.086)	5,304
4	51%	× £4,281	=	£2,183	7,487

*Average rate is arrived at by comparing the cumulative total of timing differences at the beginning of the year with the balance of the deferred tax account at that time, i.e.:

$$\frac{\text{balance on deferred tax account at beginning of current period}}{\text{total of related timing differences}} = \frac{£6,390}{£12,500} = 51.12\%$$

or:

$$\frac{£5,500}{£12,500} \times 50\% + \frac{£7,000}{£12,500} \times 52\% = 51.12\%$$

	Machine	Cost	Life	Depreciation	First-year allowance
1983	X	£9,000	4 years	£2,250	£9,000
1984	Y	£12,000	4 years	£3,000	£12,000
1985	Z	£4,500	4 years	£1,125	£4,500
1986	A	£15,000	4 years	£3,750	£15,000

			1983 £	1984 £	1985 £	1986 £
1983	X	First-year allowance	9,000	–	–	–
		Depreciation	(2,250)	(2,250)	(2,250)	(2,250)
1984	Y	First-year allowance	–	12,000	–	–
		Depreciation	–	(3,000)	(3,000)	(3,000)
1985	Z	First-year allowance	–	–	4,500	–
		Depreciation	–	–	(1,125)	(1,125)
1986	A	First-year allowance	–	–	–	15,000
		Depreciation	–	–	–	(3,750)
Net timing differences			6,750	6,750	(1,875)	4,875
Cumulative timing differences			6,750	13,500	11,625	16,500

			1987 £	1988 £	1989 £
1983	X	First-year allowance	–	–	–
		Depreciation	–	–	–
1984	Y	First-year allowance	–	–	–
		Depreciation	(3,000)	–	–
1985	Z	First-year allowance	–	–	–
		Depreciation	(1,125)	(1,125)	–
1986	A	First-year allowance	–	–	–
		Depreciation	(3,750)	(3,750)	(3,750)
Net timing differences			(7,875)	(4,875)	(3,750)
Cumulative timing differences			8,625	3,750	Nil

Liability method

	£		P & L £		Deferred taxation Per balance sheet £	
1983 Net timing difference	6,750	52%	3,510	Dr	(3,510)	Cr
1984 Adjustment (3% × £6,750)			203	Dr	(203)	Cr
Net timing difference	6,750	55%	3,713	Dr	(3,713)	Cr
	13,500		3,916	Dr	(7,426)	Cr
1985 Adjustment (5% × £13,500)			(675)	Cr	675	Dr
Net timing difference	(1,875)	50%	(938)	Cr	938	Dr
	11,625		(1,613)	Cr	(5,813)	Cr
1986 Adjustment (nil)			—		—	
Net timing difference	4,875	50%	2,437	Dr	(2,437)	Cr
	16,500		2,437	Dr	(8,250)	Cr
1987 Adjustment (5% × £16,500)			(825)	Cr	825	Dr
Net timing difference	(7,875)	45%	(3,544)	Cr	3,544	Dr
	8,625		(4,369)	Cr	(3,881)	Cr
1988 Adjustment (nil)			—		—	
Net timing difference	(4,875)	45%	(2,194)	Cr	2,194	Dr
	3,750		(2,194)	Cr	(1,687)	Cr
1989 Adjustment (nil)						
Net timing difference	(3,750)	45%	(1,687)	Cr	1,687	Dr

Deferral method: average basis

	£		P & L £		Deferred taxation Per balance sheet £	
1983 Net timing difference	6,750	52%	3,510	Dr	(3,510)	Cr
1984 Net timing difference	6,750	55%	3,713	Dr	(3,713)	Cr
	13,500				(7,223)	Cr
1985 Net timing difference	(1,875)	53.5%	(1,003)	Cr	1,003	Dr
	11,625				(6,220)	Cr

		£		Deferred taxation
			P & L	Per balance sheet
		£	£	£
brought forward		11,625		(6,220) Cr
1986 Net timing difference		4,875 50%	2,438 Dr	(2,438) Cr
		16,500		(8,658) Cr
1987 Net timing difference		(7,875) 52.47%	(4,132) Cr	4,132 Dr
		8,625		(4,526) Cr
1988 Net timing difference		(4,875) 52.48%	(2,558) Cr	2,558 Dr
		3,750		(1,968) Cr
1989 Net timing difference		(3,750) 52.48%	(1,968) Cr	1,968 Dr
		nil		nil

Corporation tax rates

$$1985: \frac{7,223}{13,500} = 53.5\%$$

$$1987: \frac{8,658}{16,500} = 52.47\%$$

$$1988: \frac{4,526}{8,625} = 52.48\%$$

$$1989: \frac{1,968}{3,750} = 52.48\%$$

If the FIFO basis is used, the following rates of corporation tax would be employed:

1983	1984	1985	1986	1987	1988	1989
52%	55%	52%	50%	55%	50%	50%

6   Principal bases for computing the tax effect of timing differences.

(a)   *'Nil provision' or 'flow through' basis:* only the tax charge of the period should be considered a liability; no provision for deferred taxation is thus made.

(b)   *'Full provision' or 'comprehensive allocation':* based on the principle that financial statements for a period should recognise the tax effect, *whether current or deferred,* of *all* transactions occurring *in that period.*

(c)   *'Partial provision'* which requires that *all current tax* should be provided and that *deferred tax* should be accounted for in respect of *'the net amount'* by which it is probable that any tax liability (or asset) will be temporarily deferred or accelerated by the operation of timing differences which *will reverse* in the foreseeable future without being replaced. Partial provision recognises that, if an enterprise is not expected to reduce its operations scale significantly, it will normally have what amounts to a hard core of timing differences so that the payment of some tax will be permanently deferred. On this basis, deferred tax has only to be provided where it is probable that tax will become payable as a result of the reversal of timing differences.

Bases 1 and 2 can be precisely quantified; however, they can both lead to a purely arithmetic approach in which certainty of calculation is given precedence over reasoned assessment of what the tax effects of transactions will actually be. Basis 3 is based on an assessment of what will actually be the position and partial provision is thus preferable (ED33).

Profit and loss account for year ended 30 June 1984

	£	£
Profit before taxation		X
Taxation (Note 1)		
Current	X	
Deferred (W2)	(9,360)	
		X
		X

Balance sheet at 30 June 1984

	£
Deferred taxation (Note 2)	14,040

Notes to accounts

1　The tax charge has been reduced by £7,800 (15,000 × 0.52) in respect of stock relief and would have been reduced by £5,200 (W3) if full provision had been made for deferred taxation.

2　Deferred taxation at 30 June 1984 (W1)

	Provided in accounts		Full potential amount	
	1984	1983	1984	1983
	£	£	£	£
Short-term timing differences	(1,560)	(2,600)	(1,560)	(2,600)
Accelerated capital allowances	15,600	26,000	374,400	390,000
	14,040	23,400	372,840	387,400

Note: Full provision is based on the principle that financial statements for a period should recognise the tax effect whether current or deferred of all transactions occurring in that period.

Partial provision requires all current tax to be provided but deferred tax is accounted for in respect of the net amount of timing differences which will reverse in the fore-seeable future.

Workings

1   Deferred taxation under SSAP 15 at 30 June 1984

(a)

Forecasts	Excess of capital allowances over depreciation £	Cumulative £
1985	(30,000)	(30,000)
1986	50,000	20,000
1987	20,000	40,000

Partial provision

The maximum cumulative reversal foreseen is £30,000 in 1985. Therefore the provision required at 30 June 1984 will be in respect of £30,000 timing differences.

(b)   Short-term timing difference on interest paid

	Timing difference £
Accumulated at 30 June 1983 (2,600 ÷ 0.52)	(5,000)
Arising during year ended 30 June 1984	2,000
Accumulated at 30 June 1984 (3,000 × 0.56 = 1,560)	(3,000)

2   Profit and loss account charge for year ended 30 June 1984

	£
Provision at 30 June 1984	14,040
Provision at 30 June 1983	23,400
Credit for the year	9,360

3   Full deferred tax in P & L account for 1984

	£
Provision at 30 June 1984	372,840
Provision at 30 June 1984	387,400
Credit for year	14,560

Therefore the tax charge would have decreased by £5,200 if full provision for deferred tax had been made.

In 'T' account form, we have for full provision:

(Note: this method ignores forecasts, thus the £26,000 provision is ignored).

Deferred taxation (full provision)

	£	P & L	£
1983		**1983**	
Short-term		Accelerated capital allowances:	
Timing differences		750,000 × 0.52	390,000
Reversing	2,600		
30/6/83 Balance b/d	387,400		
	390,000		390,000
1983/4		**1983/4**	
		1/7/83 Balance b/d	387,000
Credit to P & L for year	14,560		
Reversing timing		Short-term	
differences capital allowances		Timing differences	
£30,000 × 0.52	15,600	originating:	
		£2,000 × 0.52	1,040
		(reverses in following	
30/6/84 Balance c/d	372,840	period)	
	387,400		387,400

Deferred taxation (partial provision)

	£	P & L	1984
1983		**1983**	
Balance b/d		Balance b/d	26,000
Reversing short-term		Originating short-term	
timing differences		timing differences	
5,000 × 0.52	2,600	which *will* reverse	
		2,000 × 0.52	1,040
		(reverses in following	
		period)	
Existing balance		Anticipated 1985 reversing	
not required	26,000	timing difference on	
		capital allowances	
		£30,000 × 52%	15,600
Credit to P & L for year	9,360		
1984			
Balance c/d	14,040		
	26,000		26,000

Provision is made for all short-time timing differences and future net reversing differences foreseeable. The maximum reversal foreseen is £30,000 in 1985.

3 SSAP 6

SSAP 6 deals with the treatment of extraordinary items and prior-year adjustments. Extraordinary items are defined in the statement as items which derive from events or transactions outside the ordinary activities of the business and which are both material and expected not to recur frequently or regularly.

Examples are:

(a)   The discontinuance of a significant part of the business.
(b)   The sale of an investment not acquired with the intention of resale.
(c)   Writing off of intangibles, including goodwill, because of unusual events or developments during the period.
(d)   The expropriation of assets.

The statement goes on to say that items which, though abnormal in size and incidence, derive from the ordinary activities of the business are not extraordinary items. Such items are often called 'abnormal' or 'exceptional' items in contrast to 'extraordinary' items, but this terminology is not used in the SSAP.

Examples of abnormal items are:

(a)   Abnormal charges for bad debts and write-offs of stocks and work in progress, and research and development expenditure.
(b)   Abnormal provisions for losses on long-term contracts.
(c)   Most adjustments of prior-year taxation provisions.

Prior-year adjustments which should be adjusted against the opening balance of retained profits or reserves are rare and limited to items arising from changes in accounting policies and from the correction of fundamental errors. Prior-year adjustments (less attributable taxation) should be accounted for by restating prior years with the result that the opening balance of retained profits will be accordingly adjusted and shown separately.

The profit and loss account should disclose the profits before extraordinary items, after which the extraordinary items (less attributable taxation) should then be shown separately, finally the profit after extraordinary items should be separately disclosed.

However, the Companies Act 1948, schedule 8, paragraph 54(3), requires separate disclosure of tax on extraordinary profit or loss, and careful note should be taken of this in that SSAP 6 does not strictly come within the requirements of the Act.

A discussion paper on SSAP 6 was published in April 1983 and reviews the suitability of SSAP 6. Some of the issues considered are:

(a) Are the terms 'extraordinary' and 'exceptional' sufficiently distinguishable?
(b) Is frequency of occurrence a suitable distinguishing feature between extra-ordinary and exceptional items?
(c) Should extraordinary items be included before or after dividends in the profit and loss account?
(d) Should the standard emphasise that it is the event or transaction leading to the extraordinary items which should not recur, rather than the category of extraordinary items?

The foregoing list is not exhaustive and readers should refer to the review document.

QUESTIONS

1 Wellington Ltd, a manufacturing company, has a turnover of £12 million and pre-tax profits of £2 million before taking account of the following items:

(a) Costs of £1,500,000 incurred in terminating production at one of the company's factories.

(b) Currency exchange surplus amounting to £15,000 arising on remittance from an overseas depot.

(c) An extra £200,000 contribution by the company to the employees' pension fund.

(d) Profits of £300,000 on sale of plant and machinery written off in a previous year when production of the particular product ceased.

(e) Provision for an abnormally large bad debt of £1,000,000 arising in a trading contract.

You are required to indicate whether these items should be treated as exceptional, extraordinary or normal trading transactions within the terms of SSAP 6, giving your reasons.

15 marks

2 The draft consolidated accounts of a public company, Fuego plc, for the year ended 31 March 1982 show a profit before taxation of approximately £600,000. During the preparation of the accounts, the following matters were noted:

(a) The company repurchased £100,000 low-coupon redeemable debenture stock at 39½.

(b) The benefits payable under a newly acquired subsidiary company's pension scheme fell far short of the benefits provided by the existing group scheme. The directors decided to make a single payment of £65,000 to bring the scheme into line with that of the group.

(c) Corporation tax payable in respect of the year ended 31 March 1981 was underprovided by £62,000. The taxation payable for the year under review has been reduced by £240,000 because of tax relief on the increased value of stocks at the year end.

(d) The company purchased the minority interests in two subsidiaries. The directors wish to write off goodwill of £125,000 arising on this transaction.

(e) The company sold a property for £775,000. The property was purchased in 1969 for £600,000 and the aggregate depreciation written off since that time amounted to £125,000.

You are required to state, with reasons, how the various matters should be dealt with in the published accounts.

10 marks

3 You have ascertained the following information in relation to the accounts of Solara Ltd:

1 Year ended 31 December

	1982 £ thousands	1981 £ thousands
Profit on ordinary activities before tax (before research and development charge)	1,925	1,684
Taxation (the 1982 charge includes £36,000 relating to 1981)	485	462

2 During 1982, the company decided to change its accounting policy relating to research and development. In previous years, it had capitalised research and development and amortised it over 10 years but now all such expenditure is to be written off in the year in which it is incurred. The following figures are relevant:

	£ thousands
Balance on research and development at 1 January 1981	936
Expenditure on research and development during 1981	194
Amortisation of research and development during 1981	185
Expenditure on research and development during 1982	360

3 Newly introduced legislation led to trading difficulties in a business which was owned by Solara Ltd. The directors who had previously carried forward goodwill as a permanent asset decided to write off the full £500,000 immediately against reserves as per ED 30.

4 The retained profits brought forward at 1 January 1981 were £13,842,000.

5 The proposed dividend for both 1981 and 1982 was £250,000.

You are required to prepare the profit and loss account and statement of reserves including notes thereon for the year ended 31 December 1982. Your answer should include comparative figures and be in accordance with best accounting practice.

12 marks

4 Hudson plc is a company in the furniture retailing trade with 324 shops. It had a turnover of £78 million and pre-tax profits of £8 million in the year to 31 December 1982, tax on this profit being computed at £4 million, before taking into account the following items:

(i) As part of a programme of updating and improving shop premises, 13 shop sites were disposed of during the year at a profit of £320,000 subject to a corporation tax charge of £104,000 on the chargeable gain.

(ii) During the course of the audit of the accounts for the year to 31 December 1982 it is discovered that an error was made in the previous year's accounts whereby the closing stock of £8.7 million was brought into the accounts at £7.8 million.

(iii) During the year it was discovered that certain beds imported and distributed by the company were liable, in some circumstances, to collapse, because of a fundamental design fault. Fortunately, the company received no claims for personal injury arising from this problem, but it was necessary to recall for checking and repair all of the beds sold. The cost of this was £300,000 relating to beds sold in 1982, £500,000 relating to beds sold in 1981 and £180,000 relating to beds sold in previous years.

(iv) A revaluation of properties during the year showed surpluses totalling £4 million and deficits totalling £500,000. The company's revaluation reserve of £6.5 million includes previous revaluation surpluses of £200,000 on the properties now showing a deficit on revaluation, and revaluation surpluses of £150,000 on the properties sold during the year. It is the company's policy not to provide for deferred tax on revaluation surpluses.

(v) During the year the directors made a decision to sell all the company's investments on the Stock Exchange and in doing so realised a profit of £2 million, subject to corporation tax on the gain of £600,000.

The previous year's accounts showed a turnover of £71 million, profits of £7.5 million before tax, and a tax charge of £3.75 million with no extraordinary items or prior-year adjustments. Retained profits at 1 January 1981 were £17.25 million. The corporation tax rate in 1981 and 1982 was 50%. Dividends of £2 million were proposed each year.

You are required:

(a) To explain the appropriate treatment for each of the above items in the accounts of Hudson plc for the year ended 31 December 1982.   *10 marks*

(b) To present the profit and loss account for the year to 31 December 1982 with comparative figures in accordance with SSAP 6, and in accordance with the Companies Acts in so far as the information is available.   *5 marks*
Total 15 marks

5 The following are extracts from the draft profit and loss accounts prepared by Caroline Ltd for the year ended 31 December 1982 which you have been asked to review. The profit and loss account for the previous year is also provided.

	Notes	Year ended 31 December 1982 £	£	Year ended 31 December 1981 £	£
Profit after taxation before extraordinary items			220,000		151,000
Less: Extraordinary items					
Loss on sale of machinery	(i)	47,000		—	
Work in progress adjustment	(ii)	14,000		—	
Bad debt provision	(iii)	7,000		—	
Loss on sale of subsidiary	(iv)	18,000		14,000	
			86,000		14,000
Retained profit			134,000		137,000

	Notes	Year ended 31 December 1982 £	£	Year ended 31 December 1981 £	£
Profit brought forward as previously stated			177,000		40,000
Less: Research expenditure	(v)	45,000		27,000	
Work in progress	(ii)	12,000		–	
Bad debt provision	(iii)	10,000		–	
			67,000		27,000
			110,000		13,000
Retained profit for year			134,000		137,000
			244,000		150,000

Notes

(i) The machinery was used exclusively for producing goods which were sold through the foreign-based subsidiary companies. The enforced sale of the subsidiary companies rendered the machinery surplus to the requirements of the company.

(ii) Production overheads are charged to work in progress on the basis that work in progress is 60% completed. This basis has been used in previous year's accounts. The directors now consider that this basis is incorrect and consider that work in progress should be treated as being 50% complete, with production overheads charged accordingly. The amended basis will be used in future years. The current and previous year's adjustments have brought the closing work in progress valuation for each year into line with this new policy.

(iii) As from the current year, the company has decided to create a provision for bad debts. This is a new policy. The provision for the current year is £17,000. If the policy had been adopted last year the provision would have been £10,000.

(iv) Two subsidiary companies were located in a foreign country. In recent years the government of the country concerned nationalised all foreign-owned companies. The government paid compensation which resulted in the losses indicated in the accounts.

(v) In the current year all expenditure on research has been written off in accordance with a changed policy decision. Previously, it was written off in three equal annual instalments. The differences were as follows:

	Actual expenditure	
Year ended	for year	Charged in accounts
31 Dec 1980	£40,000	£13,000 (i.e., £40,000 × 1/3)
31 Dec 1981	£87,000	£42,000 (i.e., (£40,000 + £87,000) × 1/3)

Ignoring taxation, you are required:

(a)   To state if, in your opinion, the extraordinary items and prior-year adjustments have been correctly treated in the accounts for the year ended 31 December 1982 giving reasons for your view.   *6 marks*

(b)   To state by way of note how you would deal with the items referred to in the notes to the accounts giving reasons for your answers.   *12 marks*

Total 18 marks

ANSWERS

1 The items should be treated as follows:

(a) Costs of £1,500,000 incurred in terminating production at one of the company's factories clearly constitute an extraordinary item as defined in SSAP 6, which in fact gives this kind of expenditure as an example of an item which will normally be extraordinary in character.

(b) This gain should be treated as part of the profit of the year from ordinary activities in accordance with the provisions of SSAP 20. It is neither extraordinary nor exceptional.

(c) Contributions to the employees' pension fund will be part of the company's normal activity, but the amount of £200,000 is stated to be an 'extra' contribution, and it is material. It should therefore be disclosed as an exceptional item.

(d) The profit does not call for a prior-year adjustment since there is neither a change in accounting policy nor a fundamental error. Such a profit is generally recognised as part of the ordinary activities of the business but should be disclosed separately as an exceptional item on account of its size and incidence (see SSAP 6 discussion paper).

(e) A loss on trading debt arises from the ordinary activities of the business but since such an amount is material to the accounts it should be shown as an exceptional item.

2

(a) The profit on redemption is £60,500 which is material. It should be described as an extraordinary item since it both derives from outside the ordinary activities of the company and is not expected to recur.

(b) Since this payment relates to a *newly acquired* subsidiary it is effectively an additional cost of acquisition and therefore the best treatment for this item would be to increase the goodwill on acquisition by £65,000.

An alternative treatment that might be supported on the grounds that the additional payment is at the discretion of the directors would be as an exceptional item charged against ordinary profits (since pension arrangements are part of the ordinary activities of a company).

(c) The correction of a previous year's underprovision of corporation tax will be included in the current year's taxation charge, and separately disclosed as a note to the taxation charge.

The treatment of the reduction in the taxation payable due to the availability of stock relief would depend upon whether, in the opinion of the directors, the charge will become payable within the foreseeable future as a result of stock relief clawback. If no clawback is foreseen, then it will not be necessary to provide for any taxation in respect of the stock relief claimed but the effect of the stock relief in reducing the tax charge should be disclosed by way of note.

If on the other hand a clawback is foreseen then deferred taxation should be provided for in respect of the stock relief. (Dr profit and loss account £240,000. Cr deferred taxation £240,000.)

(d)   If the directors wish to write off goodwill immediately in accordance with ED 30 it can be written off immediately against reserves representing realised profits. Details of the accounting policy followed should be given in the notes to the accounts and the amount of goodwill written off to reserves should be shown in the accounts.

(e)   The company may treat this either as an exceptional item, or an extraordinary item, depending on the circumstances. If the company regularly sells property, then the surplus of £300,000 should be disclosed as an exceptional item. Such companies include, for example, large multi-branch retailers, since surpluses are expected to recur. If the company is selling its property as a result of a discontinuance of a significant part of the business or the sale is not expected to recur, then the gain on sale should be disclosed as an extraordinary item, net of attributable taxation.

Generally, a note should disclose the nature of all extraordinary items.

3   Profit and loss account for the year ended 31 December

	1982 £ thousands	1981 £ thousands
Turnover	X	X
Cost of sales	X	X
	X	X
Distribution expenses	X	X
Administrative expenses (Note 1)	(X + 360)	(X + 194)
Profit on ordinary activities before tax	1,565	1,490
Taxation (Note 2)	485	462
Profit after taxation before extraordinary items	1,080	1,028
Dividends	250	250
Retained profit	830	778
Statement of retained profit/reserves		
Retained profit for the year	830	778

	1982 £ thousands	1981 £ thousands
brought forward	830	778

Retained profits/reserves
at beginning of year:

	£ thousands	£ thousands
As previously reported	14,629	13,842
Prior-year adjustment (Note 3)	1,545	1,436
As restated	13,184	12,406
Retained profits/reserves at end of year	14,014	13,184

Notes

1 The items before tax are stated after charging:

	1982 £ thousands	1981 £ thousands
Depreciation	X	X
Expenditure on research and development	360	194

2 The taxation charge is UK corporation tax at 52%

	1982 £ thousands	1981 £ thousands
Current year's profits	449	462
Adjustments to prior-year	36	—
	485	462

3 Prior-year adjustments relate to the following:

(i) A change of accounting policy adopted in respect of research and development expenditure. In previous years the company capitalised such expenditure and amortised it over 10 years but now all such expenditure is written off in the year in which it is incurred.

(ii) A change of accounting policy in respect of purchased goodwill. In previous years the goodwill was retained in the accounts at original cost but it has now been decided to adopt the policy of immediate write-off as per ED 30 'Accounting for goodwill'.

The details of the prior-year adjustments are:

	1982 £ thousands	1981 £ thousands
Goodwill written off	500	500
Research and development expenditure	945	936
	1,545	1,436

(a) (i) The profit on the sale of shop premises is a material item which does not arise from the ordinary activities of the business. However, this arises as a result of a programme of updating and improving shop premises and so can be expected to recur regularly. The item is not therefore 'extraordinary', but since it is material will require disclosure because of its abnormal size and incidence.

(ii) The misstatement of stocks in the previous year's accounts would almost certainly be regarded as fundamental since it would understate the 1981 profits by £900,000 with a corresponding overstatement in profits in 1982. The item, less attributable taxation, should be treated as a prior-year adjustment, with a note explaining the nature of the adjustment.

(iii) The cost of recalling beds for checking and repair arises from the ordinary activities of the business. It does not arise either as a result of a fundamental error or change of accounting policy and so should not be treated as a prior-year adjustment. It should therefore be treated as an exceptional item, separately disclosed.

(iv) This item requires consideration of ED 16 and the Companies Act 1981 as well as SSAP 6 plus the SSAP 6 discussion paper. The revaluation surplus of £4 million must be taken direct to reserves. The revaluation deficit of £500,000 will be taken to the profit and loss account to the extent that it is not covered by previous unrealised surpluses on the same assets. Thus £200,000 will be taken to revaluation reserve and the remaining £300,000 written off to the profit and loss account, being disclosed as an exceptional item. The revaluation surplus of £150,000 realised on disposal can also be credited to the profit and loss account.

(v) From the question it would appear that the investments were not acquired with the specific intention of resale and so the profit on the sale should be treated as an extraordinary item, net of attributable taxation.

(b) **Profit and loss account for the year to 31 December**

	1982		1981	
	£	£	£	£
	thousands	thousands	thousands	thousands
Turnover		78,000		71,000
Profit on ordinary activities before tax		6,140		8,400
Taxation (W2) on profit on ordinary activities		3,164		4,200
Profit on ordinary activities after tax		2,976		4,200

	1982 £ thousands	1982 £ thousands	1981 £ thousands	1981 £ thousands
brought forward		2,976		4,200
Extraordinary items less taxation		1,400		–
Profit for the financial year		4,376		4,200
Dividends proposed		2,000		2,000
Retained profit for the year		2,376		2,200
Retained profit brought forward				
As previously reported	19,000		17,250	
Prior-year adjustment (Note 3)	450		–	
As restated		19,450		17,250
		21,826		19,450
Transfer from capital reserve on realisation of revalued properties		150		–
		21,976		19,450

Notes

1 Profit is shown after charging:

	£ thousands	£ thousands
Cost of recalling defective goods	980	–
Revaluation deficits	300	–
and after crediting:		
Surplus on sale of properties	320	–

2 **Extraordinary item**

The extraordinary item relates to the sale of investments previously held for long-term.

	1982 £ thousands	1981 £ thousands
Profit on sale of investments	2,000	–
Taxation thereon	600	–
	1,400	–

3 **Prior-year adjustment**

A prior-year adjustment has been made to correct a fundamental error in the stock figure which was understated by £900,000 at 31 December 1981. In restating the 1981 figures, profit before taxation has been increased by £900,000 and the taxation charge by £450,000.

Workings

1 Profit before taxation and extraordinary items

	£ thousands
Per question	8,000
Cost of recalling defective goods	(980)
Revaluation deficit	(300)
Surplus on sale of properties	320
Increase in value of opening stock	(900)
	6,140

2 Taxation charge

	£ thousands
Per question	4,000
Tax on surplus on sale of properties	104
Adjustment on adjustment of opening stock	(450)
Tax on costs of recalling defective goods	(490)
	3,164

5

(a)   (i)   The loss on sale of machinery is correctly treated as an extraordinary item, since it arises from the discontinuance of a (presumably) significant part of the business, the enforced sale of the foreign-based subsidiary companies, which is an event outside the ordinary activities of the business. This view accords with the suggestions made in the SSAP 6 discussion paper.

     (ii)   The work in progress adjustment is wrongly included as an extraordinary item in the statement of 1982 profits. It arises from the ordinary activities of the business and thus falls outside the definition of extraordinary items in SSAP 6, paragraph 11.

It is also wrongly included as a prior-year adjustment, since it arises neither from the correction of a fundamental error, nor from a change in accounting policy. It is merely a change in an accounting estimate and therefore should be included in the ordinary profits for the year.

    (iii)   The bad debt provision is wrongly treated as an extraordinary item in the statement of 1982 profits, since it arises from the ordinary activities of the business. It is correctly shown as a prior-year adjustment since it can be considered to be a change in accounting policy.

    (iv)   The loss on sale of subsidiaries is correctly treated as an extraordinary item, since it arises from the discontinuance of a significant part of the company's business (see (i) above).

    (v)   The additional charge for research expenditure is correctly treated as a prior-year adjustment, since it arises from a change in accounting policy. The amounts included in the restatement of the previous year's results are, however, not correct. The additional charge of £45,000 for 1981 should be included in the 1981 results and the prior-year adjustment at 1 January 1982 should be £72,000.

(b) (i)   The circumstances which resulted in the loss on sale of machinery should be described in a note to the accounts.

(ii) The work in progress adjustment should be included in the profit before extraordinary items. However, the amount of the adjustment should be disclosed in a note to the accounts because of its abnormal size and incidence.

(iii) The bad debt provision is a prior-year adjustment necessitating the re-statement of 1981 results and retained profits brought forward to 1982. This change in accounting policy should be disclosed in a note to the accounts, with the £10,000 adjustment being divided between the amount arising in 1981 and the amount arising in earlier years. The £7,000 charge for 1982 should be included in the profit before extra-ordinary items, and the amount disclosed in the note.

(iv) The circumstances causing the loss on sale of subsidiaries should be described in the note to the accounts.

(v) The change in accounting policy in relation to research expenditure should be disclosed in a note to the accounts, and the £72,000 adjustment apportioned between 1981 (£45,000) and earlier years (£27,000).

Assuming that the whole of the bad debt provision of £10,000 at 31 December 1981 arose during 1981 then the corrected statement of retained profits would be as follows:

	1982		1981	
	£	£	£	£
Retained profit for the year		122,000(W1)		82,000(W2)
Profits brought forward as previously stated	177,000		40,000	
Prior-year adjustments:				
Research expenditure	72,000		27,000	
Bad debt provision	10,000		–	
Profits brought forward as restated		95,000		13,000
Profits carried forward		172,000		95,000

Workings

1 **Retained profit for 1982**

	£
Retained profit per question	134,000
Less: Work in progress adjustment incorrectly treated as prior-year adjustment	12,000
	122,000

2 **Retained profit for 1981**

	£	£
Retained profit per question		137,000
Less: Restatement for changes in accounting policies		
Research expenditure	45,000	
Bad debt provision	10,000	
		55,000
		82,000

4 SSAP 9

INTRODUCTION

SSAP 9 was issued in May 1975 in an attempt to narrow the differences and variations in computations of the value at which stocks and work in progress are stated in financial accounts.

In summary, stocks and work in progress need to be stated at cost or, if lower, at net realisable value.

The comparison of cost and net realisable value needs to be made in respect of each major category of stock items.

The cost of stocks and work in progress should comprise that expenditure which has been incurred in the normal course of business in bringing the product or service to its present location and condition.

Such costs will include all related production overheads, even though these accrue on a time basis.

Net realisable value is defined in the statement as the amount at which it is expected that items of stocks and work in progress can be disposed of without creating either profit or loss in the year of sale; that is, the estimated proceeds of sale less all *further costs* to completion and less all costs to be incurred in marketing, selling and distributing directly related to the items in question.

The statement gives separate attention to long-term contract work in progress. Where a business carries out contracts and it is considered that their outcome can be assessed with reasonable certainty before their conclusion, then the attributable profit should be taken up, but the judgment involved should be exercised with prudence. If, however, a loss is foreseen on a contract as a whole, then prudence dictates that the whole of the loss should be provided for as soon as it is recognised. There is no one unique method of computing attributable profit and the reader's attention is drawn to the different treatments in the questions and answers.

A study of the SSAP will prove beneficial to the reader.

QUESTIONS

1 'The amount at which stocks and work in progress, other than long-term contract work in progress, is stated in periodic financial statements should be the total of the lower of cost and net realisable value of the separate items of stock and work in progress or of groups of similar items.' (SSAP 9, paragraph 26.)

You are required, in the context of that accounting standard:

(a) To define the phrase 'net realisable value'. *5 marks*

(b) To say whether 'replacement cost' is acceptable as an alternative basis of valuation and, if so, in what circumstances. *5 marks*

(c) To say whether overheads should be included in cost and if so to what extent. *5 marks*

(d) To explain *briefly* the following methods of valuing stock and work in progress:

    (i) Adjusted (discounted) selling price.
    (ii) First in, first out.
    (iii) Last in, last out.
    (iv) Base stock. *5 marks*

Note. You are not required to write on references to stock valuation in SSAP 16.

Total 20 marks

2 A company processes and sells a single product. Purchases of raw materials during the year were made at a regular rate of 1,000 tonnes at the beginning of each week. The price was £100 per tonne on 1 January 1983 and was increased to £150 per tonne on 1 July 1983 and remained constant from then until the end of the year, 31 December 1983. In addition to this a customs duty of £10 per tonne was paid throughout the year, and transport from the docks to the factory cost £20 per tonne.

Variable costs of processing were £25 per tonne; there was a capacity to process 1,500 tonnes per week and the fixed production costs for all levels of production activity up to this capacity level were £30,000 per week. One tonne of raw material is processed into one tonne of finished product and sold, at a delivered price of £240 per tonne, by a sales force whose cost was fixed at £3,000 per week. Average delivery costs to customers were £7.50 per tonne.

At the beginning of the year there were no stocks and at the end of the year there were 5,000 tonnes of raw materials and 2,000 tonnes of finished. It is expected that the costs and prices current at 31 December 1983 will continue during 1984.

You are required:

(a) To draft a statement of accounting policy on stock for the company to include in its annual accounts. *4 marks*

(b)   To calculate the value of stock at 31 December 1983 on a basis acceptable under SSAP 9.   *7 marks*

(c)   To calculate the value of raw material stock at 31 December 1983 on a LIFO basis.   *2 marks*

(d)   To comment upon the relative merits of FIFO and LIFO, and two other bases recognised under SSAP 9 for valuing stock.   *6 marks*

Total 19 marks

3   Colchester Ltd has for many years calculated the selling price of its products by adding 40% on to production cost. Relevant information for the year ended 31 December 19X4 is as follows:

Product	Spade	Shovel	Pick
Labour per unit	£4.75	£3.60	£2.80
Materials per unit	£6.20	£4.00	£2.65
Sales in units	10,000	6,250	5,000

Factory overheads	£
Factory rent	13,220
Facotry rates and insurance	4,500
Factory power (variable)	8,530
Plant maintenance (variable)	3,100
Plant depreciation	5,540
Factory canteen	3,360

You are required:

(a)   To calculate the selling price of each product assuming that factory overheads are apportioned on the basis of the number of units produced and sold (existing policy).   *5 marks*

(b)   To recalculate the selling prices assuming that the factory overheads will be apportioned using the following additional information:

(i)   All labour is paid at the same rate.
(ii)   The three products are produced on identical machines, and machine time per unit is as follows:
Spade   1.845 hours
Shovel   1.100 hours
Pick   0.750 hours   *8 marks*

(c)   To calculate the effect on profit of adopting the new policy outlined in (b) above if it is further assumed that demand for spades will fall by 500 units as a result of the new selling price.   *8 marks*

Calculate all selling prices to the nearest penny

Total 21 marks

59

4   The annual stocktaking of Ringers Ltd did not take place on the company's year end on 30 April 1983 because of staff illness. However, stock was taken at the close of business on 8 May 1983 and the resultant valuation of £23,850 was used in the preparation of the company's draft accounts for the year ended 30 April 1983 which showed a gross profit of £158,000, a net profit of £31,640 and net current assets at 30 April 1983 of £24,600.

Subsequent investigations indicated that during the period from 30 April to 8 May 1983 sales were £2,900, sales returns £340, purchases £4,200 and purchase returns £500.

In addition it was discovered that:

(i)   A quantity of stock bought in 1982 and included in the stock valuation at 8 May 1983 at a cost of £200 was, in fact, worthless. Instructions have now been given for the destruction of this stock.

(ii)   Two of the stock sheets prepared on 8 May 1983 had been overcast by £100 and £40 respectively.

(iii)   The stock valuation of 8 May 1983 included the company's office stationery stock of £1,400. (It can be assumed that the stationery did not materially change between 30 April and 8 May 1983.)

(iv)   The valuation at 8 May 1983 had not included goods, which had cost Ringers Ltd £400, sent on a sale or return basis to John Winters Ltd in February 1983. Half of these goods, in value, were bought by John Winters Ltd on 29 April 1983, but the sale has not been recorded in the draft accounts of Ringers Ltd for the year ended 30 April 1983.

Ringers Ltd achieves a uniform rate of gross profit of 20% on all sales revenue.

You are required to prepare:

(a)   A computation of Ringers Ltd's corrected stock valuation at 30 April 1983.
10 marks

(b)   A computation of Ringers Ltd's corrected gross profit and net profit for the year ended 30 April 1983, and the corrected net current assets at 30 April 1983.
10 marks
Total 20 marks

5   Carter Engineering plc undertakes a variety of manufacturing and construction work. At the end of its financial year to 30 June 1984, decisions are needed on how to deal with the following items when closing off the accounts:

(a)   A contract for A plc was commenced in February 1984 and should be completed by July 1986. The contract price is £335,000, and the original estimate of total costs of £245,000. Work in progress to date is valued at £68,000.

(b) A contract for B plc was commenced in February 1983 and should be completed by August 1984. The contract price is £480,000, and work in progress to date is valued at £340,000. It is estimated that a further £60,000 costs will be incurred before completion.

(c) The raw materials stock includes some items costing £12,000 which were bought for processing and assembly against a special order. Since buying these items the cost price has fallen to £10,000.

(d) A customer, D Ltd, ordered a special-purpose machine at an agreed price of £60,000. The manufacture was completed in October 1983 at a cost of £46,800. However, because D Ltd was then experiencing exceptional cash-flow problems, it was agreed that the sale should be on hire-purchase terms with an initial deposit of £6,000 and four half-yearly instalments of £15,000 each. By June 1984 the deposit and one instalment had been paid.

(e) E Ltd had ordered some equipment to be designed and constructed at an agreed price of £18,000. This has recently been completed at a cost of £16,800 — higher than expected, due to unforeseen problems. It has now been discovered that the design does not meet certain statutory regulations, and conversion at an estimated extra cost of £4,200 will be required. E Ltd has accepted partial responsibility and agreed to meet half of the extra cost.

You are required, for each of the above items, to say what figure you would include in stock (or work in progress) at 30 June 1984, and give a short explanation of the principle(s) or reasoning behind your answer. If appropriate, indicate any assumptions or qualifications where additional information may be required.

15 marks

6 Monsal Ltd is a manufacturing company producing and selling three products, Tipps, Lotts and Netts, all derived from the same basic raw material. Your review of the costing system has revealed that joint costs including production overheads are allocated to products for costing and stock valuation purposes on the basis of physical quantities produced. The summarised management accounts (which will form the basis of the financial statements upon which you are required to report as auditor) for the year ended 30 April 1983 are as follows:

	Tipps	Lotts	Netts	Total
Selling price	£25	£15	£30	
Sales (units)	8,000	18,000	6,000	
	£	£	£	£
Sales	200,000	270,000	180,000	650,000
Cost of sales	(127,400)	(312,000)	(108,600)	(548,000)
Gross profit (loss)	72,600)	(42,000)	71,400	102,000
Selling expenses	(12,000)	(18,000)	(12,000)	(42,000)
	60,600	(60,000)	59,400	60,000
Administration and financial expenses				(20,000)
Net profit before tax				40,000

	Tipps	Lotts	Netts
Unit cost of sales	15.93	17.33	18.10
Unit selling expenses	1.50	1.00	2.00

Your review of cost of sales and stock reveals that these headings include distribution costs to the company's own depots from which customers collect goods. You note also that stock has been valued at cost.

Required:

(a) Explain why it is part of the work of an auditor to review and test the costing system. *5 marks*

(b) Comment on the following features of the accounts of Monsal and describe what action you would take as auditor:

    (i) Costs of distribution to the company's own depots are included in cost of sales.

    (ii) The cost of sales of Lotts is £17.33 per unit and selling cost of that product is £1.00 per unit, selling price being £15 only. (You may assume that the number of Lotts on hand at 30 April 1983 is 2,500 units.)

Your answer should refer to the requirements of SSAP 9 ('Stocks and work in progress') and give calculations as appropriate. *6 marks*

(c) Show what matters you would consider if the company were to suggest changing the basis of allocation of joint costs to products for the current and preceding year from physical quantity basis to sales value basis so that cost of sales figures would read:

	£	Unit cost £
Tipps	152,000	19.00
Lotts	250,000	13.89
Netts	146,000	24.33
Total	548,000	

6 marks
Total 17 marks

7   Custom Boatbuilders are an old established firm carrying on business as manufacturers of sailing dinghies with a trade price in the range £2,000 to £5,000 and also as builders of individually designed yachts under contract.

The following data have been supplied by the firm's accountant for the year ended 30 November 1982.

| | Total for year £ | Dinghies at year end | | Contract Yachts at year end | | |
		Work in progress £	Finished stock £	Yacht X £	Yacht Y £	Yacht Z £
Direct material	500,000	20,000	40,000	20,000	32,000	5,000
Direct labour	400,000	10,000	35,000	25,000	38,000	1,000
	900,000	30,000	75,000	45,000	70,000	6,000
Overheads						
Production	800,000					
Selling	100,000					
Administration	200,000					
	2,000,000					

The following data have been provided by the management to assist in valuing the stock for inclusion in the balance sheet.

(i) The finished stock (£75,000) includes the cost of three dinghies that fail to satisfy class specifications and it is proposed to offer the three for sale at £2,000 each. The records show that the cost incurred in building the three dinghies was £9,000 (being material £5,000 and labour £4,000).

The marketing manager estimates that the remaining dinghies in finished stock will realise £200,000.

(ii) The data in respect of the yachts (X, Y, Z) being built under contract are as follows:

	Yacht X £	Yacht Y £	Yacht Z £
Estimate of final cost			
Direct material	24,000	36,000	40,000
Direct labour	30,000	42,000	25,000
	54,000	78,000	65,000
Value of work certified at year end	110,000	160,000	6,000
Progress payments received by year end	85,000	90,000	4,000
Progress payments invoiced but not received at year end	5,000	10,000	—
Final contract price	130,000	175,000	110,000

Required:

(a) Calculate the valuation of finished stock, work in progress and long-term contracts for inclusion in the balance sheet as at 30 November 1982 and show an appropriate balance sheet extract. *23 marks*

(b) Briefly discuss the relevant provisions of the Statement of Standard Accounting Practice on stock and work in progress and state any assumption you have made in calculating your valuation.

7 marks
Total 30 marks

ANSWERS

1

(a) Net realisable value is the actual or estimated selling price (net of trade but before settlement discounts) less:

    (i)   All further costs to completion; and

    (ii)   All costs to be incurred in marketing, selling and distributing the stock items.

(b) Replacement cost is the cost at which an identical asset could be purchased or manufactured.

In normal circumstances replacement cost would not be an acceptable alternative basis of valuation for stock. The standard requires the lower of cost or net realisable value.

In Appendix 3 to the standard it is recognised that 'where the value of the raw material content forms a high proportion of the total value of stock in process of production and the price of the raw materials is liable to considerable fluctuation, it is common practice to make rapid changes in selling prices to accord with the changes in the price of the raw material'. In cases of this kind the replacement cost will form the best guide to the net realisable value and can be extended as a valuation base for raw materials, stock in process of production and finished stock.

(c) SSAP 9 defines 'cost' as being the expenditure incurred in the normal course of business in bringing the product/service to its present location and condition. This 'cost' should include cost of purchase and costs of conversion. Costs of conversion are defined as including direct costs, production overhead (including those accruing wholly or partly on a time basis, i.e., fixed overheads) and 'other overheads', if any, attributable in the particular circumstances of the business in bringing the product/service to its present location and condition.

'Other overheads' which could be taken into account include:

    (i)   Distribution costs incurred in getting the stock to its present location.

    (ii)   Costs of service departments which have been apportioned between the main functions of the business, particularly those included in production overheads.

(d) (i)   The adjusted (discounted) selling price method of valuation is used primarily in retail stores which hold a large number of rapidly changing individual items, where 'cost' is calculated by deducting from stock valued at its original selling price the estimated gross profit percentage. This is acceptable under SSAP 9 as being the only practical method, in the particular circumstance, of arriving at a figure which approximates to cost.

(ii) In the first in, first out method the cost of stocks and work in progress is calculated on the basis that the quantities on hand represent the latest purchases or production.

(iii) In the last in, last out method the basis for the calculation of the cost of stocks and work in progress is that the quantities in hand represent the earliest purchases or production.

(iv) In the base stock method the basis for the calculation of the cost of stocks and work in progress is that a fixed unit value is ascribed to a predetermined number of units of stock, any excess over this number being valued on the basis of some other method. If the number of units of stock is less than the predetermined minimum, the fixed unit value is applied to the number in stock.

2

(a) **Accounting policy on stocks**

Stocks are stated at the lower of cost and net realisable value.

'Cost' is the cost incurred in bringing each product to its present location and condition. In the case of raw materials this is the purchase cost on a first-in, first-out basis. In the case of work in progress and finished goods it is the cost of direct materials and labour plus attributable overheads based on the normal level of activity.

'Net realisable value' is based on estimated selling price less further costs expected to be incurred to completion and disposal.

(b) **Value of stock at 31 December 1983 (W2)**

	£
Raw materials	900,000
Finished products and work in progress	476,666
	1,376,666

(c) **Value of raw material stock at 31 December 1983 (W3)**
Using LIFO basis £775,000

(d) The various bases of calculating stock values under SSAP 9 are:

(i) FIFO — on the basis that the quantities in hand represent the latest purchases or production.

(ii) LIFO — on the basis that the quantities in hand represent the earliest purchases or production.

(iii) Average cost — on the basis of applying to the units of stock in hand an average price computed by dividing the total cost of units by the total number of such units.

(iv) Base stock — on the basis that a fixed unit value is ascribed to a predetermined number of units of stock, any excess over this number being valued on the basis of some other method. If the number of units of stock is less than the predeterminded minimum then the fixed unit value is applied to the number in stock.

(v) Standard costs − on the basis of periodically predetermined costs calculated from management's estimates of expected levels of costs and of operations and operational efficiency and the related expenditure.

(vi) Unit cost − the cost of purchasing or manufacturing identifiable units of stock.

The standard requires management to exercise judgment to ensure that the method(s) chosen provide the fairest practicable approximation to 'actual cost': furthermore, where standard costs are used they need to be reviewed frequently to ensure that they bear a reasonable relationship to actual costs obtained during the period.

Methods such as base stock and LIFO do not usually bear such a relationship.

Unit cost, the specific tracing of expenditure direct to units, obviously will most closely fulfil the requirement of an 'actual' or historical cost; this would apply to both the balance sheet valuation and the profit and loss account calculation of cost of sales.

Where unit cost is not available the two other common methods are average cost and FIFO. Both methods are relatively simple to operate. However, although FIFO presents a reasonable approximation of actual cost for balance sheet purposes, it produces charges to the profit and loss account based on transactions (costs) further in time from the realisation dates.

Workings

1 Assume a 50-week year. 25 weeks to 30 June, and 25 weeks to 31 December. Then a trading account, quantity only, would appear as:

	Tonnes	Tonnes
Sales		43,000
Less: Cost of sales		
Raw materials:		
Purchased (1,000 tonnes per week X 50 weeks)	50,000	
In stock	5,000	
Production of finished products	45,000	
Less: Stock of finished products	2,000	
Finished products sold	43,000	

2   Using the FIFO basis:

	£ per tonne
Raw materials	
Material cost (over last five weeks)	150
Customs duty	10
Freight from docks to factory	20
	180

So the total cost of 5,000 tonnes is 5,000 × £180 = £900,000.

	£ per tonne
Finished products	
Raw material content — as above	180
Variable overheads	25
Fixed production costs	33⅓*
	238⅓

$$* \frac{\text{fixed production costs per week}}{\text{normal level of activity per week}} = \frac{£30,000}{(45,000 \text{ tonnes} \div 50)} = £33⅓ \text{ per tonne}$$

So the total cost of 2,000 tonnes is 2,000 × £238⅓ = £476,666.

3   Using the LIFO basis:

	Tonnes
Weekly — purchase	1,000
— production	900
Weekly build up of stock	100

	Tonnes	£
Raw materials		
25 weeks × 100 tonnes × £100	2,500	250,000
25 weeks × 100 tonnes × £150	2,500	375,000
	5,000	625,000
Customs duty 5,000 × £10		50,000
Freight 5,000 × £20		100,000
		775,000

3

(a)   Number of units produced = 10,000 + 6,250 + 5,000 = 21,250
Budgeted factory overheads = £38,250
Rate per unit = £38,250 ÷ 21,250 = 1.80

	Spade	Shovel	Pick
	£	£	£
Labour	4.75	3.60	2.80
Materials	6.20	4.00	2.65
Overhead	1.80	1.80	1.80
Production cost	12.75	9.40	7.25
Add 40%	5.10	3.76	2.90
Selling price	17.85	13.16	10.15

(b) Labour costs

			£
Spade	10,000 × £4.75	=	47,500
Shovel	6,250 × £3.60	=	22,500
Pick	5,000 × £2.80	=	14,000
			84,000

Canteen costs per £ labour £3,360 ÷ 84,000	=	0.04

Canteen cost per unit

Spade	4.75 × 0.04	=	0.19
Shovel	3.60 × 0.04	=	0.144
Pick	2.80 × 0.04	=	0.112

Machine time used

			Hours
Spade	10,000 × 1.845	=	18,450
Shovel	6,250 × 1.100	=	6,875
Pick	5,000 × 0.750	=	3,750
			29,075

Other production overhead costs = £38,250 − £3,360 = £34,890
Other costs per machine hour = £34,890 ÷ 29,075 = £1.20

Other costs per unit

			£
Spade	1.845 × £1.20	=	2.214
Shovel	1.100 × £1.20	=	1.32
Pick	0.750 × £1.20	=	0.90

	Spade £	Shovel £	Pick £
Labour	4.75	3.60	2.80
Materials	6.20	4.00	2.65
Canteen	0.19	0.144	0.112
Overhead	2.214	1.32	0.90
Production cost	13.354	9.064	6.462
Add 40%	5.342	3.623	2.584
Selling price (to nearest penny)	18.70	12.69	9.05

(c) All fixed costs may be ignored because they will be the same whatever the number of sales.

Cost of factory power and plant maintenance per machine hour is (£8,530 + £3,100) ÷ 29,075 = £0.40.

Cost per unit			£
Spade	1.845 × 0.40	=	0.738
Shovel	1.100 × 0.40	=	0.44
Pick	0.750 × 0.40	=	0.30

Under the existing policy:

	Spade £	Shovel £	Pick £
Selling price	17.85	13.16	10.15
Labour	(4.75)	(3.60)	(2.80)
Materials	(6.20)	(4.00)	(2.65)
Variable overhead	(0.738)	(0.44)	(0.30)
Contribution per unit	6.162	5.12	4.40

Total contribution is 10,000 × £6.162 + 6,250 × £5.12 + 5,000 × £4.40 = £115,620.

Under the proposed policy:

	Spade £	Shovel £	Pick £
Selling price	18.70	12.69	9.05
Labour	(4.75)	(3.60)	(2.80)
Materials	(6.20)	(4.00)	(2.65)
Variable overhead	(0.738)	(0.44)	(0.30)
Contribution per unit	7.012	4.65	3.30

Total contribution is 9,500 × £7.012 + 6,250 × £4.65 + 5,000 × £3.30 = £112,176.50.

Profit will fall by £115,620 − £112,176.50 = £3,443.50.

4

(a) Adjustment to stock: correction to 30 April 1983 from 8 May 1983.

		£
Stock valuation, close of business 8 May 1983		23,850
Adjustments for stock movements between 30 April and 8 May 1983:		
Deduct: Net purchase of period (£4,200 − £500)		(3,700)
		20,150
Add: Cost of goods sold in the period		
Sales: net (£2,900 − £340)	2,560	
Less: Gross profit (20% on sales)	(512)	2,048
		22,198
Adjustments required from notes (i) to (iv)		
(i) Stock write-down	(700)	
(ii) Reduction of value: overcasting (£100 + £40)	(140)	
(iii) Stationery stock: will not affect stock valuation	–	
(iv) Stock increased by cost of goods still held on sale or return basis (£400 ÷ 2)	200	(640)
Corrected value of stock at 30 April 1983		21,558

(b)

	Gross profit £	Net profit £	Net current assets £
Per draft accounts at 30 April 1983	158,000	31,640	24,600
Net reduction in value of closing stock (£23,850 − £21,558) giving a reduction of	(2,292)	(2,292)	(2,292)
Reallocation of stationery stock reduces gross profit only	(1,400)	–	–
Sales not recorded: note (iv)*			
Increase in profits	250	250	–
Increase in debtors	–	–	250
Corrected figures	154,558	29,598	22,558

*Cost of unrecorded sales is £200 which represents 80% of sales value. So the sales value is £200 × 100/80 = £250.

5 SSAP 9 states that the valuation of work in progress should include attributable profit; in calculating such attributable profit, account should be taken of the type of business concerned. Also it is necessary to define the earliest point for each particular contract before which no profit is taken up, the overriding principle being that there can be no attributable profit until the outcome of a contract can reasonably be foreseen.

(a) As far as this contract is concerned no attributable profit would be included in the valuation because:

   (i)   Only five months have elapsed out of a 30-month contract.
   (ii) Only about a quarter of the total costs have been completed and therefore the outcome cannot be reasonably foreseen.

   Consideration should be given to any foreseeable losses but as the estimated costs to completion are not provided this cannot be done.

(b) The contract with B plc is within two months of completion (out of a total of 19 months); also 85% of the total estimated costs have been incurred so the outcome of the contract can be reasonably foreseen as:

	£	£
Contract price		480,000
Less: Costs to date	340,000	
Estimated costs to completion	60,000	
	———	(400,000)
Estimated final profit on contract		80,000

   The attributable profit to be taken up 'needs to reflect the proportion of the work carried out at the accounting date and to take into account any inequalities of profitability in the various stages of a contract ... but the judgment involved should be exercised with prudence' (SSAP 9, paragraph 8).

   In this case the attributable profit would be £80,000 × 340,000/400,000 = £68,000.

(c) There is insufficient information to determine how to treat the raw materials of £12,000. If the contract for the special order is a fixed-price contract and the raw material prices used in setting the contract price were incurred then the figure of £12,000 can stand. However, if the actual cost of the raw materials purchased exceeded the cost used in setting the contract price then the excess should be written off only to the extent that it makes the contract unprofitable.

(d) In this case D Ltd has received the completed machine and it therefore would not appear within the stock valuation. However, depending on the method used for accounting for hire-purchase sales and debtors it is possible that an item could appear within current assets as stock on hire.

(e) As the equipment ordered does not comply with certain statutory regulations, further additional costs of conversion have to be incurred. Looking at the figures involved:

	£	£	£
Agreed price of equipment	18,000		18,000
Costs to date	16,800	16,800	
Costs of conversion		4,200	
		21,000	
Half costs of conversion borne by E Ltd		(2,100)	
			18,900
Expected profit	1,200		
Forseeable loss			(900)

As the current situation with this order (we are not told whether it is a long or short-term contract) is that a loss of £900 can be foreseen then that much needs to be charged against revenue in this financial year leaving a valuation of £15,900 for the work in progress.

In cases (a), (b), (c) and (e) no information is given of any payments to date.

Figures to be included in stocks would be:

	(a) £	(b) £	(c) £	(d) £	(e) £	Total £
Raw materials and consumables	–	–	12,000	–	–	12,000
Work in progress						
At cost	68,000	340,000	–	–	16,800	424,800
Provision for forseeable losses	–	–	–	–	(900)	(900)
Attributable profit on long-term contract	–	68,000	–	–	–	68,000
	68,000	408,000	–	–	15,900	491,900
Payments on account	?	?	?	–	?	?
Total	?	?	?	–	?	?

6

(a) The management accounts, according to the information given in the question, form the basis from which the financial statements are prepared. Therefore, with respect to the valuation of stocks and work in progress and the valuation of the cost of goods sold, the auditor would need to review and test the underlying costing system for the following reasons:

(i)   To check that the basis of cost determination is satisfactory. Here attention is directed to the make-up of the individual variable, semi-variable and fixed costs, ensuring that they have been based on actual costs incurred. A fully integrated financial and cost accounting system should ensure this. Further the auditor will check that the overheads have also been realistically determined and allocated on an appropriate, and consistently applied, basis to the individual product groups. To comply with SSAP 9, for stock valuation, it will be necessary to test to ensure that the overheads have been allocated on the company's normal level of activity, taking one year with another.

(ii)   To check that the costing records identify and comprise all expenditure incurred in bringing the stock and work in progress to its present location and condition; and that at the accounting date the cost and quantities of the stock and work in progress are available and can be checked against their physical existence and the basis of cost determination.

(iii)   To check that the determination of the net realisable value for each product group is linked in with the costing system to enable all future costs of production necessary to bring the stock to its saleable condition to be calculated together with costs to be incurred in marketing, selling and distribution. This is of particular importance if:

(1)   There is an increase in costs or a fall in selling price.
(2)   There is physical deterioration of stocks.
(3)   There is obsolescence of products.
(4)   There is a decision as a part of a company's marketing strategy to manufacture and sell products at a loss.
(5)   There are errors in production or purchasing.
(6)   There are stocks which are unlikely to be sold within the turn-over period normal in that company.

(b) (i)   Costs of distribution to the company's own depots are included in cost of sales. This appears to conform with SSAP 9 in that it is a cost incurred in bringing the stock to its present condition and *location*. This being so then the analysis would seem to be correct; also when looking at the 'cost' of stock held, the location of the stock and any related distribution cost will have to be considered carefully for consistency of application and prudence. Tests would need to be made by the auditor on the way these costs were calculated. The procedures adopted by the company for allocation of transport and other distribution costs to cost of sales/stocks should also be reviewed.

(ii)   SSAP 9 requires stock to be valued at the lower of cost and net realisable value. In this company's case, and particularly the Lotts, the following would apply:

	£/unit
Cost, after being satisfied that joint costs have been allocated on a consistently applied basis	17.33

Selling price, ascertained by examining post balance
sheet events, i.e., the sale of Lotts after 30 April 1983   15.00
Deduct: Selling costs, assuming these to be wholly
incurred between 30 April 1983 and the date of sale
and allocated over normal level of activity   1.00

Net realisable value per unit   14.00

In this instance the stock of Lotts would be valued, in accordance with
SSAP 9, at 2,500 × £14.00 = £35,000.

The effect of this change in valuation would be an adjustment of
2,500 × (£17.33 − £14.00) = £8,325, as shown below:

	Lotts £	Total £
Cost of sales	(320,325)	(556,325)
Gross profit	(50,325)	93,675
Net profit before tax		31,675

(c)   If the company adopted the new basis of allocation of joint costs to products
then the revised management accounts would read:

	Tipps	Lotts	Netts	Total
Selling price	£25	£15	£30	
Sales (units)	8,000	18,000	6,000	
	£	£	£	£
Sales income	200,000	270,000	180,000	650,000
Cost of sales	(152,000)	(250,000)	(146,000)	(548,000)
Gross profit	48,000	20,000	34,000	102,000
Selling expenses	(12,000)	(18,000)	(12,000)	(42,000)
	36,000	2,000	22,000	60,000

Administration and financial expenses   (20,000)

   40,000

The reallocation of the joint costs produces an analysis of the gross profit by
products and shows them all to be profitable; while at the same time the total
profit earned by the company would remain at £40,000.

One valuation problem does, however, disappear — that of valuing the Lotts
at their net realisable value of £14.00 per unit. By using the new basis the cost
is £13.89, which is 11p below the net realisable value.

As an auditor or director you would need to satisfy yourself that the accounting policy was appropriate to the circumstances of the financial circumstances of the company as required by company law and good accounting practice.

The Companies Act 1981 and SSAP 2 both define the fundamental accounting concept of consistency; whilst this needs to be maintained one year with another it does not preclude a change, such as is proposed by the company, providing that proper notes are made within the financial statement showing:

(i)   Detail of change in accounting policy.
(ii)   The effect on profit of the year to be disclosed.
(iii)   The effect on prior years to be accounted for as a prior-year adjustment, in accordance with SSAP 6.

7

(a) **Extracts from balance sheet**

Stocks	£	£
Raw materials and consumables		N/A
Work in progress, at cost		50,000
Long-term contracts, at cost	249,000	
Attributable profits	6,500	
Foreseeable losses	(4,000)	
	251,500	
Less payments on account	(194,000)	
		57,500
Finished products		134,000
		241,500
Provisions for liabilities and charges		
Other provisions		1,000

(b) Cost is defined in relation to the different categories of stocks and work in progress as being that expenditure which has been incurred in the normal course of business in bringing the product or service to its present location and condition. This expenditure should include, in addition to cost of purchase, such costs of conversion as are appropriate to that location and condition and would include:

(i)   Direct labour and direct expenses.
(ii)   Production overheads, based on the normal level of activity.
(iii)   Other overheads, if any, attributable in the particular circumstances of the business in bringing the product to its present location and condition.

(i) and (ii) apply in this question.

Net realisable value is the actual/estimated selling price less:

(i)   All further cost to completion.
(ii) All cost to be incurred in marketing, selling and distribution.

It is assumed that if the yachts are offered for sale at £2,000 no further costs to completion will be incurred and there will be no marketing costs. NRV is to be applied to individual items of stock whenever possible even though the total cost for a particular group is less than its NRV.

Workings

Production overhead recovery base

An appraisal of the information available indicates that the examiner was expecting the production overhead recovery to be based on direct labour, i.e. £800,000 to £400,000 (being £2 for every £1 of direct labour).

There would, however, be other acceptable alternatives, i.e., based on direct material or total direct costs. Whichever base is selected would need to be applied consistently.

It would appear that the sailing dinghies have been weighted far more towards direct materials during the earlier stages of construction whereas on completion there is no great difference.

Long-term contracts X and Y appear to be incurring more direct labour at their current stage of completion and also at their anticipated completion whilst the reverse is true for long-term contract Z.

A recovery rate of £2 production overheads to £1 direct labour gives the following:

		Finished stock		Long-term contracts			
	WIP	Below standard	Other	X	Y	Z	Total
	£	£	£	£	£	£	£
Direct material	20,000	5,000	35,000	20,000	32,000	5,000	117,000
Direct labour	10,000	4,000	31,000	25,000	38,000	1,000	109,000
	30,000	9,000	66,000	45,000	70,000	6,000	226,000
Production overheads	20,000	8,000	62,000	50,000	76,000	2,000	218,000
	50,000	17,000	128,000	95,000	146,000	8,000	444,000
Write down to net realisable value	–	(11,000)	–	–	–	–	(11,000)
Long-term contracts							
Attributable profits	–	–	–	Nil	6,500	N/A	6,500
Foreseeable losses	–	–	–	N/A	N/A	(5,000)	(5,000)
	50,000	6,000	128,000	95,000	152,500	3,000	434,500
Progress payments receivable	–	–	–	90,000	100,000	4,000	194,000

Determination of attributable profits and foreseeable losses

	X		Y		Z	
	£	£	£	£	£	£
Final contract price		130,000		175,000		110,000
Estimated costs to completion						
Direct materials	24,000		36,000		40,000	
Direct labour	30,000		42,000		25,000	
Production overheads	60,000		84,000		50,000	
		114,000		162,000		115,000
Estimated final profit		16,000		13,000		–
Estimated final loss		–		–		(5,000)

Stage of completion
Value of work certified to date
as a percentage of the final
contract price (to nearest whole
number)

£110,000/£130,000   £160,000/£175,000   £6,000/£110,000
= 85%   = 91%   = 5%

Attributable profits

SSAP 9 emphasises that many businesses carry out contracts where the outcome cannot reasonably be assessed before the conclusion of the contract and in such a case no profit should be taken up; further no attributable profit can be taken up until the outcome of the contract can be assessed with reasonable certainty.

Contract Y is closer to completion than contract X and the outcome of contract Y could be assessed with more reasonable certainty than that of contract X.

Therefore, on the above assumption, no attributable profit will be taken into account for contract X but a maximum profit of £13,000 could be attributed to contract Y.

The concept of prudence leads to the following determination of the profit/(loss) earned to date:

	£	£
Work certified to date		160,000
Costs to date		
Direct material	32,000	
Direct labour	38,000	
Production overheads	76,000	146,000
'Profit' earned to date		14,000

Clearly it would be imprudent to take credit for a profit of £14,000 when it is reasonably certain that the final profit will be £13,000. Furthermore prudence requires that the profit taken into account should be restricted to the amount represented by:

$$\text{final profit} \times \frac{\text{cash received to date}}{\text{final contract price}} = £13,000 \times \frac{£90,000}{£175,000} = £6,685 \text{ (to the nearest pound) say } £6,500$$

Foreseeable losses

SSAP 9 requires that foreseeable losses are provided for in full as soon as they become apparent; even before work has commenced. Therefore £5,000 needs to be provided for in full.

Loss-making contracts

Provision for a foreseeable loss should be deducted from the cost of the contract work in progress at the balance sheet date, unless the amount of the loss exceeds the costs incurred to date on that contract less progress payments received, in which case the excess should be shown as a provision among the liabilities on the balance sheet. For contract Z:

	£
Costs to date	8,000
Progress payments received	4,000
	4,000

Therefore there is a limit of £4,000 on the amount by which the valuation can be written down. The remaining £1,000 should be shown as a provision.

5 SSAP 12 and SSAP 19

INTRODUCTION

SSAP 12, 'Accounting for depreciation', was first issued in December 1977, and was revised in November 1981.

Depreciation is the measure of the wearing out, consumption or other loss of value of a fixed asset whether arising from use, effluxion of time or obsolescence through technological and market changes.

When there is a revision of the estimated useful life of an asset, the unamortised cost should be charged over the revised remaining useful life.

Where there is a change from one method of depreciation to another the unamortised cost of the asset should be written off over the remaining useful life on the new basis commencing with the period in which the change is made. The effect should be separately disclosed in the year of change, if material.

A review of SSAP 12 was issued in February 1983. The main points for discussion were:

(a)   The principles behind depreciation should remain the same in all accounts.
(b)   That historical cost accounts should not be 'purified' by prohibiting the incorporation therein of asset revaluations.
(c)   That current cost principles should be used as the basis for any revaluations.

This list is not exhaustive and the reader should refer to the discussion paper.

SSAP 12 does not apply to investment properties.

SSAP 19, 'Accounting for investment properties', was issued in 1981 in order to recognise that a different treatment is required where a significant proportion of the fixed assets of an enterprise is held not for consumption in the business operations but as investments, the disposal of which do not materially affect any manufacturing or trading operations of the enterprise.

Investment property which should not be charged to depreciation as set out in SSAP 12 is defined as an interest in land and/or buildings:

(a)   In respect of which construction work and development have been completed; and

(b) Which is held for its investment potential, any rental income being negotiated at arm's length.

The following are exceptions from the definition:

(a) A property which is owned and occupied by a company for its own purposes is not an investment property.
(b) A property let to and occupied by another group company is not an investment property for the purposes of its own accounts or the group accounts.

Readers are advised to refer directly to both SSAP 12 and SSAP 19.

QUESTIONS

1

(a) Define the terms 'depreciation' and 'obsolescence'.   *3 marks*

(b) What three factors are involved in assessing depreciation and allocating it to accounting periods?   *2 marks*

(c) Opinions differ with regard to the depreciation of:

    (i)   Freehold land and buildings.
    (ii)   Wasting assets (i.e. those subject to depletion).

What are the requirements of Statement of Standard Accounting Practice No 12 ('Accounting for depreciation') in this regard? What arguments are put forward by those opposed to SSAP 12?   *7 marks*

(d) In what circumstances may/ought a company to revalue fixed assets for balance sheet purposes? When is it necessary for the value of fixed assets to appear in the directors' report?   *8 marks*

Total 20 marks

2 'Depreciation is the part of the cost of the fixed asset consumed during its period of use by the firm' (Frank Wood, *Business Accounting*).

You are required:

(a) To comment critically on the above definition within a brief discussion of the objective of providing for depreciation. You may, in so doing, quote the definition which appears in SSAP 12, or use your own comparable words.   *5 marks*

(b) To state with reasons, whether you agree or disagree with the statement 'depreciation provides for the replacement of fixed assets'.   *5 marks*

(c) To state briefly the various suggestions which have been made to overcome the limitations of charging historical cost depreciation in an inflationary period.   *5 marks*

You are not required to comment on methods of calculating the depreciation charge (e.g. straight-line, reducing balance, sum of the digits, etc.).

Total 15 marks

3 At 1 July 1983 the fixed asset balances of Wellington Ltd comprised the following:

	Original cost £	Depreciation £	Net £
Freehold land and buildings	296,000	–	296,000
Plant and equipment	395,200	238,100	157,100
Vehicles	32,000	18,400	13,600

The straight-line rates of depreciation based on cost, used to that date were 10% p.a. for plant and equipment, and 12½% for vehicles. It is the company's practice to make a full year's charge on new items in the year of purchase. The following additional information is relevant to the calculation of depreciation for the year to 30 June 1984:

(i) An item of equipment bought in September 1979 for £84,000 is now recognised to have a useful life of at least 20 years.

(ii) It has been decided to charge depreciation on the freehold buildings at 2% p.a. The buildings represent £180,000 of the £296,000 shown above, and were all completed in August 1970.

(iii) A vehicle purchased in January 1980 for £4,000 was traded in at a value of £1,800 in part exchange for a new vehicle costing £6,400.

(iv) Included with the equipment is an item which originally cost £72,000 and which is already fully depreciated but not expected to last for very much longer. Otherwise all items of equipment are less than 10 years old, and all vehicles less than eight years old.

Required:

(a) Prepare a schedule of fixed asset movements and balances suitable for inclusion in the company's published accounts for the year to 30 June 1984. Include a clear indication of the amount to be charged against the year's profits and the balances to be shown in the balance sheet.   *12 marks*

(b) A director suggests that to make a change in the annual depreciation for item (i) is against the accounting conventions of consistency and prudence. How would you respond?   *6 marks*

(c) Comment briefly on the requirements of the Companies Act 1981 in respect of depreciation of tangible fixed assets, comparing them with relevant SSAPs.
     7 marks
     Total 25 marks

4   Goneril plc and Regan plc are manufacturing companies and Cordelia plc is a property investment company. All three companies have recently acquired and disposed of freehold properties which were identical in every respect. Details of the properties are as follows:

3 June 1982   —   Each company bought its property for £300,000. The buildings element in the cost of each property was estimated at £120,000 with an estimated useful life of 40 years.

30 June 1983   —   Each property was revalued at £380,000 (including buildings element £160,000). The estimated useful life at this date was revised to 50 years.

30 June 1984   –   Each property was revalued at £290,000 (including buildings element £100,000).

29 June 1985   –   Each property was sold for £320,000.

Goneril plc and Regan plc both use their properties for their business operations and both provided a full year's depreciation (straight-line) in the year of acquisition and none in the year of disposal. Goneril plc always incorporates property revaluations into its historical cost accounts, whereas Regan plc never does.

Cordelia plc leased its property to produce a rental income negotiated at arm's length.

All three companies have accounting periods ending on 30 June.

You are required:

(a)   To show how the properties would be dealt with in the historical cost accounts (1983 to 1985) of each company. The rental income of Cordelia plc should be ignored. You should answer in accordance with all relevant SSAPs and EDs.   *15 marks*

(b)   To outline the treatment of investment properties as put forward in SSAP 10.
    5 marks
    Total 20 marks

5   'When a depreciating asset is first acquired, the accountant should try to forecast the net relevant cash flow pattern.'

(a)   Explain what you understand by the 'net relevant cash flow pattern'.   *10 marks*

(b)   Explain why such a forecast may be necessary.   *10 marks*
    Total 20 marks

ANSWERS

1

(a) (i) Depreciation is defined in SSAP 12 as 'the measure of the wearing out, consumption or other loss of value of a fixed asset whether arising from use, effluxion of time or obsolescence through technology and market changes'.

(ii) Obsolescence is the process whereby the asset permanently loses value usually as a result of changes in technology or a shift in the market demand.

(b) The factors involved in assessing depreciation and its allocation to accounting periods are as follows:

(i) Cost (or valuation, where an asset has been revalued).

(ii) Nature of the asset and the length of its expected useful life to the business.

(iii) Estimated residual value.

(c) (i) SSAP 12 does not generally require that depreciation be charged on the land element of freehold land and buildings. The exceptions are the following cases:

1 Freehold land subject to depletion by, for example, the extraction of minerals.

2 Freehold land whose value is adversely affected by considerations such as the desirability of its location should be written down to reflect permanent diminution in value.

Paragraph 12 of SSAP 12 requires that buildings should be depreciated according to the same criteria as other fixed assets because they 'have a limited life which may be materially affected by technological and environmental changes'.

It is specifically stated that it is not appropriate to omit charging depreciation of a fixed asset on the grounds that its market value is greater than its net book value (paragraph 10).

(ii) Depreciation must be applied to wasting assets, i.e. those subject to depletion such as mines, in a similar manner to other assets. The additional requirement to depreciate land has been dealt with in (c) (i) above.

The arguments against SSAP 12 relate mainly to the requirements to depreciate freehold buildings. These can be summarised as follows:

1 If buildings are included on the basis of historical cost and depreciated, the effect will be to reduce shareholders' funds and net assets at a time when the capital value of the buildings may well be increasing. Paragraph 10 of SSAP 12 deals with this argument by suggesting that the land and buildings could be revalued to reflect appreciation in their value and then requiring that depreciation be charged on the revalued amount.

2 Some feel that it is impracticable or at least arbitrary to split the cost or valuation of land and buildings between site value and bricks and mortar.

3 Breweries, banks and insurance companies have in some cases complained that depreciation of their properties is not required since they continuously incur maintenance expenditure on their properties in order to extend the useful lives almost indefinitely. It is contended that it is illogical to reduce shareholders' funds (profit) twice by charging both for maintenance and also for depreciation.

(d) There is no legal requirement that companies must revalue their fixed assets. In fact, to incorporate a revaluation in the accounts represents a departure from the historical cost convention. However, a company *may* incorporate valuations of its fixed assets in its accounts. The Companies Act 1948, schedule 8, paragraphs 29–34, specifies certain disclosure requirements, essentially quantifying the difference.

SSAP 16, which applies to listed and large unlisted companies, requires fixed assets, investments and stocks to be included at 'value to the business' in the supplementary current cost accounts. With this exception it is a matter for the discretion of the directors of the company whether or not the fixed assets should be revalued in the main accounts.

Where the valuation of fixed assets differs materially from their book value, it is likely that a revaluation will provide more information about the asset backing of the company and therefore enhance the true and fair view. This is particularly relevant for businesses such as property companies and investment trusts where asset values are of considerable significance to investors.

When a company acquires a subsidiary, SSAP 14 requires that valuations of all the assets of the subsidiary at the date of acquisition should form the basis of consolidated accounts.

SSAP 19 requires that investment properties should not be subject to periodic charges for depreciation on the basis set out in SSAP 12 (except any property held on a lease with an unexpired period of less than 20 years) and that they should be shown in the balance sheet at their open market values.

Where investment properties represent a substantial proportion of the total assets of a major enterprise, the valuation would normally be carried out:

(i)   Annually by persons holding a recognised professional qualification and having recent post-qualification experience in the location and category of the properties concerned.

(ii)   At least every five years by an external valuer.

Section 16 of CA 1967 states *inter alia* that where the market value of the company's interests in land differs substantially from the amount at which they are included in the balance sheet, the directors should indicate the difference if they are of the opinion that the matter is of sufficient significance to be drawn to the attention of either shareholders or debenture holders.

2

(a)   SSAP 12 defines depreciation as 'the measure of the wearing out, consumption or other loss of value of a fixed asset whether arising from use, effluxion of time or obsolescence through technology or market changes'.

The quotation from Wood is too narrow in its meaning and it differs from the SSAP 12 definition in the following ways:

(i)   Wood refers to 'cost' and does not implicitly recognise the presence of an inflationary environment as the term 'value' in the SSAP definition does. Further, there are situations in historical cost accounts when fixed assets are revalued, depreciation being calculated on the new value. SSAP 12 recognises this but Wood's quotation talks of 'cost' only.

(ii)   'Effluxion of time' and 'obsolescence' are acknowledged by SSAP 12 in addition to 'use' as matters which give rise to loss of value which must be measured by depreciation. For example, leases lose value in a predetermined manner, mines lose value through depletion, computers because of technological and market changes.

In stable economic periods the objective of providing depreciation to spread the expenditure incurred in acquiring the asset over its effective lifetime has been generally accepted. The allocation should be charged regardless of whether a profit or loss has been incurred if a 'true and fair' view is to be determined. Note that under the Companies Act 1981 the 'true and fair view' takes precedence.

SSAP 12 requires that when an asset is revalued, or the estimate of its useful life is altered, it is the new value which is to be spread over the remaining useful life of the asset. Thus the phrase 'expenditure in acquiring the asset' in the above paragraph would need modification to recognise 'replacement costs' or 'value to the business' of assets.

While SSAP 12, therefore, implicitly recognises the importance of replacement costs, it has nothing to say on the treatment of repair costs in relation to depreciation charges and is also silent on the desirability of allowing for the cost of capital in depreciation calculations.

To conclude, it may be said that an objective of depreciation is to make a charge against profit for the use of assets during the period. Depreciation based on replacement cost charges the current price for assets used up in production.

(b) Whether or not depreciation has a secondary objective of providing a fund for the assets' replacement is a matter of some contention. Some would categorically deny that any such fund is provided. The depreciation charge is not synonymous with cash and unless an equivalent amount to the debit to the profit and loss account is set aside in a specific investment 'fund' for the replacement of the assets, then it will be fortuitous only if sufficient cash is available at the required time. The effect of the charge for depreciation in periods of profitability is to prevent that proportion of profit being distributed as dividend. Profit equals cash at one moment of time only, i.e. when the cash sale is effected or the debtor collected. That cash is then reinvested and becomes part of the generality of assets, e.g. increased stock, lower current liabilities, extra fixed assets. It will be seen, therefore, that the 'fund' representing the accumulated depreciation is in the form of general additional assets. To the extent that it provides security for borrowing to replace the related fixed assets, then it may be said that a secondary objective of depreciation is to provide for the assets' replacement. Ensuring that there is sufficient cash available to replace fixed assets as and when necessary is, however, a problem of cash management rather than of depreciation.

A fundamental question is whether assets should be replaced from funds generated from current operations. Should selling prices be sufficiently high not only to provide adequate profit, but also the replacement of assets? Alternatively, should they only provide sufficient profit plus recovery of costs actually incurred? If the latter, then it should be borne in mind that the extra funds required in an inflationary period will need to come from external borrowing. It comes down to the question whether current or future customers should pay for the future plant etc.

Depreciation may be viewed, then, as an amount set aside out of profits equal to the proportion of the original investment used up during the year. Thus capital depletion is avoided. However, the 'fund', invested in the general assets of the business can be used for other matters than replacement, e.g. it could be used to buy different assets or even be repaid to shareholders, if enough of the general assets were turned into cash at the appropriate moment. Depreciation based on historical cost replaces the funds used up in money terms, but depreciation based on replacement cost replaces those funds in 'real' terms and maintains the purchasing power of the original investment.

(c) The following are suggestions to overcome the limitations of historical cost depreciation in inflationary periods.

During the inflation of the early 1950s, both the ACCA and ICMA effectively recommended charging depreciation against profit based on replacement costs.

The ICAEW, however, recommended that the profit and loss account continue to be charged with historical cost depreciation, and that any additional replacement costs be appropriated from reserves.

Subsequently, under provisional SSAP 7, the CPP method was used to adjust the 'value' of fixed assets for the general fall in the purchasing power of money. Depreciation was charged as a percentage of the CPP values.

Under RCA (or CCA) fixed assets are revalued to their replacement cost (or value to the business) and the depreciation provision is charged in the profit and loss account based on the revalued figure. Backlog depreciation is taken from the amount of the fixed asset revaluation.

The 'Hyde guidelines' require a profit and loss inflation statement to supplement the historical accounts. The depreciation adjustment therein is the difference between the revised current year depreciation charge (based on current costs) and the historical cost depreciation charge. There is no requirement for backlog depreciation.

3

(a) **Tangible fixed assets**

	Freehold land and buildings £	Plant and equipment £	Vehicles £	Total £
Cost				
1 July 1983	296,000	395,200	32,000	723,200
Disposal			(4,000)	(4,000)
Addition			6,400	6,400
30 June 1984	296,000	395,200	34,400	725,600
Depreciation 1 July 1983				
As previously stated	—	238,100	18,400	256,500
Prior-year adjustment	46,800	—	—	46,800
As restated	46,800	238,100	18,400	303,300
Disposal			(2,000)	(2,000)
Charge for year	3,600	27,070	4,300	34,970
30 June 1984	50,400	265,170	20,700	336,270
Net book value				
30 June 1983	249,200	157,100	13,600	419,900
30 June 1984	245,600	130,030	13,700	389,330

Depreciation to be charged in profit and loss account

	£
As above	34,970
'Loss' on disposal of vehicle	200
	35,170

The total depreciation would be allocated to the appropriate holdings within the published profit and loss account; the Companies Act 1981 gives the option of one of four formats to be adopted by the reporting company.

Workings

			£
1 Prior-year adjustment: depreciation of freehold buildings			
13 years at 2% on £180,000			46,800

2 Depreciation on plant and equipment

	£		£
Item cost	84,000	50,400/16 years	3,150
Item cost	72,000		Nil
Balance cost	239,200	at 10%	23,920
	395,200		27,070

	£
3 Loss on sale of motor vehicle: cost 1 January 1980	4,000
Depreciation (4 years at 12½% p.a.)	2,000
	2,000
Sale proceeds	2,000
Loss on sale	1,800
	(200)

(b) The change in the annual depreciation for item (i) complies with SSAP 12 paragraph 17 which states that the depreciation charge should be adjusted if changing circumstances result in a revision of the original estimate of an asset's useful life. The overriding principle is that of matching revenue and expense, which, applied to fixed assets, means apportioning the cost less any residual value over the life of the assets as equitably as possible. Due regard has been given to the prudence concept by taking account of the minimum expected life of 20 years. Consistency cannot overrule the matching principle where the circumstances are sufficiently clear to show that a change in the annual charge is necessary: it is a desirable but secondary concern. If the change made a significant difference to the company's results, the effect would be noted.

(c) The Companies Act 1981 requires that depreciation shall be provided on all fixed assets with a limited useful economic life so as to write off the purchase price or production cost less any estimated residual value systematically over the asset's useful economic life. This requirement is similar to that contained in SSAP 12. SSAP 19 requires that investment properties shall not be depreciated. Such a policy is prima facie contrary to the requirements of the Act, but the requirement of SSAP 19 not to depreciate such properties is considered to be authority that such a policy is necessary for the accounts to give a true and fair view in which case the detailed requirements of the Act may be overridden. Such a departure from the accounting rules and its effect must be disclosed.

The following disclosures are required under the Act with regard to depreciation for each class of fixed asset:

(i)   Cumulative amounts for depreciation at the beginning and end of the year.
(ii) Provisions made in respect of current year.
(iii) Adjustments in respect of disposals.
(iv) Any other adjustments.
(v)   Accounting policy.

SSAP 12 requires additionally disclosure of:

(i) Depreciation method.
(ii) Useful lives or depreciation rate.

4

(a)   **Goneril plc**

Extracts from balance sheets for years ended 30 June

	1982 £	1983 £	1984 £	1985 £
Freehold land and buildings				
Land at cost/valuation	180,000	220,000	190,000	–
Buildings at cost/valuation	120,000	160,000	100,000	–
	300,000	380,000	290,000	–
Less: Accumulated depreciation	3,000	–	–	–
	297,000	380,000	290,000	–
Asset revaluation reserve	–	86,000(3)	–	–

Extracts from profit and loss accounts for years ended 30 June

	1982 £	1983 £	1984 £	1985 £
Depreciation of freehold buildings	3,000(1)	3,000(1)	3,200(2)	–
Loss on revaluation	–	–	800(3)	–
Profit on sale	–	–	–	30,000(4)

Notes

1 For years ended 30 June 1982 and 30 June 1983:
   cost ÷ useful life = £120,000 ÷ 40   =   £3,000 p.a.

2 For year ended 30 June 1984:
   valuation ÷ useful life = £160,000 ÷ 50   =   £3,200 p.a.

3 Revaluation at 30 June 1983:
   surplus = revaluation less (cost less depreciation to
   30 June 1983) = £380,000 − (£300,000 − £6,000)   =   £86,000

   Revaluation at 30 June 1984:
   deficit (loss) = revaluation 1984 less
   (revaluation 1983 less depreciation to 30 June 1984,
   1 year) = £290,000 − (£380,000 − £3,200)   =   £86,800
   set off against balance brought forward on
   asset revaluation reserve   =   £86,000

   Deficit (loss) written off to P & L account   £800

4 Profit on sale
   sale proceeds less revaluation to 30 June 1984
   = £320,000 − £290,000   =   £30,000

Regan plc

Extracts from balance sheets as at 30 June

	1982 £	1983 £	1984 £	1985 £
Freehold land and buildings				−
Land at cost	180,000	180,000	180,000	−
Buildings at cost	120,000	120,000	120,000	−
	300,000	300,000	300,000	−
Less: accumulated depreciation	3,000	6,000	8,280	−
	297,000	294,000	291,720	−

Extracts from profit and loss accounts for years ended 30 June

	1982 £	1983 £	1984 £	1985 £
Depreciation: Freehold buildings	3,000(1)	3,000(1)	2,280(2)	−
Profit on sale	−	−	−	28,280(3)

Notes

1 For years ended 30 June 1982 and 1983:
    cost ÷ useful life = £120,000 ÷ 40   =   £3,000 p.a.

2 For year ended 30 June 1984:
    net book value ÷ useful life
    = £120,000 − £6,000 ÷ 50   =   £2,280 p.a.

3 Profit on sale = sale proceeds less net book value
    at 30 June 1984 = £320,000 − £291,720   =   £28,280

Cordelia plc

Extracts from balance sheets as at 30 June

	1982 £	1983 £	1984 £	1985 £
Freehold land and buildings				
Land at cost/valuation	180,000	220,000	190,000	–
Buildings at cost/valuation	120,000	160,000	100,000	–
	300,000	380,000	290,000	–
Investment property revaluation reserve	–	80,000(1)	–	–

Extracts from profit and loss accounts for years ended 30 June

	1982 £	1983 £	1984 £	1985 £
Loss on revaluation	–	–	10,000(1)	–
Profit on sale	–	–	–	30,000(2)

Notes

1 Revaluation at 30 June 1983:
    surplus = revaluation 1983 less
    cost = £380,000 − £300,000   =   £80,000
  Therefore, to non-distributable reserve   =   £80,000
  Revaluation at 30 June 1984:
    deficit (loss) = revaluation 1984 less
    revaluation 1983 = £290,000 − £380,000   =   £90,000
  Less: Transferred from investment property
    revaluation reserve   =   £80,000

  Net loss on revaluation to P & L account   =   £10,000

2 Profit on sale:
    sale proceeds less revaluation 1984
    = £320,000 − £290,000   =   £30,000

(b)   Investment properties should not be subject to periodic charges for depreciation except for properties held on a lease which should be depreciated on the basis set out in SSAP 12 at least over the period when the unexpired term is 20 years or less.

Investment properties should be included in the balance sheet at their open market value.

Investment properties should be valued:

(i)   Annually by persons holding a recognised professional qualification and having recent post-qualification experience in the location and category of the properties concerned; and

(ii)   At least every five years by an external valuer.

5

(a)   SSAP 12 requires that 'depreciation should be allocated to accounting periods so as to charge a fair proportion to each accounting period during the expected useful life of the asset'. However, the standard does not specify any particular method of allocation.

The net relevant cash flows of an asset can be one of the methods used in allocating the consumed part of the asset to the accounting periods covering its estimated useful life.

'Net' means that both receipts and payments are to be considered. 'Relevant' means that only receipts and payments that are affected by the age and usage of the asset are considered.

In determining the net relevant cash-flow pattern the following will have to be taken into consideration:

(i)   Anticipated changes in price levels of the future cash flows.
(ii)   Capital outlay both initial and future (if applicable).
(iii) Maintenance and repair payments, which are affected by the asset's age and usage.
(iv)   Proceeds of sale.
(v)   An interest charge based on the finance required to cover the capital outlay. The interest rate being either that of a specific loan to buy the asset or the company's cost of capital.

(b)   SSAP 12's definition of depreciation says that the loss in value results from 'use, effluxion of time or obsolescence through technology and market changes'.

As with any method of calculating the annual depreciation allocation of an asset's cost, a good deal of subjectivity is involved; this applies to the determination of the 'net relevant cash-flow pattern'. However, it is argued that the net relevant cash-flow pattern will aid management in predicting the optimum life of an asset, the optimum life being the period of usefulness of the asset until the point when it is worth while to replace the asset. The optimum life of an asset will be affected by obsolescence through technological and/or market changes, and may not be as long as the period to the physical expiration of the asset.

Once the net relevant cash-flow pattern and optimum life have been established, then the appropriate accounting policy needs to be adopted.

The forecast of net relevant cash-flow pattern is useful as an aid in determining the consumed cost of an asset to be charged against revenue in an accounting period to determine profit under current accounting practice. It would not be required, for example, if cash-flow accounting was the major reporting medium.

6   SSAP 13

INTRODUCTION

SSAP 13, 'Accounting for research and development', was issued in December 1977. The questions set in this chaper are considered adequate to cover the scope and pervasiveness of the statement. Nevertheless, readers are recommended to study the SSAP.

QUESTIONS

1   You are required to discuss fully and explain the matters considered in SSAP 13 relating to research and development.

20 marks

2   The financial controller of Arthur plc has approached you as the company's auditors for advice in respect of the treatment he should apply to various matters concerning research and development expenditure which are detailed below:

(a)   Expenditure on applied research amounting to £600,000 which is the first annual instalment of the cost of the applied research on a specified project. The controller informs you that the expenditure will be repeated in each of the next two years, and that management are optimistic about the successful development and sale of the resultant new product.

(b)   Contribution to a research foundation amounting to £100,000 which is for pure research related to the field in which Arthur plc operates.

(c)   Expenditure on the development of a specified project amounting to £200,000. The controller advises you that the management view the project with enthusiasm and there is sufficient evidence to show that profitable returns will result from the sale of the new product in the near future.

(d)   Research and development expenditure related to a patent granted for the manufacture and sale of a product amounting to £250,000 which includes £3,000 of fees paid to the Patent Office and to a patent agent.

(e)   Costs incurred in the acquisition of specialised knowledge relating to a specified process amounting to £40,000.

You are required to advise the financial controller on the accounting treatment of each of the five items.

20 marks

3   During the course of a year Venture Ltd incurred expenditure on many research and development activities. Details of three of them are given below:

Project 3
To develop a new compound in view of the anticipated shortage of a raw material currently being used in one of the company's processes. Sufficient progress has been made to suggest that the new compound can be produced at a cost comparable to that of the existing raw material.

Project 4
To improve the yield of an important manufacturing operation of the company. At present, material input with a cost of £100,000 per annum becomes contaminated in the operation and half is wasted. Sufficient progress has been made for the scientists to predict an improvement so that only 20% will be wasted.

98

Project 5
To carry out work, as specified by a creditworthy client, in an attempt to bring a proposed aerospace product of that client into line with safety regulations.

Costs incurred during the year were:

Project	3	4	5
	£	£	£
Staff salaries	5,000	10,000	20,000
Overheads	6,000	12,000	24,000
Plant at cost (life 10 years)	10,000	20,000	5,000

You are required:

(a)   To define the following:

    (i)   Pure research expenditure.
    (ii)   Applied research expenditure.
    (iii)   Development expenditure.   *5 marks*

(b)   To state the circumstances in which it may be appropriate to carry forward research and development expenditure to future periods.   *8 marks*

(c)   To show how the expenditure on projects 3, 4 and 5 would be dealt with in the balance sheet and profit and loss account in accordance with SSAP 13.
12 marks
Total 25 marks

ANSWERS

1 SSAP 13 recognises the term 'research and development' as covering a wide variety of activities, but acknowledges three broad 'blanket' categories of activities; namely pure research which is defined as work directed primarily towards the advancement of knowledge; applied research which is defined as work directed primarily towards exploiting pure research, other than work defined as development expenditure; and development which is defined as work directed towards the introduction or improvement of specific products or processes.

Because the dividing line between the above definitions may often be vague, strict conditions are laid down for deferring R & D expenditure. Firstly, because the reference periods, for which expenditure on pure and applied research has been incurred, generally cannot be identified for receiving the benefits of such expenditure, it is recommended that such expenditure be written off in the period in which they are incurred.

Development expenditure is considered separately but should also be written off in the period in which it is incurred unless all the following conditions are met:

(a) There is a clearly defined project.

(b) The related expenditure can be separately identified.

(c) There is reasonable certainty about the technical feasility of the project and its ultimate commercial viability considered in the light of such factors as likely market conditions (including competing products), public opinion, consumer and environmental legislation.

(d) If further development costs are to be incurred on the same project, the aggregate of such costs together with related production, selling and administration costs, are reasonably expected to be more than covered by related future revenues.

(e) Adequate resources exist, or are reasonably expected to be available, to enable the project to be completed and to provide any consequential increases in working capital.

In the foregoing circumstances, development expenditure may be deferred to the extent that its recovery can reasonably be regarded as assured, its amortisation commencing with commercial production.

In choosing a deferral policy, regard should be given to:

(a) Whether the company's planning and forecasting systems have been successful in the past.
(b) Policies followed by companies in similar industries.
(c) Materiality of the amounts involved.

2

(a) SSAP 13 requires that the expenditure of £600,000 incurred on applied research must be written off as it is incurred.

(b) SSAP 13 requires that expenditure of £100,000 incurred on pure research must be written off.

(c) SSAP 13 requires that expenditure on the development of a specified project amounting to £200,000 may be deferred if it meets the conditions laid down within the SSAP.

(d) R & D expenditure incurred in relation to a patent granted for the manufacture and sale of a product amounting to £250,000 may also be deferred if it meets the conditions laid down within SSAP 13. In amortising the expenditure, attention should be given to the fact that patents have a maximum life of 20 years.

(e) Although the acquisition of specialised knowledge in relation to a specified process is not mentioned in the SSAP specifically, it would appear to be the better view that such expenditure could be deferred if it meets the conditions that apply to development expenditure.

3

(a) (i) Pure research expenditure is an original investigation undertaken in order to gain new scientific or technical knowledge or understanding, not directed towards any specific practical objective.

(ii) Applied research expenditure is on original investigation undertaken in order to gain new scientific or technical knowledge directed towards a specific practical objective.

(iii) Development expenditure relates to the use of scientific or technical knowledge in order to produce new or substantially improved materials, devices, products, processes, systems or services prior to the commencement of commercial use or production.

(b) Expenditure on fixed assets for the purpose of research and development should be capitalised and depreciated over its estimated useful life. Expenditure fully recoverable under a firm contract from a customer should, in so far as it has not been reimbursed at the balance sheet date, be carried forward as work in progress.

All other expenditure on pure and applied research must be written off in the year it is incurred. Development expenditure should normally be written off in the year in which it is incurred but may be written off under the following conditions:

(i) There must be a clearly defined project, expenditure on which should be separately identifiable.

(ii)   The project must be technically feasible and commercially viable, bearing in mind market conditions and legal requirements.

(iii) Total revenues from the project must be reasonably expected to cover total costs.

(iv)   There must be good reason to believe that adequate resources exist, or will become available, to carry through the project.

The policy chosen in respect of development expenditure must be applied consistently.

(c) Projects 3 and 4 both fall within the scope of development expenditure, while project 5 will be included in work in progress. Treatment of projects 3 and 4 will depend:

(i)   On whether the projects meet the criteria for deferral laid down by SSAP 13.

(ii)   On whether the company has chosen to adopt a deferral or a write-off policy in respect of such expenditure.

Expenditure on projects 3, 4 and 5 will therefore be reflected in the accounts as follows:

(i)   The balance sheet will include £35,000 additions to plant.
(ii)   The balance sheet will, if the deferral method is used, include a note as follows:

	£	£
Deferred development expenditure at the beginning of the year		X
Development expenditure incurred (including £36,000 relating to projects 3 and 4)	X	
Development expenditure amortised	X	X
Deferred development expenditure at the end of the year		X

(iii) The amount for work in progress in the balance sheet will include £44,500 in respect of project 5, less any payments on account received.

(iv)   The figure for depreciation shown in the published profit and loss account will include £3,500 relating to fixed assets used on projects 3, 4 and 5.

(v)   The notes on the company's accounting policies will include a note on the policy adopted in respect of research and development expenditure and on stock and work in progress.

1 Projects 3 and 4: deferred expenditure

	3 £	4 £	Total £
Salaries	5,000	10,000	15,000
Overheads	6,000	12,000	18,000
Depreciation	1,000	2,000	3,000
	12,000	24,000	36,000

2 Project 5: work in progress

	£
Salaries	20,000
Overheads	24,000
Depreciation	500
	44,500

7 SSAP 3

INTRODUCTION

Earnings per share (EPS) is defined as the earnings in pence attributable to each equity share, based on the consolidated profit of the period after tax and after deducting minority interests and preference dividends, but before taking into account extraordinary items, divided by the number of equity shares in issue and ranking for dividend in respect of the period.

In the field of financial reporting, the price-earnings ratio and thus the EPS are perhaps the ratios most widely used as a guide in performance analysis.

EPS is based on the number of shares in issue and ranking for dividend in respect of the reference period.

The basic earnings per share (BEPS) is worked out using a time basis in computing the average number of shares in the period if shares have been issued in that period. An adjustment to such a computation is required where the share issue was a rights issue.

Bonus issues

An issue of bonus shares spreads the earnings over a greater number of shares but does not affect the earnings capacity. Therefore, the EPS should be based on the number of shares ranking for dividend after the issue.

Issue of shares at full market price

An issue of shares at full market price should increase the earnings capacity but spread it over a greater number of shares. Therefore, the EPS should be based on the average number of shares in issue weighted on a time basis.

Rights issue

A rights issue should increase the earnings capacity. To the extent that the shares are issued at a discount, a rights issue is equivalent to a bonus issue but otherwise a rights issue is equivalent to an issue at full market price. In order to calculate the EPS it is necessary:

(a)   To adjust the comparative figure of EPS.

(b)   To calculate the number of shares in that part of the issue which equates to a discount on market value.

(c)   To calculate the average number of shares in issue weighted on a time basis to the extent that the rights issue equates to an issue at full market price.

The comparative figure of EPS is equal to:

previous EPS × theoretical ex rights price ÷ actual cum rights price

The weighted average number of shares (current period) is equal to:

proportion of shares in issue before the rights issue × actual cum rights price ÷ theoretical ex rights price

This adjusts for the bonus element. Note that no adjustment is made for the proportion in issue after the rights issue.

Dilution

Dilution occurs where a company has an existing obligation to issue new shares. If new shares have been issued but they do not yet rank for dividend then the fully diluted EPS is calculated by including those shares in the total number of shares as though they had ranked for dividend from the date of issue.

If there are options to subscribe for new equity shares then it is necessary to compute the fully diluted EPS by:

(a)   Estimating the prospective effect on earnings.

(b)   Estimating the prospective effect on the number of shares in issue.

With regard to earnings:

(a)   If there is a right to convert loan stock or preference share capital into equity shares then add back the prospective savings in interest (net of tax) or preference dividends.

(b)   If there is an option to subscribe for cash the prospective earnings of the fund should be estimated as though invested in 2½% Consolidated Stock purchased at the price ruling at the end of the day before commencement of the reference period.

If the fully diluted EPS is greater than the basic EPS then the fully diluted EPS should be disclosed.

Questions in this chapter

The questions in this chapter deal with most, if not all, of the possible 'mechanics' that the reader may be confronted with.

Further reading

Although the major points have been outlined above it would still be beneficial to read SSAP 3.

106

QUESTIONS

1 The following is the consolidated profit and loss account of Kingswear plc for the year ended 31 December 1983:

	£	£
Net profit after all expenses including debenture interest		2,300,000
Less:		
Corporation tax on the profits for the year at 52%	1,100,000	
Irrecoverable ACT	100,000	
		1,200,000
		1,100,000
Less: Extraordinary item after adjusting for corporation tax		80,000
		1,020,000
Less:	£	
Dividends: Preference, paid	120,000	
Ordinary interim, paid	200,000	
Ordinary final, proposed	400,000	
		720,000
Retained profits for the year		300,000
Add: Balance brought forward		150,000
Retained profits, carried forward		450,000

On 1 January 1983, there were in issue 10 million £1 ordinary shares and 2 million 6% £1 preference shares. In addition, the company had in issue £1,250,000 10% convertible debentures carrying conversion rights into ordinary shares as follows:

Date	Price per share
On 30 June 1983	£1.10
On 30 June 1984	£1.25
On 30 June 1985	£1.75
On 30 June 1986	£1.90

No debenture holders took up the option to convert on 30 June 1983.

No debenture or share issues took place during the year ending 31 December 1983.

You are required:

(a) To define earnings per share as applicable to a group of companies having minority interests, either as in SSAP 3, or in your own comparable words.

2 marks

(b) To write, briefly, of your understanding of:
   (i) the 'net' basis
   (ii) the 'nil' basis
   of calculating earnings per share.

4 marks

(c) To calculate and state the basic earnings per share for the year ending 31 December 1983 using:
  (i)   the 'net' basis,
  (ii) the 'nil' basis.   *4 marks*

(d) To calculate and state the fully diluted earnings per share on the 'net' basis for the year ended 31 December 1983.   *4 marks*
                                                              Total 14 marks

2 The draft consolidated profit and loss account of the Nursery Rhymes Group for the year ended 31 December 1984 was as follows:

	£ thousands	£ thousands
Operating profit		6,620
Share of profits less losses of associated companies		290
		6,910
Interest paid		1,507
Profit before taxation		5,403
Taxation		
Parent company and subsidiaries	2,309	
Associated companies	140	
		2,449
Profit attributable to parent company shareholders before extraordinary items		2,645
Extraordinary items		
Expenses of rights issue		103
Profit attributable to parent company shareholders after extraordinary items		2,542
Dividends paid or proposed		1,012
Profit retained		1,530

A note dealing with parent company taxation explained that the charge of £2,309,000 included adjustments to prior years (credit of £274,000) and irrecoverable advance corporation tax on dividends of £56,000.

The issued share capital of the parent company was as follows:

	1984 £	1983 £
4.2% Cumulative preference shares of £1 each	1,000,000	1,000,000
Ordinary shares of £0.25 each	7,658,000	5,875,000

Changes in the ordinary share capital during the year were:

(i) On 5 May 816,000 shares were issued at a premium of £0.20 on the acquisition of Bobby Ltd.

(ii) On 14 June the company made a rights issue of one share for every four held at a price of £0.35 per share.

(iii) On 11 November 237,200 shares were issued at a premium of £0.35 in part consideration for the acquisition of Teddy Bears Picnic Ltd.

Options to subscribe for 730,000 shares were granted to directors and senior executives on 31 March 1984. These options will be exercisable at £0.60 per share between 1 April 1987 and 31 March 1990.

The closing price of 2½% Consols on 31 December 1983 was £13.16. The market price of the ordinary shares immediately before the rights issue was £0.45 per ordinary share.

You are required:

(a) To calculate the basic earnings per share and the fully diluted earnings per share for the year ended 31 December 1984.   *12 marks*

(b) To outline the adjustments required to earnings per share of previous years so that they can be compared with earnings per share for the current year.
                                                                     3 marks
                                                               Total 15 marks

3   The following information relates to an offer by Super plc to acquire the whole of the issued share capital of Roads plc.

The terms of the offer were:

For every 100 ordinary shares of 10p each fully paid of Roads plc:

  13 ordinary shares of £1 each of Super plc.
  13 ordinary share warrants of Super plc.
  £2 cash.

For every 100 ordinary shares of 10p each 1p paid of Roads plc (a further 66p was payable on each share):

  3 ordinary shares of £1 each of Super plc.
  3 ordinary share warrants of Super plc.

The market prices and dividends paid for the shares at the last practicable date were:

	Market price	Dividend including tax credit
Super plc		
ordinary shares of £1 each	480p	16.5p
ordinary warrants	150p	nil
Roads plc		
ordinary shares of 10p each fully paid	64p	13.5%
ordinary shares of 10p each 1p paid	not quoted	nil

The share capital of Super plc is:

Authorised		Issued and fully paid
£		£
19,000,000	Cumulative preference shares of £1 each	19,000,000
134,534,443	Ordinary stock units of £1 each	134,534,443
3,400,049*	Ordinary shares of £1 each	–
8,065,508	Unclassified shares of £1 each	–
165,000,000		153,534,443

*Reserved to satisfy in full the rights comprised in the company's existing ordinary share warrants.

Super plc intends to increase its authorised share capital to £200,000,000.

Full implementation of the offer would result in the issue of 8,931,599 ordinary stock units and the same number of warrants. The warrants entitle holders to acquire ordinary stock on a basis of £1 stock unit for 1 warrant of Super plc at £4 per £1 stock unit for cash or by the surrender of £4 nominal of Super plc's 8½% loan stock.

There is £80 million of loan stock outstanding at the present time.

Summarised latest profit and loss accounts

	Super plc £ thousands	Roads plc £ thousands
Income from trading	58,000	2,141
Interest payable	10,000	–
	48,000	2,141
Taxation	19,000	899
	29,000	1,242
Preference dividends	2,000	–
	27,000	1,242
Ordinary dividends	16,000	455
Retained	11,000	787

Despite the existing low taxation charge it is estimated that any additional income will be taxed at 40%.

You are required to calculate to one decimal place of a penny:

(a) The financial effects of the offer on a holder of 100 fully paid and 100 partly paid shares in Roads plc. *12 marks*

(b) The earnings per share of Super plc before and after the proposed acquisition. *13 marks*

Total 25 marks

4 Part of a listed company's consolidated profit and loss account is shown below:

Chasewater plc

Consolidated profit and loss account (extract) for the year ended 30 June 1981

	£	£
Group net profit before taxation		500,000
Taxation		270,000
Group net profit after taxation		230,000
Minority interests in subsidiaries		20,000
Attributable to shareholders in Chasewater plc		210,000
Extraordinary items (after taxation)		11,000
Net profit for year		221,000
Dividends (net)		
Preference	25,000	
Ordinary	100,000	
		125,000
Retained earnings for year		96,000

Issued share capital (fully paid), 1 July 1980: 250,000 10% cumulative preference shares of £1 each, and 4,000,000 ordinary shares of 25p each.

Loan capital, 1 July 1980: £500,000 7% convertible debentures (convertible into 200 ordinary shares per £100 debenture, with proportionate increases for subsequent rights issues).

Changes during the year ended 30 June 1981:
1 October 1980   Rights issue of ordinary shares (ranking for dividend 1980–81: 1 for 4 at £0.90 per share; market price before issue, £1.00.
1 January 1981   Conversion of £100,000 of 7% convertible debentures.
1 March 1981   Bonus issue of ordinary shares, 1 for 3.

Basic earnings per share for the year ended 30 June 1980 were 4.0p.

Corporation tax, 52%; income tax basic rate, 30%.

You are required:

(a)   To compute the company's basic earnings per share for the current year, and its comparative BEPS for the previous year.   *10 marks*

(b)   To compute the company's fully diluted earnings per share for the current year only, and to state, with reasons, whether it ought to be published.
10 marks
Total 20 marks

111

1

(a)   SSAP 3 defines earnings per share as:

       The profit in pence attributable to each equity share, based on the consolidated profit of the period after tax and after deducting minority interests and preference dividends, but before taking into account extraordinary items, divided by the number of equity shares in issue and ranking for dividend in respect of the period.

(b)   (i)   In determining earnings per share on the net basis, the charge for taxation used in determining earnings includes:

       (1) any irrecoverable advance corporation tax (ACT);
       (2) any unrelieved overseas tax arising from the payment or proposed payment of dividends.

    (ii)   In determining earnings per share on the nil basis, the charge for taxation used in determining earnings generally excludes (1) and (2) in (b) (i) above (except in so far as these arise in respect of preference dividends).

(c)   (i)   The basic EPS on the net basis is 9.8p.
    (ii)   The basic EPS on the nil basis is 10.8p.

Workings

	'Net' basis		'Nil' basis	
	£ thousands	£ thousands	£ thousands	£ thousands
Net profit before taxation		2,300		2,300
Less: Corporation tax at 52%	1,100		1,100	
Irrecoverable ACT	100		–	
		1,200		1,100
Profit attributable to shareholders		1,100		1,200
Less: Preference dividends		120		120
Profit attributable to ordinary shareholders *A*		980		1,080
		thousands		thousands
Number of £1 ordinary shares in issue throughout year *B*		10,000		10,000
BEPS = *A* ÷ *B*		9.8p		10.8p

(d) Fully diluted EPS on the net basis is 9.45p.

Note. This would not be disclosed as the difference from BEPS is less than 5% of the BEPS.)

	£ thousands	£ thousands
Profit attributable to ordinary shareholders per workings for basic EPS		980
Increase in profit, on dilution, on conversion of loan stock		
Loan stock convertible £1,250,000		
Interest thereon at 10%	125	
Less tax thereon at 52%	65	
		60
		C 1,040

Number of £1 ordinary shares in issue throughout the year		10,000
Increase in number of shares on dilution		
Loan stock convertible £1,250,000 at £1.25 per share		1,000
		D 11,000
Fully diluted EPS = $C \div D$		9.45p

2

(a) Basic earnings per share is 9.33p

Fully diluted earnings per share is 9.26p.

(b) The earnings per share of previous years will require adjustment in respect of the bonus element of the rights issue. As per SSAP 3, this will require the reciprocal of the factor calculated in relation to the rights issue at less than full market value, i.e.:

$$\frac{\text{theoretical ex rights price}}{\text{actual cum rights price}} = \frac{43}{45}$$

The adjusted figure will be:

previous earnings per share $\times$ 43/45

Workings

1 Number of shares

SSAP 3 requires that where a rights issue is made during the year at less than full market price, the weighted average share capital should be adjusted by taking the proportion of the capital in issue before the rights issue and applying the following factor:

$$\frac{\text{actual cum rights price on the last day of quotation cum rights}}{\text{theoretical ex rights price}}$$

In this example the factor is established as follows:

	£
Value of shareholding before rights issue: 4 shares at £0.45	1.80
Cost of rights issue: 1 share at £0.35	0.35
Value of holding after rights issue: 5 shares worth	2.15
Therefore ex rights share price is 2.15/5	0.43

The required factor will be 45/43 and it will adjust for the bonus element included in the rights issue.

As required by SSAP 3 the weighted average share capital is calculated as follows, using shares issued and ranking for dividend:

Period of year	Days × Shares issued (in thousands) × Rights factor	Shares/days (in thousands of shares)
1 January to 5 May	125 × 23,500 × 45/43	3,074,128
6 May to 14 June	40 × 24,316 × 45/43	1,017,879
15 June to 11 November	150 × 30,395	4,559,250
12 November to 31 December	50 × 30,632.2	1,531,610
		10,182,867

Weighted average = 10,182,867 × 1,000/365 = 27,898,266

2 **Earnings**

	£ thousands
Profit after tax, after minority interest but before extraordinary items	2,645
Less: Preference dividends	42
Earnings for ordinary shareholders	2,603

3 Basic EPS = £2,603,000/27,898,266 = 9.33p (to 2 decimal places)

	£	£
4 Earnings, see 2 above		2,603,000

Add: assumed yield of 19% on proceeds
of share option from 31 March onwards

	£	£
19% × 730,000 × £0.60 × 9/12	62,415	
Less: Corporation tax at 52%	32,456	29,959
		2,632,959

The assumed yield is calculated using the closing market price of 2½% Consolidated Stock on the day before the start of the period.

In this case £13.16 would give a return of £2.50 or a yield of 2.50/13.16 = 19% (to 2 decimal places).

	£
Number of shares	27,898,000
Add: option rights (assuming exercised from date of issue) 730,000 × 9/12	547,500
	28,445,500

Fully diluted EPS = £2,632,959/28,445,500 = 9.26p (to 2 decimal places).

As the dilution is not material (i.e. more than 5%) it would not be necessary to disclose the fully diluted earnings per share.

3

(a)   Valuation of Roads plc fully paid shares

Market value per share	64p
Market value of 100 shares	£64.00

	£
When converted into Super plc shares	
Market value of 13 ordinary shares: 480p × 13	62.40
Market value of 13 ordinary share warrants: 150p × 13	19.50
Cash	2.00
For every 100 fully paid ordinary shares of 10p each	83.90

Income (including tax credit) on 100 fully paid ordinary shares of 10p each of Roads plc: 100 × 13.5% × £0.1	£1.35
Income (including tax credit) on 100 fully paid ordinary shares of Roads plc after the offer: 13 × 16.5p	£2.145

Valuation of Roads plc partly paid shares

100 shares, 1p each paid up to date	£1.00
Market value not available.	
Contingent liability: 100 × 66p	£66.00

When converted into Super plc shares

	£
Market value of 3 ordinary shares: 480p × 3	14.40
Market value of 3 ordinary share warrants 150p × 3	4.50
	18.90

Income, after offer: 16.5p × 3   49.5p

The capital position of a holder of 100 fully paid and 100
  partly paid shares will be enhanced under the terms of the
  offer by: (£83.90 − £64.00) + (£18.90 − £1.00)   £37.80

Income of the holder will be increased by:
  214.5p − 135p + 49.5p   £1.29

The contingent liability of £66 will disappear.

(b)

	Basic EPS	Fully diluted EPS
Before proposed acqution of Roads plc	20.1p	20.1p
After proposed acquisition of Roads plc	19.7p	19.7p

Workings

1 EPS before proposed acquisition of Roads plc

	Ordinary £1 stock units
Already in issue (use for BEPS), A	134,534,443
Number to be issued if all warrants converted	3,400,049
(Use for FDEPS), B	137,934,492

	£ thousands	£ thousands
Profits available to the ordinary shareholder after taxation and preference dividends (use for BEPS), C		27,000
Increase in profits, on dilution, with cancellation of loan stock		
Loan stock cancelled on conversion of warrants (4 × 3,400,049) = £13,600,196		
Interest thereon at 8½%	1,156	
Less tax at 40%	462	694
(Use for FDEPS), D		27,694

BEPS $= C \div A = 20.069$p   (to 3 decimal places)
FDEPS $= D \div B = 20.078$p   (to 3 decimal places)

2 **EPS after proposed acquisition of Roads plc, assuming 100% acceptance of the offer**

	£	Ordinary £1 stock units
Already in issue		134,534,443
To be issued on acceptance of offer		8,931,599
(Use for BEPS), A		143,466,042
Number to be issued if all warrants converted		
Warrants already in issue	3,400,049	
To be issued on acceptance of offer	8,931,599	12,331,648
(Use for FDEPS), B		155,797,690

	£ thousands	£ thousands
Profits available to ordinary shareholders after taxation and preference dividend (consolidated figure)		
(Use for BEPS), C		28,242
Increase in profits, on dilution, with cancellation of loan stock		
Loan stock cancelled on conversion of warrants ($4 \times 12,331,648$) = £49,326,592		
Interest thereon at 8½%	4,193	
Less tax at 40%	1,677	2,516
(Use for FDEPS), D		30,758

BEPS $= C \div A = 19.685\text{p}$ (to 3 decimal places)
FDEPS $= D \div B = 19.742\text{p}$ (to 3 decimal places)

4

(a) Basic EPS, year ended 30 June 1981: £185,000/5,450,630 = 3.39p (to 2 decimal places). Basic EPS, year ended 30 June 1980, adjusted for comparability $4\text{p} \times 0.98 \times 3/4 = 2.94\text{p}$.

(b) Fully diluted EPS, year ended 30 June 1981: £200,120/6,538,630 = 3.06p (to 2 decimal places). This figure should be disclosed because it is less than 95% of the corresponding basic EPS.

Workings

	Basic EPS £	Diluted EPS £
Earnings attributable to shareholders	210,000	210,000
Less: Preference dividend	(25,000)	(25,000)

	Basic EPS	Diluted EPS
	£	£
brought forward	185,000	185,000

Add: Debenture interest saving (net of tax at 52%)

400,000 at 7% for 1 year × 48%	–	13,440
100,000 at 7% for ½ year × 48%	–	1,680
	185,000	200,120

Movement on share capital during year		Number issued	Number in issue
1 Jul 1980	Issued ordinary shares	–	4,000,000
1 Oct 1980	Rights issue: 1 for 4	1,000,000	5,000,000
1 Jan 1981	Conversion £100,000 7% convertible debentures	204,000*	5,204,000
1 Mar 1981	Bonus issue: 1 for 3	1,734,667	6,938,667

Calculation of theoretical ex rights price

	£
Market value of 4 million ordinary shares at £1.00	4,000,000
Rights issue proceeds: 1 million ordinary shares at £0.90	900,000
	4,900,000

Theoretical ex rights price = £4,900,000/5,000,000 = £0.98 per share

Calculation of number of shares in issue in accordance with SSAP 3

Portion of period	Fraction of year × Shares in issue × Rights factor		Number of shares for EPS
1 July to 30 Sep 1980	(3/12) × 4,000,000 × 1/0.98	=	1,020,408
1 Oct to 31 Dec 1980	(3/12) × 5,000,000	=	1,250,000
1 Jan to 28 Feb 1981	(2/12) × 5,204,000	=	867,333
1 Mar to 30 Jun 1981	(4/12) × 6,938,667	=	2,312,889
			5,450,630

Dilution: Conversion of £400,000 7% convertible debenture stock at 272 per £100*	1,088,000
	6,538,630

*Conversion rates for 7% convertible debentures on 1 July 1980: 200 ordinary shares per £100.

On 1 October 1980 (including bonus element of rights issue): 200 × 1/0.98 = 204 ordinary shares per £100.

On 1 March 1981 (including bonus issue of 1 for 3): 204 × 4/3 = 272 ordinary shares per £100.

8 SSAPs 2, 4, 17 and 18

INTRODUCTION

This chapter covers the following SSAPs:

SSAP 2: Disclosure of accounting policies
SSAP 4: The accounting treatment of government grants
SSAP 17: Accounting for post balance sheet events
SSAP 18: Accounting for contingencies

In respect of SSAP 2, it is recommended that the reader appreciates the differences and definitions of: fundamental accounting concepts (that is, the broad basic assumptions which underlie the periodic financial accounts of business enterprises), accounting bases (that is, the methods which have been developed for expressing or applying fundamental accounting concepts to financial transactions and items), and accounting policies (that is, the specific accounting bases judged by business enterprises to be most appropriate to their circumstances and adopted by them for preparing their financial accounts).

SSAP 4 standardises the accounting treatment of capital-based grants. Three principal treatments are identified in the statement:

(a) To credit to P & L account the total amount of the grant immediately.
(b) To credit the amount of the grant to a non-distributable reserve.
(c) To credit the amount of the grant to revenue over the useful life of the asset by either:

  (i)   Reducing the cost of the acquisition of the fixed asset by the amount of the grant;
        or
  (ii) treating the amount of the grant as a deferred credit, a portion of which is transferred to revenue annually.

Treatment (c) is recommended by the statement because its effect on the company's reported earnings under the methods listed is progressive over the life of the asset.

SSAP 17 defines post balance sheet events as those events, both favourable and unfavourable, which occur between the balance sheet date and the date on which the financial statements are approved by the board of directors.

Post balance sheet events are further classified as adjusting events and non-adjusting events. Adjusting events are post balance sheet events which provide additional evidence of conditions existing at the balance sheet date. They include events which because of statutory or conventional requirements are reflected in financial statements. Non-adjusting events are post balance sheet events which concern conditions which did not exist at the balance sheet date.

SSAP 18 deals with contingencies. The statement defines a contingency as a condition which exists at the balance sheet date, where the outcome will be confirmed only on the occurrence or non-occurrence of one or more uncertain future events. A contingent gain or loss is a gain or loss dependent on a contingency.

QUESTIONS

1 On 1 January 1982 Syrup Ltd purchased a machine costing £200,000 with an estimated life of 10 years and no residual value. An investment grant of £30,000 was received relating to this asset one month after purchase. Syrup Ltd makes its accounts up to 31 December.

You are required to show the differing accounting methods of treating the grant which are acceptable under SSAP 4 by showing:

(a) The relevant balance sheet figures at 31 December.
(b) The relevant profit and loss account figures at 31 December.

15 marks

2 The following events occurred after 31 December 1982, which was the year end of Thorenson Ltd, but before the accounts had been approved by the directors. State in each case, how you would expect such events to be dealt with in the published accounts for the year ended 31 December 1982.

(a) On 20 February 1983 one of the three major plants of Thorenson Ltd was destroyed by fire, the loss being estimated at £500,000 only £400,000 of which was covered by insurance. *4 marks*

(b) Stock retailed by Thorenson Ltd had been selling in the market at £5 per item on 31 December 1982. This price had prevailed for two weeks prior to the year end following an official market report that predicted vastly enlarged supplies. The stock cost Thorenson £6 per item and is normally turned-over once per month. The normal retail price throughout 1982 had been £9 per item. On 4 January 1983 the selling price returned to its former level of £9 per item following public disclosure of an error in the official calculations of the prior December, correction of which destroyed the expectations of excessive supplies. This stock has been valued in the draft accounts at the net realisable value of £5 on 31 December 1982 as this was lower than the cost per item of £6. *4 marks*

(c) Thorenson had a claim for damages from a customer. The claim has been outstanding for two years and has been reflected in the accounts as a contingent liability. On 15 February 1983 Thorenson Ltd paid a substantial amount to the customer in an out-of-court settlement. *4 marks*

(d) The assets and liabilities of an overseas subsidiary, Tully Ltd were translated into sterling in the balance sheet at the rates ruling at 31 December 1982 but since then the value of sterling has increased by some 16% against the overseas currency. *4 marks*

Total 16 marks

3 Spring Surprise Ltd's main product is a mousetrap. The company have recently embarked on an export drive to the USA.

Their sales campaign has been concentrated in the state of California where they have advertised their products as 'A girl's best friend'. Unhappily they have found

121

themselves, in that litigious nation, subject to several lawsuits. You are required to state the accounting treatment and disclosure which is required in respect of each of these items in the accounts.

(a) Mr G. Washington has lost his thumb as a result of handling a mousetrap with an excessively powerful spring, and is suing the company for £5,000. The company's legal advisers are of the opinion that this claim is reasonable in amount and that no defence can be put forward.   *3 marks*

(b) The Californian Women's Liberation Group claims that the company's advertising is offensive to the dignity of women and are claiming £10,000,000 as damages. The company's legal advisers are of the opinion that the outcome of this action will depend upon which judge happens to hear the case, there being a 70% chance that the company will be held free of blame and a 30% chance that the company will be required to pay damages in full.   *3 marks*

(c) Mr A. Lincoln, a keen self-publicist, is suing the company for £1,000,000,000 on the grounds that he is widely known to have a great fear of mice, and the company's advertising has caused him to be accused of effeminacy in this respect. The company's legal advisers are of the opinion that the risk of any court upholding this claim is negligible.   *3 marks*

Total 9 marks

4 SSAP 2, 'Disclosure of accounting policies', states that there are four fundamental accounting concepts which have general acceptability.

(a) State and briefly explain each of these four fundamental concepts.   *8 marks*

(b) State and briefly explain any three other accounting concepts.   *6 marks*

(c) In what circumstances might you abandon one of the concepts stated in either part (a) or part (b) when preparing a financial statement?   *6 marks*

Total 20 marks

5 The report *Setting Accounting Standards* (Accounting Standards Committee 1981), affirmed that accounting standards are necessary and will continue to be necessary in order to complement statutory regulations.

Do you agree with the statement? State your reasons.

20 marks

6 You have recently been appointed as accountant to Enoon Ltd, a footwear manufacturing company, which is the United Kingdom subsidiary of a Ruritanian company. The draft financial statements have been prepared for Enoon Ltd for the year ended 31 December 1982, and the company has followed the policies of the parent company in preparing such statements. As the newly appointed accountant you are asked by the directors to examine the financial statements prepared by the previous accountant and to comment on them. The accounting policies described as the first note to the financial statements are as follows:

(a) **Turnover**
Turnover represents sales less returns during the year including VAT.

(b) **Research and development expenditure**
Research and development expenditure is written off over a period of five years commencing in the year in which it is incurred.

(c) **Depreciation**
No depreciation is provided on freehold land and buildings. Leasehold land and buildings and other fixed assets are written off over the period of their estimated useful lives.

(d) **Stock and work in progress**
Stock and work in progress are valued at the lower of cost and net realisable value. Cost of raw materials and work in progress is calculated on a LIFO basis, only direct costs being taken into account, while finished goods include a relevant proportion of overheads.

(e) **Investment grants**
Investment grants received are credited to a capital reserve account and transferred to the profit and loss account over a period of five years.

(f) **Goodwill**
Goodwill is stated at cost and not amortised on an annual basis.

(g) **Deferred taxation**
It is not the company's policy to provide for deferred taxation.

(h) **Expansion and reorganisation**
The company has made a number of new acquisitions in recent years and has been involved in internal reorganisation and rationalisation following this policy of expansion. All reorganisation costs, together with surpluses and deficits on the disposal of properties and businesses, are dealt with in the capital reserve.

Comment briefly on each of the above accounting policies which have been adopted by the company, referring to any conflicts with accounting standards, legislation or normal conventions.

20 marks

ANSWERS

1

Method 1: reduce the cost of the acquisition of the fixed asset by the amount of the grant

Balance sheet at 31 December 1982

	Cost	Depreciation	Net
	£	£	£
Machine	170,000	17,000	153,000

Profit and loss account 31 December 1982

	£
Depreciation	17,000

Method 2: treat the grant as a deferred credit, a portion of which is transferred to revenue annually

Balance sheet at 31 December 1982

	Cost	Depreciation	Net
	£	£	£
Machine	200,000	20,000	180,000

	£	£
Deferred credit		
Government grant	30,000	
Less: Transfer to profit		
and loss account	3,000	27,000

(The net effect on net assets is £153,000 as in the first method.)

Profit and loss account 31 December 1982

	£
Depreciation	20,000 (Debit)
Government grant	3,000 (Credit)

(The net effect is £17,000 as in the first method.)

2

(a) This event does not concern any condition which existed at the balance sheet date. Therefore it is not necessary for any adjustment to be made to the balance sheet in respect of this. However, the company will incur a loss of £100,000 due to the fire in the next financial period which could be material.

If it is material the matter should be disclosed by way of a note to the financial statements.

(b) This event does have a direct bearing upon the balance sheet and should be recognised in the stock valuation at 31 December 1982. Stock should be valued at the lower of cost or net realisable value. The cost per item is £6 and the NRV is £5 at that date. However, subsequent events clearly indicate that the NRV is £9 rather than £5, the latter being an abnormally low price due to erroneous calculations. No loss should be made on the stock and therefore the NRV can be taken as £9. However, since cost of £6 is lower than £9 cost will be used for valuation purposes at 31 December 1982. If any stock has been sold between 31 December 1982 and 4 January 1983 at the price of £5 then this stock will have to be valued at £5.

(c) The out-of-court settlement provides additional evidence of conditions existing at the balance sheet date. The financial statements at 31 December 1982 should therefore be adjusted to reflect the liability and the profit and loss charge should be separately disclosed if material.

(d) This is a non-adjusting event since it does not concern conditions existing at the balance sheet date. If it is deemed to be material it should be disclosed by way of a note to the financial statements.

3 The accounting treatment and disclosure requirements for contingencies are dealt with in SSAP 18, 'Accounting for contingencies'.

(a) Since it is almost certain that the company will have to meet the claim in full, then the full amount of the loss should be provided for in the accounts.

(b) In this case it seems probable that the action will fail, but the possibility of it succeeding is still far from remote. In such cases SSAP 18 requires disclosure of the existence of the contingent liability. The disclosure required is:

    (i) The general nature of the legal action.
    (ii) An explanation that the outcome depends on the attitude taken by the courts of the state of California.
    (iii) A statement that the financial effect of the contingency is estimated at £10,000,000.
    (iv) An explanation of the tax implications where necessary for a proper understanding of the financial position of the business.

(c) In this case the possibility of loss is so remote that no disclosure is required.

4

(a) SSAP 2, 'Disclosure of accounting policies', lists the four fundamental concepts as:

    (i) Going concern. This is the assumption that the business will continue in operational existence for the foreseeable future.

(ii)   Accruals concept. Revenue and costs are recognised on an accruals basis and not a cash basis, matched where possible, and dealt with in the profit and loss account of the period to which they relate.

(iii)   Consistency. Similar items are dealt with consistently both within each accounting period and between accounting periods.

(iv)   Prudence. Revenue and profits are not anticipated; provision is made for all known liabilities.

(b)   (i)   Business entity. This is the assumption that the business can be separately identified from its owners and that financial statements are prepared from this perspective.

(ii)   Money measurement. Only those assets and liabilities capable of being expressed in monetary terms are included in financial statements.

(iii)   Materiality. This principle states that the way an item is treated in the accounts should depend upon its materiality, i.e. its 'relative significance'. For example, small items of capital expenditure may sometimes be treated as revenue.

(c)   Examples of circumstances where concepts may be abandoned are:

(i)   A firm which has adopted a FIFO method of valuing stock for a number of years may decide that AVCO would be a preferable method of stock valuation. If they decide to adopt this new policy the consistency concept has been abandoned. There must of course be a note to the effect in the accounts.

(ii)   There are a number of circumstances where the prudence concept will override the accruals concept. For example, research and development costs may possibly all be written off as incurred even though some benefit will result in future, although such benefit may not be accurately quantified.

(iii)   The materiality concept may override the accrual concept when for example, small items of capital expenditure which may be of use in more than one accounting period are written off as incurred.

5   The main points which may be discussed are as follows:

(a)   The reasons for establishing the ASC and SSAPs were set out in the 'Statement of intent on accounting standards in the 1970s' (ICAEW 1970). These were:

(i)   To encourage uniformity of practice.
(ii)   To ensure disclosure of accounting bases.
(iii)   To ensure disclosure of departures from accounting bases.
(iv)   To involve interested bodies in the discussion of exposure drafts before promulgating a standard.
(v)   To seek to improve legislation and the regulations of other bodies.

(b)   The legal regulations on financial reporting are not concerned, in the main, with accounting methods. This is the province of the accounting profession and standards are methods of accounting approved by the ASC.

(c)   Whether standards should become part of the statutory regulations rather than complementing them (some standards are now embodied in the Companies Act 1981).

(d)   Whether standardisation can exist without a conceptual framework.

(e)   Whether standardisation necessarily leads to the best accounting method being adopted. Are any standards the result of pressure groups lobbying the ASC?

(f)   Whether it is possible to apply standards to all industries, however different they may be. There may be rejection problems, and if so what powers of enforcement does the ASC have?

(g)   Whether standards are too rigid, possibly restricting the scope of directors to prepare financial statements as they see the underlying economic events.

(h)   Whether standards should be abandoned and instead the financial statements should simply disclose the bases used in preparing the statements so that they can be understood.

(i)   Whether the impact of standards is weakened by the fact that auditors on a number of occasions have agreed with firms who have not complied with them.

6

(a)   SSAP 5, 'Accounting for value added tax', states that turnover should be shown excluding VAT. If it is desired to show the gross turnover including VAT this can be done but in this case the VAT must be disclosed separately. The policy clearly conflicts with SSAP 5.

(b)   The accounting policy conflicts with SSAP 13, 'Accounting for research and development expenditure'. This SSAP does not allow such expenditure to be carried forward over a five-year period. All pure and applied research expenditure should be written off as incurred, and development expenditure can only be carried forward if it meets the stringent criteria outlined in SSAP 13.

(c)   There is a conflict with SSAP 12, 'Accounting for depreciation'. This SSAP requires the freehold buildings to be depreciated as opposed to land which need not be depreciated. Consequently the value of the freehold must be split between land and buildings. It is also necessary to provide more information regarding depreciation. It is necessary to provide a breakdown of all fixed assets into each major category (e.g. plant and machinery, long leaseholds, short leaseholds, etc.) and for each class to show the depreciation method used, the useful lives or rates used, the total depreciation for the period and the gross amount of depreciable assets together with the accumulated depreciation.

(d) This policy conflicts with SSAP 9, 'Stocks and work in progress', which does not allow the LIFO basis for valuation of materials in the United Kingdom. Also work in progress does not include overheads which conflicts with SSAP 9. The latter requires the inclusion in the valuation of all related production overheads, both fixed and variable, which have been incurred in the normal course of business in bringing the product to its present location and condition. Prime cost is unacceptable. The term 'relevant proportion of overheads' is vague and could be expanded and some elaboration could be given on 'net realisable value'.

(e) There is a conflict with SSAP 4, 'The accounting treatment of government grants'. Such grants (if for capital expenditure) can either be deducted from the cost of the fixed asset or treated as a deferred credit with a portion transferred to revenue on an annual basis over the life of the asset. They cannot be taken to a capital reserve.

(f) There is no SSAP on the subject but the policy conflicts with ED 30, 'Accounting for goodwill'. Purchased goodwill cannot be carried forward in the balance sheet as a permanent item. It can either be written off immediately on acquisition directly against reserves representing the realised profits or it can be amortised through the profit and loss account on a systematic basis over its estimated useful economic life, not exceeding 20 years. Non-purchased goodwill should never appear in a balance sheet.

(g) SSAP 15, 'Accounting for deferred taxation', requires that deferred taxation should be provided for on all short-term timing differences. It should also be accounted for in respect of the tax effects arising from all other originating timing differences of material amount other than any tax effects which, based on certain criteria laid down in the SSAP, can be demonstrated with reasonable probability to recur in the future. The directors cannot simply decide that their policy is not to provide for deferred taxation. They can, however, decide that no provision is necessary, after considering all factors involved including materiality. If none is considered necessary the notes to the financial statements must clearly explain the position.

(h) The policy adopted here conflicts with SSAP 6, 'Extraordinary items and prior-year adjustments'. This SSAP attempted to abolish reserve accounting, and all profits and losses should be reflected in the profit and loss account apart from unrealised surpluses on fixed asset revaluations, which can go direct to reserves. From the facts of this case it would appear to be that these items should be treated as exceptional (assuming they are material). (See the Discussion Paper, 'Review of SSAP 6'.)

9 Issue and redemption of securities

INTRODUCTION

Sections 45 to 55 in part 3 of the Companies Act 1981 deal with the powers of incorporated companies to issue and redeem shares. In order to be able to cope with problems of this nature, various key points are extracted and summarised below in order that solutions to problems may be more meaningful.

(a)   Any premium payable on redemption must be paid out of distributable profits (Companies Act 1981, s. 45(5)(b)).

(b)   If the redeemable shares were issued at a premium initially, then by s. 45(6) of the 1981 Act, any premium payable on redemption must be paid out of the proceeds of a fresh issue of shares up to an amount equal to the lesser of

    (i)   the aggregate of premiums received by the company when redeemable shares were originally issued; or

    (ii) the amount on the share premium account including any sum transferred to that account in respect of premiums on the new shares.

This is complicated in two ways from the point of view of interpretation. Firstly, the share premium account may only be used when a fresh issue of shares occurs and when the shares being redeemed were issued at a premium. Secondly, there are, in fact, three constraints on the amount of share premium that may be used; that is, the proceeds of the fresh issue itself, the aggregate of premiums received by the company when the redeemable shares were originally issued, or the amount on the share premium account including any sum transferred to that account in respect of premiums on the new shares. It is the least of these three amounts that is the constraining factor. One final note of caution on this matter is that it is the better view to use only the amount of the share premium relating to the shares actually being redeemed which were originally issued at a premium, rather than use say the whole of the premium in respect of the original issue, when only a part of the class of shares in question are being redeemed and not the whole of the class.

(c)   Where any shares of a company are redeemed or purchased wholly out of profits the amount by which the company's share capital is reduced on cancellation, shall be transferred to the capital redemption reserve (Companies Act 1981, s. 53(1)).

(d)   Where a fresh issue of shares is effected for redemption of shares, and the proceeds of issue are less than the aggregate nominal value of shares redeemed, then the difference is transferred to capital redemption reserve, which can only be used to pay up unissued shares or for issuing fully paid bonus shares to members (Companies Act 1981, s. 53(2) and (3)).

(e)   POOC + DP + PNI = price of redemption
Where: POOC = payments out of capital which is the same as the permissible capital payment (PCP).
DP = distributable profits.
PNI = proceeds of a new issue of shares.

A private company limited by shares or limited by guarantee and having a share capital may, if authorised to do so by its articles, make a payment in respect of the redemption or purchase, under s. 45 or (as the case may be) under s. 46 of this Act, of any of its own shares otherwise than out of distributable profits of the company or the proceeds of a fresh issue of shares (Companies Act 1981, s. 54(1)).

The payment permitted is calculated in accordance with the formula stated above (Companies Act 1981, s. 54(2) and (3)).

(f)   Where the permissible capital payment is less than the nominal value of the shares redeemed, then the difference will go to the capital redemption reserve (Companies Act 1981, s. 54(4)).

(g)   Where the permissible capital payment is greater than the nominal value of the shares redeemed, then one may reduce: the capital redemption reserve, share premium, fully paid share capital or unrealised profits accounts which are in credit; there would appear to be no sequential order of reduction preferred by the Act.

Part 3 (s. 39 to 45) of the Companies Act 1980 deals with the restrictions on distribution of profits and assets.

(a)   A company shall not make a distribution except out of profits available for the purpose (Companies Act 1980, s. 39(1)). A company's profit available for distribution are its accumulated, realised profits, so far as not previously utilised by distribution or capitalisation, less its accumulated, realised losses, so far as not previously written off in a reduction or reorganisation of capital duly made.

(b)   A company cannot apply unrealised profit in paying up debentures or any amounts unpaid on any of its issued shares (Companies Act 1980, s. 39(3)).

(c)   For the purposes of the above, any provision, other than one in respect of any diminution in value of a fixed asset appearing on a revaluation of *all* the fixed assets of the company, shall be treated as a realised loss (Companies Act 1980, s. 39(4)).

130

(d)   If a fixed asset is revalued upwards, then the increased depreciation charge (compared with the original depreciation) can be treated as a realised profit (Companies Act 1980, s. 39(5)).

(e)   A public company may only make a distribution of profits where:

(i)   The net assets of the company are greater than the aggregate of the company's called-up share capital and its undistributable reserves;
(ii)   The distribution does not reduce the net assets to less than that aggregate (Companies Act 1980, s. 40(1)).

(f)   For the purposes of section 40(1) of the Companies Act 1980, the undistributable reserves of a company are:

(i)   The share premium account.
(ii)   The capital redemption reserve.
(iii) The amount by which the company's accumulated, unrealised profits, so far as not previously utilised by any capitalisation of a description to which this paragraph applies, exceeds its accumulated unrealised losses, so far as not previously written off in a reduction or reorganisation of capital duly made; and
(iv)   Any other reserve which the company is forbidden from distributing by any enactment, other than one contained in part 3 of the Companies Act 1980, by its memorandum or articles.

Paragraph (iii) applies to every description of capitalisation except a transfer of any profits of the company to its capital redemption reserve on or after 22 December 1980.

In effect, a capital maintenance test has been introduced; this means that public companies must now write off revaluation losses when computing their distributable profit.

Investment companies

An investment company must be a listed public company (Companies Act 1980, s. 41(3)).

For an investment company, an 'asset ratio' test has been introduced in deciding whether it can make a distribution of profits, that is, the aggregate of its assets is at least equal to one and a half times its liabilities, where 'liabilities' includes any provisions (Companies Act 1980, s. 41).

The requirements for an investment company to fall to be classified as such are:

(a)   That the business of the company consists of investing its funds mainly in securities, with the aim of spreading investment risk and giving members of the company the benefit of the results of the management of its funds.

(b) That none of the company's holdings in companies, other than companies which are for the time being investment companies, represents more than 15% by value of the investing company's total investments.

(c) That distribution of the company's capital profits is prohibited by its memorandum or articles of association.

(d) That the company has not retained, otherwise than in compliance with part 3 of the Companies Act 1980, in respect of any accounting reference period more than 15% of the income it derives from securities.

(e) That the company has given notice to the Registrar that it is intended to be an investment company.

QUESTIONS

1 In accordance with its articles, Milner Ltd is to redeem £5,000 of preference shares at par by making an issue of £5,000 of ordinary shares at par for the purpose.

The summarised balance sheet of Milner Ltd before the above transactions are effected, is as follows:

	£
Net assets (excluding bank)	18,750
Bank	6,250
	25,000

	£
Ordinary shares	12,500
Preference shares	5,000
Profit and loss	7,500
	25,000

You are required to show the balance sheet of Milner Ltd after the above transactions are completed.

10 marks

2 In accordance with its articles, Hudson Ltd is to redeem £40,000 of ordinary shares at par with no new issue of shares to provide funds for the purpose.

The summarised balance sheet of Hudson Ltd before the above transaction is effected, is as follows:

	£
Net assets (excluding bank)	150,000
Bank	50,000
	200,000

	£
Ordinary shares	140,000
Profit and loss	60,000
	200,000

You are required to show the balance sheet of Hudson Ltd after the above transaction is completed.

10 marks

3 In accordance with its articles, Mellor Ltd is to redeem £11,000 of preference shares at par by issuing £6,600 of ordinary shares at par and utilising distributable profits as required.

The summarised balance sheet of Mellor Ltd before the above transactions are effected, is as follows:

	£
Net assets (excluding bank)	41,250
Bank	13,750
	55,000

	£
Ordinary shares	27,500
Preference shares	11,000
Profit and loss	16,500
	55,000

You are required to show the balance sheet of Mellor Ltd after the above transactions have been completed.

10 marks

4 In accordance with its articles, Boothroyd Ltd is to redeem £45,000 of preference shares, which were originally issued at par, at a premium of 20%. No new issue of shares will be made for the purpose.

The summarised balance sheet of Boothroyd Ltd before the above transaction is effected, is as follows:

	£
Net assets (excluding bank)	168,750
Bank	56,250
	225,000

	£
Ordinary shares	101,250
Preference shares	45,000
Share premium	11,250
Profit and loss	67,500
	225,000

You are required to show the balance sheet of Boothroyd Ltd after the above transaction has occurred.

15 marks

5 Three private limited companies, A Ltd, B Ltd and C Ltd whose summarised balance sheets are shown below are to redeem £17,000 of preference shares (which were originally issued at a premium of 25%) at a premium of 30%.

Company A issues £20,400 of ordinary £1 shares at par. Company A has also used £2,125 of the share premium account for the purposes of a bonus issue.

Company B issues £17,000 of ordinary £1 shares at a premium of 25%.

Company C issues £13,600 of ordinary £1 shares at a premium of 55%.

	A Ltd	B Ltd	C Ltd
	£	£	£
Sundry net assets (excluding bank)	63,750	63,750	63,750
Bank	21,250	21,250	21,250
	85,000	85,000	85,000
	£	£	£
Ordinary share capital	41,225	39,100	39,100
Preference share capital	17,000	17,000	17,000
Share premium	1,275	3,400	3,400
Profit and loss	25,500	25,500	25,500
	85,000	85,000	85,000

You are required to show each company's balance sheet after the above transactions.

20 marks

6   The summarised balance sheet of Mortimer Ltd is as follows:

	£
Sundry net assets (excluding bank)	156,250
Bank	162,500
	318,750
	£
Ordinary share capital	187,500
Non-distributable reserves	75,000
Profit and loss	56,250
	318,750

You are required to show the balance sheets of Mortimer Ltd after the following transactions:

(a)   In accordance with its articles, Mortimer Ltd redeems £75,000 of its shares at par, there being no new issue of shares for the purpose.   *10 marks*

(b)   Instead of (a), Mortimer Ltd redeems £75,000 of its shares at a premium of 100%, there being no new issue of shares for the purpose.   *10 marks*

Total 20 marks

7 The following figures relate to the shareholders' funds of five companies at 31 December 1983.

	Venus plc £ thousands	Pluto plc £ thousands	Mars plc £ thousands	Saturn Ltd £ thousands	Jupiter Ltd £ thousands
Capital and reserves					
Called-up share capital:					
£1 ordinary share	240	240	240	240	240
Share premium account	60	60	60	60	60
	300	300	300	300	300
Profit and loss account	100	100	100	10	10
	400	400	400	310	310

On 1 January 1984, each of the five companies purchases 40,000 of its own £1 ordinary shares. The details are as follows:

(i) Venus plc purchases its shares at 200p each. The shares were originally issued at a premium of 25p each.

(ii) Pluto plc purchases its shares at 90p each.

(iii) Mars plc purchases its shares at 200p each. The shares were originally issued at a premium of 25p each. The company partly finances the purchase by an issue at par of 6,000 8% redeemable preference shares of £1 each.

(iv) Saturn Ltd, as a private company, purchases its shares partly out of capital at a price of 200p each.

(v) Jupiter Ltd, also a private company, purchases its shares partly out of capital at a price of 90p each.

You are required to show the balance sheets of each of the above companies immediately after the transactions have been effected.

20 marks

8

(a) The Companies Act 1981, s. 54, has now created an authority for private limited companies to redeem or purchase their own shares out of capital in certain circumstances. Sections 45 to 55 of the Companies Act 1981 deal with these circumstances.

You are required to identify *any four* matters under ss. 45 to 55 to which a private limited company must pay special attention before a redemption or purchase is undertaken and further define what you understand by 'permissible capital payment'.

10 marks

(b) Two unrelated private companies, Hermes Ltd and Invincible Ltd have identical balance sheets as at 31 March 1982 as follows:

	Hermes Ltd £	Invincible Ltd £
Ordinary shares	3,000	3,000
Preference shares	5,000	5,000
Non-distributable reserves	4,000	4,000
Profit and loss	3,000	3,000
	15,000	15,000
Net assets (excluding bank)	5,000	5,000
Bank	10,000	10,000
	15,000	15,000

Hermes Ltd redeems the preference shares at par without any fresh issue of
shares.

Invincible Ltd redeems all its preference shares at a premium of 75% without
any fresh issue of shares.

You are required to show the balance sheet of each of the companies after
the redemption, together with your workings and reasoning.   *10 marks*
Total 20 marks

9   The Companies Act 1980 has made far-reaching changes in the law relating to
the determination of profits available for distribution.

Discuss.

20 marks

ANSWERS

1 A recommended sequential approach to these types of problem is to ask the following questions:

(a) Does a payment out of capital arise?

In this problem the answer to this is no as there are sufficient distributable profits and the proceeds of a new issue which are more than sufficient to cover the price of redemption.

(b) Is there any premium payable on redemption?

The answer is no.

(c) Are the shares redeemed wholly out of profits?

The answer is no.

(d) Are the proceeds of the fresh issue less than the aggregate nominal value of the shares redeemed?

The answer is no.

As capital is maintained, the summarised balance sheet after the transactions will be as follows:

	£
Net assets	18,750
Bank	6,250
	25,000

	£
Ordinary shares	17,500
Profit and loss	7,500
	25,000

2 Following the sequential approach of the answer to question 1:

(a) Does a payment out of capital arise? The answer is no because there are sufficient distributable profits to cover the redemption.

(b) Is there any premium payable on redemption? The answer is no.

(c) Are the shares redeemed wholly out of profits? The answer is yes. Thus s. 53(1) is applied which requires a transfer to capital redemption reserve, equal to the amount by which the company's share capital is reduced on cancellation.

Thus the balance sheet will appear as follows:

	£	
Net assets	150,000	
Bank	10,000	
	160,000	

	£	
Ordinary shares	100,000	(£140,000 − £40,000 redeemed)
Capital redemption reserve	40,000	(transferred from P & L)
Profit and loss	20,000	(£60,000 − £40,000 to capital redemption reserve)
	160,000	

3 Following the sequential approach as in the previous answers:

(a) Does a payment out of capital arise? The answer is no as the distributable profits alone, not including the fresh issue of shares, are sufficient to cover the redemption.

(b) Is there any premium payable on redemption? The answer is no.

(c) Are the shares redeemed wholly out of profits? The answer is no.

(d) Are the proceeds of the fresh issue less than the aggregate nominal value of the shares redeemed? The answer is yes. Thus s. 53(2) is activated and the difference between the aggregate nominal value of the shares redeemed and the proceeds of the fresh issue is transferred to capital redemption reserve:

	£
Nominal value of shares redeemed	11,000
Proceeds of fresh issue	6,600
Required transfer to capital redemption reserve	4,400

The summarised balance sheet of Mellor Ltd after the transactions will be as follows:

	£	
Net assets	41,250	
Bank	9,350	(£13,750 + £6,600 − £11,000)
	50,600	

	£	
Ordinary shares	34,100	(£27,500 + £6,600)
Preference shares	Nil	
Capital redemption reserve	4,400	
Profit and loss	12,100	(£16,500 − £4,400)
	50,600	

4

(a) Does a payment out of capital arise? The answer is no.

(b) Is there any premium payable on redemption? The answer is yes.

(c) Is a fresh issue of shares to be effected? The answer is no. Thus any premium payable on redemption must be paid out of distributable profits (Companies Act 1981, s. 45(5)(b)). The amount of the premium is $20\% \times £45,000 = £9,000$.

(d) Are the shares redeemed wholly out of profits? The answer is yes. Thus s. 53(1) must be applied, under which the amount by which the company's share capital is reduced on cancellation, shall be transferred to the capital redemption reserve. The company's share capital will be reduced by £45,000 and this amount will be transferred to the capital redemption reserve.

The balance sheet of Boothroyd Ltd after the transaction will be as follows:

	£	
Net assets (excluding bank)	168,750	
Bank	2,250	$(£56,250 - 1.2 \times £45,000)$
	———	
	171,000	
Ordinary shares	101,250	
Preference shares	Nil	
Share premium	11,250	
Capital redemption reserve	45,000	(From P & L £45,000)
Profit and loss	13,500	$(£67,500 - £45,000$ to capital
	———	redemption reserve $- £9,000)$
	171,000	

In summary; s. 45(5)(b) is applied, that is, the premium must be met out of distributable profits, this premium will go to redemption account. Section 53(1) is applied, that is, transfer from P & L to capital redemption reserve, being the nominal value of the shares redeemed.

Redemption account

	£		£
Cash book	54,000	Preference share capital	45,000
		P & L	9,000
	———		———
	54,000		54,000

Profit and loss

	£		£
Redemption	9,000	Balance b/d	67,500
Capital redemption reserve	45,000		
Balance c/d	13,500		
	67,500		67,500

5 Following the sequential approach as in the previous examples.

A Ltd

(a) Does a payment out of capital arise? The answer is no: the profit and loss account balance is sufficient by itself.

(b) Is there any premium payable on redemption? The answer is yes. Section 45(6) must be applied.

  (i) The proceeds of the issue are £20,400.
  (ii) The aggregate of premiums received by the company when the redeemable shares were originally issued was £3,400.
  (iii) The amount on the share premium account is now £1,275.

  The premium payable on redemption is $0.3 \times £17,000$ which equals £5,100. Under s. 45(6), the least amount of (i), (ii) and (iii), which is £1,275, can be used to offset the amount which comes from the profit and loss acount, that is, £3,825.

(c) Are the shares redeemed wholly out of profits? No.

(d) Are the proceeds of the fresh issue less than the nominal value of the shares redeemed? No.

The balance sheet of A Ltd after the transactions have been effected will therefore be:

	£
Sundry net assets (excluding bank)	63,750
Bank ($£21,250 + £20,400 - (1.3 \times £17,000)$)	19,550
	83,300

	£
Ordinary Shares ($£41,225 + £20,400$)	61,625
Profit and loss ($£25,500 - £3,825$)	21,675
	83,300

B Ltd

(a) Does a payment out of capital arise? No.

(b) Is there a premium payable on redemption? Yes. Section 45(6) must be applied.

(i)	The proceeds of the fresh issue are: 1.25 × £17,000	=	£21,250
(ii)	The premiums received when redeemable shares issued	=	£3,400

(iii)	The amount on the share premium account	=	£3,400
	Plus premium on fresh issue	=	£4,250
			£7,650

The premium payable on redemption is 0.3 × £17,000 = £5,100. £3,400 of the share premium account can be used for redemption purposes and £1,700 will come from P & L.

(c) Are the shares redeemed wholly out of profits? No.

(d) Are the proceeds of the fresh issue less than the nominal value of the shares redeemed? No.

The balance sheet of B Ltd can now be prepared:

	£
Sundry net assets (excluding bank)	63,750
Bank (£21,250 + £17,000 × 1.25 − £17,000 × 1.3)	20,400
	84,150

	£
Ordinary shares (£39,100 + £17,000)	56,100
Share premium (£3,400 + £4,250 − £3,400)	4,250
Profit and loss (£25,500 − £1,700)	23,800
	84,150

C Ltd

(a) Does a payment out of capital arise? No.

(b) Is there a premium payable on redemption? Yes, the premium payable is 0.3 × £17,000 = £5,100. Section 45(6) must be applied and £3,400 on the share premium account may be used in the redemption.

(c) Are the shares wholly redeemed out of profits? No.

(d) Are the proceeds of the fresh issue less than the nominal value of the shares redeemed? No.

The balance sheet of C Ltd after the transactions will therefore be as follows:

	£
Sundry net assets (excluding bank)	63,750
Bank (£21,250 + £21, 080 − £22,100)	20,230
	83,980

	£
Ordinary shares (£39,100 + £13,600)	52,700
Share premium (3,400 + £7,480 − £3,400)	7,480
Profit and loss (£25,500 − £1,700)	23,800
	83,980

6

(a) Does a payment out of capital arise? Yes

POOC + DP + PNI = Redemption price

where: POOC = payment out of capital
           DP   = distributable profits
           PNI   = proceeds of a new issue

Thus POOC = redemption price − DP − PNI
              = £75,000 − 56,250 − nil = £18,750

Thus £18,750 = payment out of capital = permissible capital payment.

Section 54(2) and (3) must be applied, where the permissible capital payment is less than nominal value of shares redeemed, the difference is transferred to capital redemption reserve. As £18,750 is less than £75,000, then £56,250 is transferred to capital redemption reserve.

Is there any premium payable on redemption? No.

Are the shares redeemed wholly out of profits? No, since a permissible capital payment arises, and s. 53(1) is overridden by s. 54.

The balance sheet of Mortimer Ltd will appear thus:

	£
Sundry net assets (excluding bank)	156,250
Bank (£162,500 − £75,000)	87,500
	243,750

	£
Ordinary share capital (£187,500 − £75,000)	112,500
Non-distributable reserves (£75,000 + £56,250)	131,250
	243,750

(b) Does a payment out of capital arise? Yes

POOC = redemption price − DP − PNI

$$= £150,000 - 56,250 - nil = £93,750$$

Section 54 must be applied. The permissible capital payment is greater than nominal value of shares redeemed, i.e. £93,750 is greater than £75,000. The difference of £18,750 can reduce non-distributable reserves (s. 54(5)).

Balance sheet of Mortimer appears thus:

	£
Sundry net assets (excluding bank)	156,250
Bank (£162,500 − £150,000)	12,500
	168,750

	£
Ordinary share capital (£187,500 − £75,000)	112,500
Non-distributable reserves (£75,000 − £18,750)	56,250
	168,750

7   Firstly, note that permissible capital payments are not allowed as far as public limited companies are concerned.

(a)   Venus plc purchases 40,000 shares for £80,000. As no fresh issue of shares occurs for the purpose, the existing share premium account cannot be used. Any premium payable on redemption must therefore be paid out of distributable profits (s. 45(5)(b)). Since the shares are redeemed wholly out of profits, the amount by which the company's share capital is reduced on cancellation, shall be transferred to the capital redemption reserve (s. 53(1)).

(b)   Pluto plc purchases its shares at 90p each. Section 53(1) must be applied. Further, the discount of 10p per share will be passed to capital redemption reserve thus reducing the amount to be transferred from P & L.

(c)   Mars plc purchases its shares at 200p each. As a fresh issue of shares, 6,000 8% redeemable preference shares, are issued, the share premium account can be used under s. 45(6).

(i)   Proceeds of a fresh issue = £6,000.
(ii)   Premium received in respect of shares being cancelled is equal to £60,000 × 40,000/240,000 = £10,000.
(iii) No premium arises on preference shares issued.

Where a fresh issue of shares is effected for the redemption and the proceeds of issue (£6,000) are less than the aggregate nominal value of the shares redeemed (£40,000), the difference is to be transferred to capital redemption reserve.

(d)   Saturn Ltd purchases its shares partly out of capital at 200p each.
PCP = redemption price − DP − PNI
Where: PCP = permissible capital payment

DP = distributable profits
PNI = proceeds of a new issue
So PCP = £80,000 − £10,000 − nil = £70,000
Where PCP is greater than nominal value of shares redeemed (£70,000 is greater than £40,000), the difference can reduce the share premium account (s. 54(5)).

(e) Jupiter Ltd purchases its shares partly out of capital at 90p.
PCP = redemption price − DP − PNI
    = £36,000 − £10,000 − nil = £26,000
Where PCP is less than nominal value of shares redeemed (£26,000 is less than £40,000), the difference must be transferred to capital redemption reserve (s. 54(4)).

The balance sheets of the companies after the transactions will be as follows:

	Venus plc £ thousands	Pluto plc £ thousands	Mars plc £ thousands	Saturn Ltd £ thousands	Jupiter Ltd £ thousands
Capital and reserves					
8% preference shares	−	−	6	−	−
Ordinary shares	200	200	200	200	200
Share premium	60	60	54	30	60
Capital redemption reserve	40	40	34	nil	14
	300	300	294	230	274
Profit and loss	20	24	32	nil	nil
	320	324	326	230	274

8

(a) Matters to be given attention before a private limited company redeems or purchases its own shares:

(i) Check authority in articles of association.
(ii) Redeemable shares cannot be issued for the purposes of redemption when there are no issued shares of the company which are not redeemable.
(iii) Shares cannot be redeemed unless they are fully paid.
(iv) The terms of redemption must provide for payment on redemption.
(v) Within the period of 28 days beginning with the date on which any shares purchased by a company under section 46 of CA 1981, are delivered to the company, the company shall deliver to the Registrar of Companies for registration a return in the prescribed form stating, with respect to the shares of each class purchased, the number and nominal value of those shares and the date on which they were delivered to the company.
(vi) A payment out of capital must be approved by special resolution.
(vii) The directors must make a statutory declaration.
(viii) The statutory declaration must be accompanied by an auditors' report addressed to the directors.

This list is not exhaustive.

(b)

	Hermes Ltd Before £	Hermes Ltd After £
Net assets (excluding bank)	5,000	5,000
Bank	10,000	5,000
	15,000	10,000
	£	£
Capital and reserves		
Preference shares	5,000	nil
Ordinary shares	3,000	3,000
Capital redemption reserve	nil	3,000
Non-distributable reserve	4,000	4,000
Profit and loss	3,000	nil
	15,000	10,000

PCP = redemption price − DP − PNI
Where PCP = permissible capital payment
     DP   = distributable profits
     PNI = proceeds of a new issue
So PCP = £5,000 − £3,000 − nil = £2,000

Where the permissible capital payment is less than nominal value of shares redeemed (£2,000 is less than £5,000), the difference must go to capital redemption reserve (s. 54(4)).

	Invincible Ltd Before £	Invincible Ltd After £
Net assets (excluding bank)	5,000	5,000
Bank	10,000	1,250
	15,000	6,250
	£	£
Capital and reserves		
Preference shares	5,000	nil
Ordinary shares	3,000	3,000
Capital redemption reserve	nil	nil
Non-distributable reserve	4,000	3,250
Profit and loss	3,000	nil
	15,000	6,250

PCP = redemption price − DP − PNI
    = £8,750 − £3,000 − nil = £5,750

Where the permissible capital payment is greater than the nominal value of shares redeemed, then non-distributable reserves can be reduced by the difference.

Although s. 53(1) states that a redemption wholly out of profits requires the nominal value of shares redeemed to go to capital redemption reserve, this does not apply here because the redemption is not wholly out of profits.

9 Part 3 (ss. 39 to 45) of the Companies Act 1980, deals with the restrictions on the distribution of profits and assets. Section 39(1) forbids a company from making a distribution except out of profits available for the purpose. A company's profits available for distribution are its accumulated, realised profits, so far as not previously utilised by distribution or capitalisation, less its accumulated realised losses, so far as not previously written off in a reduction or reorganisation of capital duly made.

A company cannot apply unrealised profit in paying up debentures or any amounts unpaid on any of its issued shares (s. 39(3)).

For the purposes of the above, any provision, other than one in respect of any diminution in value of a fixed asset appearing on a revaluation of *all* the fixed assets of the company, shall be treated as a realised loss (s. 39(4)). Thus a revaluation deficit on the revaluation of *all* fixed assets is not to be treated as a realised loss. However, if all the fixed assets are not revalued, then any deficit will presumably be treated as a realised loss. If a fixed asset is revalued upwards, then the increased depreciation charge (compared with the original depreciation) can be treated as a realised profit (s. 39(5)).

A public company may only make a distribution of profits where (s. 40(1)):

(a)   The net assets of the company are greater than the aggregate of the company's called-up share capital and its undistributable reserves;

(b)   The distribution does not reduce the net assets to less than the aggregate.

For the purpose of this section, the undistributable reserves of a company are:

(a)   The share premium account.

(b)   The capital redemption reserve.

(c)   The amount by which the company's accumulated, unrealised profits, so far as not previously utilised by any capitalisation of a description to which this paragraph applies, exceed its accumulated, unrealised losses, so far as not previously written off in a reduction or reorganisation of capital duly made.

(d)   Any other reserve which the company is forbidden from distributing by any enactment, other than one contained in part 3 of the Companies Act 1980, or by its memorandum or articles.

Paragraph (c) applies to every description of capitalisation except a transfer of any profits of the company to its capital redemption reserve on or after 22 December 1980.

In effect, a capital maintenance test has been introduced; this means that public companies must now write off revaluation losses when computing their distributable profit.

Some points are worthy of mention in respect of the effect of the Companies Act 1980, on investment companies.

Firstly, an investment company must be a listed public company (s. 41(3)).

For an investment company, an 'asset ratio' test has been introduced in deciding whether it can make a distribution of profits, that is, the aggregate of its assets is at least equal to one a half times its liabilities, where 'liabilities' includes any provisions (s. 41).

The requirements for an investment company to fall to be classified as such are:

(a)   That the business of the company consists of investing its funds mainly in securities, with the aim of spreading investment risk and giving members of the company the benefit of the results of the management of its funds.

(b)   That none of the company's holdings in companies, other than companies which are for the time being investment companies, represents more than 15% by value of the investing company's total investment.

(c)   That distribution of the company's capital profits is prohibited by its memoradum or articles of association.

(d)   That the company has not retained, otherwise than in compliance with part 3 of the Companies Act 1980, in respect of any accounting reference period more than 15% of the income it derives from securities.

(e)   That the company has given notice to the Registrar that it is intended to be an investment company.

10   Preparation of financial statements for publication

INTRODUCTION

The Companies Act 1981 introduced a number of formats for company balance
sheets and profit and loss accounts and required that a company should adopt one
of the laid-down formats for its annual accounts. This is the first time that there has
been a requirement in law as to the way in which financial statements have to be
presented. There are two formats for the balance sheet, one horizontal and one
vertical, and four for the profit and loss account, two horizontal and two vertical.
In addition to the specified formats the Companies Act 1981 added to and changed
the requirements of previous Companies Acts. Unfortunately there is as yet no
consolidated Act and consequently in order to ensure that companies comply with
the statutory requirements for disclosure in their published accounts one has to be
aware of the disclosures required by the Companies Acts from 1948 to 1981
inclusive. Five questions appear in this chapter on published accounts, the last
question also requiring a directors' report. All questions incorporate aspects of
various Statements of Standard Accounting Practice as published accounts must
not only comply with the law but with generally accepted accounting principles.
The answers have used format 1 for both the balance sheet and the profit and
loss account as it is felt that this is the format which is most likely to be encountered.

QUESTIONS

1   From the information given below you are required to prepare for Brighton Metals Ltd a forecast profit and loss account for the year ended 30 June 1983 and a balance sheet at that date, both statements to comply, as far as the information is given, with the Companies Acts 1948 to 1981. (Ignore comparative figures.)

35 marks

Trial balance of Brighton Metals Ltd as at 30 June 1982

	Dr £	Cr £
Ordinary shares of £1 each		200,000
14% redeemable preference shares (redeemable 1 January 1983 at 110)		100,000
General reserve		40,000
Profit and loss account		52,000
12% debentures (repayable 31 March 1983)		100,000
Tax payable 1 January 1984		40,000
Creditors		60,000
Tax payable 1 January 1983		60,000
Proposed final ordinary dividend		21,000
Bank overdraft		80,000
VAT		18,000
Wages accrued		2,000
Distribution expenses accrued		3,000
Administration expense accrued		4,000
ACT payable on proposed final dividend		9,000
Long leasehold factory	360,000	
Plant and machinery (cost £500,000)	150,000	
Office equipment (cost £100,000)	50,000	
Motor vehicles (cost £240,000)	60,000	
Stock	100,000	
Debtors	60,000	
ACT recoverable	9,000	
	789,000	789,000

The budget controller obtained the following additional details about proposed cash movements during the year ended 30 June 1983 of Brighton Metals Ltd.

(a)   Share capital. There is to be a rights issue of one ordinary share for every two shares held. The offer price is to be 80p per share. The difference between offer price and par value is to be transferred out of general reserve.

(b)   Loan capital. There is to be an issue on 31 March 1983 of £160,000 of 10% loan stock, repayable in 1986. The issue price is to be £95.

(c) Fixed assets:

   (i)   The long leasehold factory is to be sold on 31 December 1982 for £500,000 and leased back at a rental of £40,000 per annum, payable half yearly in arrears. The tax liability on the capital gain is estimated at £42,000.
   (ii) An office block is to be purchased costing £280,000.
   (iii) Machinery costing £140,000 which has been depreciated by £30,000 is to be sold for £30,000.
   (iv) New plant and machinery is to be purchased for £184,000. VAT is recoverable.
   (v)   Vehicles are to be purchased for £69,000. VAT is recoverable.

(d) Working capital:

   (i)   Estimated payments will be as follows:

	£
Paid to creditors	670,000
Paid to employees	246,000
Paid for distribution costs	172,000
Paid for administration expenses	188,800
Paid for 1981 audit fee	10,000
VAT	47,000

   Note: the leaseback charge of £20,000, the debenture interest and the loan interest to 30 June 1983 are included in the administration expense.

   (ii) Estimated receipts will be:

	£
Received from debtors	1,464,000

   (iii) Accruals and stocks at 30 June 1983:

	£
Stock will increase by	20,000
Creditors at 30 June 1983 will total	80,000
Debtors will increase by	10,000
Wages accrued	6,000
Distribution costs accrued	2,000
Administration expenses accrued	6,000
Tax due on loan interest	1,200

(e) A dividend of £35,000 is proposed for 1982/3.

(f) Taxation:

   (i)   The corporation tax estimate for 1982/83 is £43,000.
   (ii) ACT is calculated at 3/7 of dividend declared.
   (iii) VAT is calculated at 15%. Assume all stock purchases, new plant and vehicles were subject to VAT which is recoverable. The VAT content of distribution expenses was £18,000 and the VAT content of administration expenses was £20,000.

(g)   Depreciation charges for the year 1982/83:

New office block £20,000
Plant and machinery 25% of reducing balance
Vehicles 25% of reducing balance
Office equipment 20% of reducing balance.

2   Sails Ltd, a trading company, has an authorised share capital of £5,000,000 divided into 2,000,000 8% preference shares of £1 each and 6,000,000 ordinary shares of 50p each. Draft accounts for the year ended 30 April 1983 have been prepared as as follows:

Profit and loss account

	£ thousands		£ thousands
Cost of sales	3,964	Turnover	8,500
Distribution costs	827		
Administrative expenses	676		
Corporation tax at 52% (payable 1 January 1985)	650		
Depreciation	315		
Market research: amount written off	848		
Audit fee	18		
Directors' remuneration	86		
Bad debt provision	516		
Net profit for year	600		
	8,500		8,500

Balance sheet at 30 April 1983

	£ thousands		£ thousands	£ thousands
Share capital (all fully paid)		Freehold land and		
Preference	2,000	buildings, at cost		1,600
Ordinary	2,500	Equipment and		
Profit and loss account	2,164	fittings at cost	1,260	
Corporation tax	1,342	Less: Depreciation	840	
Creditors	1,022			420
				2,020
		Balance at bank		4,207
		Stocks		1,716
		Debtors		1,085
	9,028			9,028

You also obtain the following information:

(1) Of the directors' remuneration, all of which was included in the administrative expenses, the non-executive chairman received £2,000, the managing director £24,000 and the remaining three directors equal amounts.

(2) Depreciation has been charged at 25% on cost of equipment and fittings by the straight-line method. All equipment and fittings have been purchased within the last three years. The only alteration to fixed assets was the acquisition of the freehold land and buildings on 1 May 1982 when the value of the land was estimated at £600,000. The directors have agreed that the accounts should conform with the requirements of SSAP 12. Depreciation on equipment and fittings should be included in cost of sales, and that on buildings in administrative expenses.

(3) In previous years the stocks have been valued for accounts purposes at cost on FIFO basis but the administration costs of maintaining this system have become unreasonably high. As the physical stock records are maintained at selling price for control purposes the directors decided on 30 April 1982 to discontinue the recording of stock records at cost. The stock as on 30 April 1983 has been valued at selling price less 45% for the purposes of the accounts. The effect of using this method of valuing the stock as on 30 April 1982 would have been to increase its value by £4,000 and it is estimated that the value of the closing stock has been increased by £5,000 compared with the previous method.

(4) The bad debt provision in the profit and loss account includes an amount of £485,000 in respect of a customer who has been adjudicated bankrupt.

(5) In the profit and loss account the charge of £848,000 in respect of market research on new product lines includes £526,000 carried forward from previous years in accordance with SSAP 13. Whilst market research costs were previously written off over the expected life of the line, the directors have now decided to write off the full expenditure in the year in which it is incurred.

(6) Cost of sales includes £150,000 in respect of uninsured flood damage.

(7) The directors recommend the payment of the preference dividend for the year and an ordinary dividend of 8p per share.

You are required to prepare the company's profit and loss account, balance sheet, and notes thereon for the year ended 30 April 1983 in accordance with generally accepted accounting principles and in a form suitable for presentation to members.

Corresponding figures are not required and the information given may be taken as if it included all that is necessary to satisfy the requirements of the Companies Acts 1948 to 1981.

22 marks

3 Assembly Ltd, which has an authorised share capital of 10,000,000 ordinary shares of 50p each, is a manufacturing company making up its accounts to 30 September in each year. An extended trial balance extracted from the company's records on 30 September 1983 showed the following:

	Revenue accounts £	£	Balance sheet £	£
Advertising	39,960			
Audit fee	7,875			
Balance at bank			1,753,942	
Creditors				357,037
Debtors			167,400	
Discounts on sales for prompt settlement	25,702			
Doubtful debt provision				16,065
Factory power	213,157			
Flood loss	262,500			
General expenses:				
Factory	11,925			
Office	53,047			
Insurance	5,344			
Issued ordinary share capital, fully paid				1,500,000
Light and heat	20,880			
Office furniture, at cost			120,750	
Packing and delivery	30,720			
Plant and machinery at cost			384,487	
Production director's salary	23,437			
Profit and loss account, as on 30 September 1982				259,815
Provision for depreciation to 30 September 1982				
On plant and machinery				173,220
On office furniture				63,060
Provision for unrealised profit on stock, as on 30 September 1982				40,972
Purchases	1,355,752			
Rent and rates	28,080			
Repairs to plant	11,827			
Salaries:				
Office (8 employees)	69,457			
Sales		3,688,042		
Sales director's salary	26,250			
Stocks on hand as on 30 September 1982				
Raw materials	92,565			
Finished goods	450,697			
carried forward	2,729,175	3,688,042	2,426,579	2,410,169

154

	Revenue accounts		Balance sheet	
	£	£	£	£
brought forward	2,729,175	3,688,042	2,426,579	2,410,169
Wages:				
Factory (93 employees)	795,157			
Work in progress as on				
30 September 1982	147,300			
Stocks on hand as on				
30 September 1983				
Raw materials		63,187	63,187	
Finished goods		541,365	541,365	
Work in progress as on				
30 September 1983		137,220	137,220	
Surplus for year	758,182			758,182
	4,429,814	4,429,814	3,168,351	3,168,351

You also obtain the following information:

(1) Finished goods are transferred to trading account at cost plus 10% and this basis is used in valuing year-end stocks for management accounts.

(2) Seven-eights of rent and rates, light and heat and insurance are to be allocated to the factory.

(3) The doubtful debt provision is to be adjusted to 5% of debtors.

(4) Depreciation is to be provided on cost of plant and machinery at 25% and on office furniture at 20%.

(5) The flood loss represents uninsured losses incurred when an outside warehouse storing finished goods was flooded during severe weather conditions.

(6) Provision is to be made for corporation tax of £330,000 based on a rate of 52%, after allowing for the uninsured flood loss.

(7) The directors propose to pay an ordinary dividend of 10p per share for the year.

You are required to prepare so far as the information given allows:

(a) Detailed manufacturing, trading and profit and loss accounts for the year ended 30 September 1983, showing the net profit before taxation for presentation to the directors.   *10 marks*

(b) Financial statements for the year ended 30 September 1983, in accordance with generally accepted accounting principles and in a form suitable for presentation to members, as far as the information is provided in the question.   *18 marks*

Corresponding figures are not required.

Ignore the requirement to disclose accounting policies, and a sources and application of funds statement.

Total 28 marks

4 Building Blocks Ltd manufacture blocks for the building trade and this is their only product. The summarised trial balance of Building Blocks Ltd on 31 March 1983 was:

	£	£
Share capital authorised, issued and fully paid		20,000
Profit and loss account as on 31 March 1982		6,200
Plant and machinery, at cost	6,000	
Depreciation of plant and machinery		3,000
Motor vehicles, at cost	3,200	
Depreciation of motor vehicles		1,400
Freehold land and buildings, at cost	18,000	
Depreciation of freehold buildings		1,600
Trading profit: half-year to 30 September 1982		3,900
Trading profit: half-year to 31 March 1983		3,686
Distribution expenses	2,200	
Administration expenses	900	
Directors' remuneration	2,500	
Auditors' remuneration	400	
Office equipment and furnishings, at cost	1,000	
Depreciation of office equipment and furnishings		300
Balance at bank	2,680	
Debtors	4,900	
Creditors		2,644
Stocks at 31 March 1983 at cost:		
Cement and aggregate	304	
Blocks	646	
	42,730	42,730

The make-up of the trading profit for each of the half-years was:

	To 30 September 1982		To 31 March 1983	
	Blocks	£	Blocks	£
Sales	780,000	23,400	756,000	24,192
Cost of production:				
Labour		11,000		12,540
Cement		3,300		3,590
Aggregate		2,200		2,284
Plant expenses and production overheads		2,520		2,458
carried forward		19,020		20,872

156

	To 30 September 1982		To 31 March 1983	
	Blocks	£	Blocks	£
brought forward		19,020		20,872
Depreciation of plant and machinery		150		150
Depreciation of freehold buildings		80		80
	770,000	19,250	784,000	21,102
Opening stocks of blocks	12,000	300	2,000	50
	782,000	19,550	786,000	21,152
Closing stocks of blocks	2,000	50	24,000	646
	780,000	19,500	762,000	20,506
Trading profit		£3,900		£3,686

You ascertain in respect of the year to 31 March 1983 that:

(1) During the year an adjoining plot of open ground was purchased freehold for £1,500.

(2) There were no changes in the other fixed assets during the year.

(3) The apparent shortage of blocks arose through the use of blocks to build a wall around the side of the newly acquired land during January 1983.

(4) No separate records were kept of the cost of building the wall. Blocks, cement and aggregate were taken from stock, and labour normally engaged on production was used, men being transferred from production to wall building and back as available.

(5) The only variations in the direct costs of production were that from 1 October 1982 wages were increased by 10%, and the price of cement was increased by 5%, these being the first changes for 12 months.

(6) Motor vehicles are to be depreciated by 25% on the reducing-balance basis.

(7) Office equipment and furniture are to be depreciated by 10% on cost.

(8) Freehold buildings are depreciated by 2%: the cost of the land at 1 April 1982 was £8,500. Depreciation should not be charged on the wall.

(9) A bad debt of £211 is to be written off.

(10) Provision is to be made for a dividend of 3% for the year.

(11) No corporation tax liability arises for the year nor does Building Blocks Ltd expect any to arise next year.

You are required to prepare, in accordance with the Companies Acts and SSAPs as far as the information permits, the profit and loss account for the year ended 31 March 1983, the balance sheet as on that date, and notes to the accounts.

Assume basic-rate income tax to be 30%, and ignore the requirement to disclose accounting policies.

30 marks

5 Serpell plc is an established engineering company. The following trial balance at 31 March 1983 has been extracted:

		£ thousands	£ thousands
Share capital			500
Share premium			150
Profit and loss at 1 April 1982			1,523
Capital redemption			50
10% debentures, redeemable 1990 (secured by floating charge)			300
Land and buildings:	At cost	2,010	
	Accumulated depreciation		60
Plant and machinery:	At cost	500	
	Accumulated depreciation		210
Motor vehicles:	At cost	120	
	Accumulated depreciation		50
Goodwill:	At cost	150	
	Accumulated depreciation		10
Investment: 25,000 £1 ordinary shares in Rail plc		30	
Stocks at 1 April 1982:	Raw materials	50	
	Work in progress	75	
	Finished goods	150	
Purchases ledger control			210
Sales ledger control		300	
Rates prepayment		4	
Cash in hand		2	
Cash at bank			42
Wages accrual			2
Expenses accrual			6
Bank loan, repayable 1986 (interest 2% above base rate)			75
Sales			5,125
Purchases, including factory wages		4,100	
Distribution costs		200	
Administrative expenses (including £300 SDP donation)		610	
Debenture interest		30	
Dividend income, net			7
Bank interest: Overdraft		5	
Loan		7	
Extraordinary income: surplus on disposal of investment			30
Corporation tax		2	
Auditors' fees		5	
		8,350	8,350

You are told the following additional information.

(1) Stocks at 31 March 1983 were

	£
Raw materials	45,000
Work in progress	79,000
Finished goods	170,000

(2) Directors received the following remuneration

	£
Mr A (chairman)	35,000
Mr B	22,000
Mr C	41,000
Mr D	15,000
Mr E	nil

All directors were additionally paid fees of £1,500 each, and had pension contributions paid by the company on their behalf of £2,000 each. Mr D worked for the company overseas during the year, returning only for the monthly board meetings.

All emoluments have already been charged to the appropriate expense account.

(3) Corporation tax of £25,000 is to be provided: the existing balance being due to an underprovision in the previous year.

(4) Depreciation has already been provided as follows

	£	Estimated useful life
Land	nil	
Buildings	10,000	50 years
Plant and machinery	35,000	20 years
Motor vehicles	20,000	5 years
Goodwill	7,500	20 years

(5) During the year, plant was purchased for £20,000, and freehold land and buildings for £1,000,000. A holding of shares of Superdrug plc, a fixed-asset investment, was bought for £42,000 and sold for £72,000 during the year. Tax of £9,000 is payable on the surplus. This is in addition to that provided in (3) above.

(6) Staff were employed during the year as follows

	Factory	Distribution	Administrative
Average number employed	120	10	35
Remuneration (including pension costs)	£1,350,000	£97,500	£317,000

One salesman earned £31,500 during the year.

(7) All directors have held 20,000 shares in the company throughout the year, and Mr A was trustee of a trust that held a further 10,000 shares.

(8) There was an issue of 150,000 shares at £2 during the year to fund the purchase of land and buildings.

You are required to prepare the following in accordance with the requirements of the Companies Acts in a form suitable for presentation to the members:

(a)   The profit and loss account.

(b)   The balance sheet.

(c)   The notes required in respect of:

      (i)   Directors and staff.
      (ii)   Fixed assets.
      (iii) Accounting policies.

(d)   The directors' report.

Assume a rate of income tax of 30%.

35 marks

ANSWERS

1

Profit and loss account for the year ended 30 June 1983 of Brighton Metals Ltd.

		£
Turnover* (W1)		1,440,000
Cost of sales* (W2)		960,000
Gross profit		480,000
Distribution cost (W3)	183,000	
Administration expenses (W4)	217,000	400,000
Trading profit		80,000
Interest payable (W4)		13,000
Profit on ordinary activities before tax		67,000
Taxation		43,000
Profit on ordinary activities after tax		24,000
Extraordinary item		
Sale of freehold	140,000	
Less: Tax	42,000	98,000
		122,000
Dividend		
Preference dividend paid	7,000	
Ordinary dividend proposed	35,000	42,000
Retained profit		80,000

*Brighton Metals Ltd is a medium-sized company and so these items could be omitted from the accounts filed with the Registrar.

Balance sheet as at 30 June 1983

	£ thousands	£ thousands	£ thousands
Fixed assets			
Tangible assets			
Land and buildings		260	
Plant and machinery		150	
Office equipment		40	
Vehicles		90	540
carried forward			540

	£ thousands	£ thousands	£ thousands
brought forward			540
Current assets			
Stocks	120		
Debtors			
Trade debtors	70		
Other debtors: ACT (W5)	15		
Cash at bank and in hand (W9)	151	356	
Creditors: amounts falling due within one year			
Bank overdraft	—		
Trade creditors	80		
Other creditors (W7)	82		
Accruals	14		
Proposed dividend	35	211	
Net current assets			145
Total assets less current liabilities			685
Creditors: amounts falling due after more than one year			
Loans		160	
Other creditors (W8)		73	233
			452
Capital and reserves			
Called-up share capital		300	
General reserve		20	
Profit and loss account		132	
			452

Notes to the accounts

1 Profit for year after charging:

	£
Cost of sales	
Depreciation	50,000
Loss on sale of plant	80,000
Distribution costs	
Depreciation	30,000
Administration costs	
Depreciation	30,000
Auditors' remuneration	10,000
Interest payable	
Interest on debentures repaid 31 March 1983	9,000
Interest on loan repayable under five years	4,000

2 Tangible fixed assets

	Land and buildings £	Plant £	Office equipment £	Vehicles £	Total £
Cost					
At 1 July 1982	360,000	500,000	100,000	240,000	1,200,000
Additions	280,000	160,000	–	60,000	500,000
Disposal	(360,000)	(140,000)	–	–	(500,000)
At 30 June 1983	280,000	520,000	100,000	300,000	1,200,000
Depreciation					
At 1 July 1982	–	350,000	50,000	180,000	580,000
Charged in P & L	20,000	50,000	10,000	30,000	110,000
Adjust for disposal		(30,000)	–	–	(30,000)
	20,000	370,000	60,000	210,000	660,000
Net book amounts					
30 June 1982	360,000	150,000	50,000	60,000	620,000
30 June 1983	260,000	150,000	40,000	90,000	540,000

3 Share capital

	1983 £	1982 £
Authorised, allotted, issued, fully paid		
14% preference shares of £1 each		
(redeemable 1 January 1983 at 110)	–	100,000
Ordinary shares of £1 each	300,000	200,000

4 Reserves: Profit and loss account

	£
Balance at 1 July 1982	92,000
Less: Capitalisation:	20,000
Rights issue of 1 ordinary share for every 2 held at offer price of 80p per share, 20p per share being issued as a bonus from reserves	72,000
Retained profit for the year	80,000
	152,000

5 Dividends

	1983 £	1982 £
Final 11.66p per share (10.5p)	35,000	21,000
Preference (14p per share)	7,000	14,000

6   Loan capital

	£
Repayable in full in less than five years	
10% loan stock 1986	160,000

Note. The answers are in format 1 of the 1981 Companies Act. The other formats are acceptable.

Workings

		VAT	
	£	£	£
1 **Turnover**			
Debtors at 30 June 1982	60,000		
Cash received	1,646,000		
	1,586,000		
Debtors at 30 June 1983	70,000		
	1,656,000	216,000	1,440,000
2 **Cost of sales**			
Purchases			
Creditors at 30 June 1982	60,000		
Cash payments	670,000		
	610,000		
Creditors at 30 June 1983	80,000		
	690,000	90,000	600,000
Wages			
Accrued at 30 June 1982	2,000		
Paid	246,000		
	244,000		
Accrued at 30 June 1983	6,000		
	250,000	—	250,000
Depreciation			
Plant cost	520,000		
Depreciation to 30 June 1982	320,000		
Book value	200,000		
25% of balance			50,000
Loss on sale			80,000
			980,000
Less: Stock increase			20,000
			960,000

		VAT	
	£	£	£
3 Distribution cost			
Accrued at 30 June 1982	3,000		
Paid	172,000		
	169,000		
Accrued at 30 June 1983	2,000		
	171,000	18,000	153,000
Depreciation			
Cost of vehicles	300,000		
Less depreciation	180,000		
	120,000		
25% of balance			30,000
			183,000
4 Administration			
Accrued at 30 June 1982	4,000		
Paid	198,800		
	194,800		
Accrued at 30 June 1983 (£6,000 + £1,200)	7,200		
	202,000	20,000	182,000
Depreciation			
Cost of office equipment	100,000		
Depreciation	50,000		
	50,000		
20% of balance			10,000
Office premises per question			20,000
Premium on redemption	10,000		
Discount on issue	8,000		18,000
			230,000

Total made up of:

	£
Administration expenses	217,000
Interest on debentures	9,000
Interest on loan	4,000

5   ACT on £35,000 dividend = £15,000

6 VAT

	£	£
Accrued at 30 June 1982		18,000
Sales		216,000
		234,000
Purchases	90,000	
Distribution	18,000	
Administration	20,000	
Plant	24,000	
Vehicles	9,000	161,000
		73,000
Cash paid		47,000
Accrued at 30 June 1983		26,000

7 Other creditors (due within one year)

	£ thousands
Tax	40
VAT (W6)	26
ACT	15
	81
Income tax	1
	82

8 Other creditors (due after more than one year)

	£ thousands
1982/83 tax	43
ACT paid	3
	40
Extraordinary	42
	82
Less: ACT	9
	73

9 Cash at bank and in hand

	£	£	£
Overdraft at 30 June 1982			80,000
Cash from debtors			1,646,000
carried forward			1,566,000

	£	£	£
brought forward			1,566,000
Less:			
Creditors		670,000	
Wages		246,000	
Administration		198,800	
Distribution		172,000	
Office block		280,000	
Plant		184,000	
Vehicles		69,000	
Preference shares		110,000	
Debentures		100,000	
VAT		47,000	
ACT		9,000	
Dividend 1981/82		21,000	
Preference 1982/83		7,000	
Tax	60,000		
Add: ACT	3,000	63,000	(2,176,800)
Add:			
Sale of plant		30,000	
Freehold sale		500,000	
Loan		152,000	
Rights issue		80,000	
			762,000
			151,200

2

Profit and loss account for the year ended 30 April 1983 of Sails Ltd

	Note	£ thousands	£ thousands
Turnover	1(a)		8,500
Cost of sales			4,451
Gross profit			4,049
Distribution costs			827
Administrative expenses			1,316
Profit on ordinary activities	2		1,906
Tax on profit on ordinary activities	3		728
Profit on ordinary activities after taxation			1,178
Extraordinary loss	4		72
Profit for the financial year			1,106
Dividends	5		560
Retained profit for the year			546
carried forward			546

167

	Note	£ thousands	£ thousands
brought forward			546

Retained profits brought forward

	Note	£ thousands	£ thousands
As previously stated		1,564	
Prior-year adjustment	1(d)	526	
			1,038
Retained profits carried forward			1,584

Balance sheet as at 30 April 1983

	Note	£ thousands	£ thousands
Fixed assets: tangible assets	6		2,000
Current assets			
Stocks		1,716	
Debtors	7	1,325	
Cash at bank and in hand		4,207	
		7,248	
Creditors: amounts falling due within one year	8	2,514	
Net current assets			4,734
Total assets less current liabilities			6,734
Creditors: amounts falling due after more than one year	9		650
			6,084
Capital and reserves			
Called-up share capital	10		4,500
Profit and loss account			1,584
			6,084

. . . .) Directors
. . . .)

Notes to the accounts

1 Accounting policies

(a) Turnover represents the amount received and receivable in respect of goods and services provided in the year.

(b) Depreciation has been provided on a straight-line basis to write off the cost of the assets over their estimated useful lives as follows:

Freehold building   50 years (assumed)
Equipment and fittings   5 years

(c) Stocks are valued on a 'first in, first out' basis at selling price less gross profit. In previous years stocks were valued at cost. The effect of this change in policy on the accounts is immaterial.

(d) Market research costs are written off in the period in which they are incurred. In previous years, they were capitalised and written off over the expected life of the product line to which they are related. The effect of this change in policy is shown as a prior-year adjustment to retained profits brought forward.

2 Operating profit is arrived at after charging the following:

	£ thousands	£ thousands
Depreciation		335
Auditors' remuneration		18
Directors' emoluments		
Fees	2	
Other	84	
		86
Exceptional bad debt		485
Market research costs		322

Directors' emoluments	
Your chairman received	£2,000
Your highest-paid director received	£24,000
Three other directors received emoluments in the range £15,001 – £20,000	

3 Taxation comprises UK corporation tax at 52% based on the profit for the year.

4 Extraordinary charge

	£ thousands
Loss due to uninsured flood damage	150
Tax thereon	78
	72

5 Proposed dividends are as follows:

	£ thousands
Preference shares (8p per share)	160
Ordinary shares (8p per share)	400
	560

6 Fixed assets

Cost	Freehold land and buildings £ thousands	Equipment and fittings £ thousands	Total £ thousands
At 1 May 1982	–	1,260	1,260
Additions	1,600	–	1,600
At 30 April 1983	1,600	1,260	2,860
Accumulated depreciation			
At 1 May 1982	–	525	525
Provision for year	20	315	335
At 30 April 1983	20	840	860
Net book value			
At 1 May 1982		735	735
At 30 April 1983	1,580	420	2,000

7 Debtors

	£ thousands
Trade debtors	1,085
Prepayments and accrued income: Advance corporation tax recoverable after more than one year	240
	1,325

8 Creditors: amounts falling due within one year

	£ thousands	£ thousands
Trade creditors		1,022
Other creditors including taxation and social security		
Corporation tax	692	
Advance corporation tax	240	
Proposed dividend	560	
		1,492
		2,514

9 Creditors: amounts falling due after more than one year

	£ thousands
Other creditors including taxation and social security: corporation tax payable 1 January 1985	650

10 Share capital

	Authorised £ thousands	Issued and fully paid £ thousands
8% £1 preference shares	2,000	2,000
50p ordinary shares	3,000	2,500
	5,000	4,500

11 The accounts were approved by the board of directors on . . . . . .

Workings

1 **Cost of sales**

	£ thousands
Balance per profit and loss account	3,964
Depreciation	315
Research and development	322
	4,601
Less: Flood damage	150
	4,451

2 **Administrative expenses**

	£ thousands
Balance per profit and loss account	676
Audit fee	18
Directors' remuneration	86
Bad debt provision	516
Depreciation	20
	1,316

3 **Tax on profit on ordinary activities**

	£ thousands
Balance per profit and loss account	650
Add: Tax on extraordinary item (52% × £150,000)	78
	728

3

(a) **Manufacturing, trading and profit and loss account for the year ended 30 September 1983**

	£	£
Raw materials		
Stocks as on 30 September 1982	92,565	
Purchases	1,355,752	
	1,448,317	
Stocks as on 30 September 1983	(63,187)	
		1,385,130
Wages		795,157
Prime cost		2,180,287
carried forward		2,180,287

171

	£	£	£
brought forward			2,180,287
Indirect expenses			
Factory power		213,157	
Rent and rates (W1)		24,570	
Light and heat (W1)		18,270	
Insurance (W1)		4,676	
General expenses		11,925	
Production director's salary		23,437	
Plant: Repairs		11,827	
Depreciation (W2)		96,122	
			403,984
Factory cost of production			2,584,271
Work in progress as on			
30 September 1982		147,300	
Work in progress as on			
30 September 1983		(137,220)	10,080
Factory cost of finished goods			2,594,351
Add: Profit margin (10%)			259,435
Transferred to trading account			2,853,786
Sales			3,688,042
Cost of goods sold			
Stocks as on 30 September 1982		450,697	
Transferred from manufacturing			
account		2,853,786	
		3,304,483	
Stocks as on 30 September 1983		541,365	
			2,763,118
Gross profit			924,924
Establishment costs			
Rent and rates (W1)	3,510		
Light and heat (W1)	2,610		
Insurance (W1)	688		
Depreciation on office			
furniture (W2)	24,150		
		30,938	
Administration and general costs			
General expenses	53,047		
Salaries	69,457		
Audit fee	7,875		
		130,379	
carried forward		161,317	924,924

	£	£	£
brought forward		161,317	924,924
Selling and distribution costs			
Advertising	39,960		
Packing and delivery	30,720		
Sales director's salary	26,250		
		96,930	
Financial costs			
Discount on sales for prompt settlement	25,702		
Doubtful debt provision no longer required	(7,695)		
		18,007	
			276,254
Net profit			648,670
Factory profit (from manufacturing account)			259,435
			908,105
Less: Increase in provision for unrealised profit (W4)			8,243
Net profit before extraordinary item			899,862
Extraordinary item before taxation: Flood loss			262,500
Net profit for the year before taxation and after extraordinary item			637,362

(b) **Profit and loss account for the year ended 30 September 1983**

Notes		£	£
1	Turnover		3,688,042
	Cost of sales (W10)		2,511,926
	Gross profit		1,176,116
	Distribution costs*		96,930
	Administrative expenses		179,324
2	Profit before taxation on ordinary activities		899,862
3	Tax on profit on ordinary activities (W5)		466,500
	Profit after taxation on ordinary activities		433,362
4	Extraordinary charge		126,000
	Profit for the financial year		307,362
	Dividends proposed: 10p per share		300,000
5	Retained profit for the year		7,362

*Note that advertising and sales director's salary have been classified as a distribution cost.

Balance sheet as at 30 September 1983

Notes		£	£
	Fixed assets		
6	Tangible assets		148,685
	Current assets		
7	Stocks	692,557	
8	Debtors	287,601	
	Cash at bank and in hand	1,753,942	
		2,734,100	
9	Creditors: amounts falling due within one year	1,115,608	
	Net current assets		1,618,492
	Total assets less current liabilities		1,767,177
	Capital and reserves		
10	Called-up share capital		1,500,000
5	Profit and loss account		267,177
			1,767,177

Notes on the accounts

These notes form part of the financial statements.

1 Turnover represents the total amounts receivable in respect of goods supplied net of returns and excludes value added tax.

2 Profit before taxation is arrived at after charging:

	£
Depreciation: Plant and machinery	96,122
Office furniture	24,150
Audit fee	7,875
Directors' emoluments: Fees	—
Other	49,687

The emoluments of the chairman were £X.

The emoluments of the highest paid director were £26,250. One other director's emoluments were between £20,001 and £25,000.

3 Taxation

	£
Corporation tax on profit for the year at 52%	466,500

4 Extraordinary item

	£
Uninsured losses arising from flood	262,500
Less: Attributable taxation	136,500
	126,000

5 Profit and loss account

	£
At 30 September 1982	259,815
Retained for year	7,362
At 30 September 1983	267,177

6 Fixed assets (this schedule would normally give further information about additions, sales etc. but details are not given in the question).

	Plant and machinery £	Office furniture £	Total £
Cost	384,487	120,750	505,237
Accumulated depreciation	269,342	87,210	356,552
At 30 September 1983	115,145	33,540	148,685

7 Stocks

	£
Raw materials and consumables	63,187
Work in progress	137,220
Finished goods and goods for resale (W9)	492,150
	692,557

8 Debtors

	£
Trade debtors less bad debts provision (W3)	159,030
Prepayments and accrued income: ACT receivable after more than one year (W8)	128,571
	287,601

9 Creditors: amounts falling due within one year

	£
Trade creditors	357,037
Other creditors including taxation and social security: taxation (W8)	458,571
Proposed dividend	300,000
	1,115,608

10 Share capital

   Authorised: 10,000,000 ordinary shares of 50p each
   Issued and fully paid: 3,000,000 ordinary shares of 50p each.

11 The average number of employees during the year was as follows:

Factory	Office	Total
93	8	101

   Their aggregate remuneration amounted to £864,614.

Workings

1 Allocation of expenses

	Total £	Factory £ (7/8)	Office £ (1/8)
Rent and rates	28,080	24,570	3,510
Light and heat	20,880	18,270	2,610
Insurance	5,344	4,676	668
	54,304	47,516	6,788

2 Depreciation charge for the year

	£
Plant and machinery 25% × £384,487	96,122
Office furniture 20% × £120,750	24,150
	120,272

3 Provision for doubtful debts

	£
Provision required as on 30 September 1983 5% × £167,400	8,370
Less: Provision per trial balance	16,065
Provision no longer required	(7,695)

4 Provision for unrealised profit

	£
Provision required as on 30 September 1983 £541,365 × 10/110	49,215
Less: Provision as on 30 September 1982	40,972
Increase in provision for the year	8,243

5 Taxation

	£
Corporation tax to be provided	330,000
Add: Tax saving attributable to extraordinary item 52% × £262,500	136,500
Taxation on ordinary profits	466,500

6 Extraordinary item

	£
Flood loss before tax effects	262,500
Less: Tax saving attributable thereto (W5)	136,500
Extraordinary item net of attributable taxation	126,000

7 Debtors

	£
Per trial balance	167,400
Less: Provision for doubtful debts (W3)	8,370
	159,030

8 Corporation tax payable

	£
Corporation tax on income (£466,500 − £136,500)	330,000
ACT on proposed dividend (£300,000 × 30/70)	128,571
	458,571

9 Stock of finished goods

	£
Per trial balance	541,365
Less: Provision for unrealised profit (W4)	49,215
	492,150

10 Cost of sales

	£	£
Factory cost of finished goods		2,594,351
Add: Opening stock of finished goods	450,697	
Less: Unrealised profit	40,972	409,725
		3,004,076
Less: Closing stock of finished goods	541,365	
Less: Unrealised profit	49,215	492,150
		2,511,926

Profit and loss account for the year ended 31 March 1983

	Note	£
Turnover		47,592
Cost of sales (W1)		39,531
Gross profit		8,061
Distribution costs (W2)		2,650
Administrative expenses (W3)		4,111
Profit on ordinary activities	1	1,300
Tax on profit on ordinary activities	2	257
Profit on ordinary activities after taxation		1,043
Dividend	3	600
Retained profit for the year		443
Retained profits brought forward		6,200
Retained profits carried forward		6,643

Balance sheet as at 31 March 1983

	Note	£	£
Fixed assets: tangible assets	4		21,835
Current assets			
Stocks (W5)		940	
Debtors: trade debtors		4,689	
Cash at bank and in hand		2,680	
		8,309	
Creditors: amounts falling due within one year	5	3,501	
Net current assets			4,808
Total assets less current liabilities			26,643
Capital and reserves			£
Called-up share capital	6		20,000
Profit and loss account			6,643
			26,643

Notes to the accounts

1 Profit on ordinary activities is arrived at after charging:

	£
Directors' remuneration	2,500
Depreciation	1,010
Auditors' remuneration	400

2 Tax on profit on ordinary activities. The tax charge consists of advance corporation tax deemed to be irrecoverable.

3 The directors propose to pay a dividend of 3% for the year.

4 Fixed assets

	Freehold land and buildings £	Plant and machinery £	Motor vehicles £	Office equipment and furnishings £	Total £
Cost at 1 April 1982	16,500	6,000	3,200	1,000	26,700
Additions	1,985	–	–	–	1,985
Cost at 31 March 1983	18,485	6,000	3,200	1,000	28,685
Depreciation at 1 April 1982	1,440	2,700	1,400	300	5,840
Provision for year	160	300	450	100	1,010
At 31 March 1983	1,600	3,000	1,850	400	6,850
NBV at 31 March 1983	16,885	3,000	1,350	600	21,835
NBV at 1 April 1982	15,060	3,300	1,800	700	20,860

The following depreciation rates are used:

Freehold buildings	2% on cost
Plant and machinery	5% on cost
Motor vehicles	25% on written-down value
Office equipment and furnishings	10% on cost

5 Creditors: amounts due within one year

	£	£
Trade creditors		2,644
Other creditors including taxation and social security:		
Advance corporation tax	257	
Proposed dividend	600	
		857
		3,501

6 Called-up share capital

<table>
<tr><td></td><td>£</td></tr>
<tr><td>Authorised, issued and fully paid</td><td>20,000</td></tr>
</table>

Workings

1 **Cost of sales**

	£
Per trading accounts	40,006
Cost of wall capitalised (W4)	(485)
Overvaluation of stock (W5)	10
	39,531

2 **Distribution costs**

	£
Per profit and loss account	2,200
Depreciation on vehicles (25% × £1,800)	450
	2,650

3 **Administrative costs**

	£
Per profit and loss account	900
Directors' remuneration	2,500
Auditors' remuneration	400
Depreciation on office equipment (10% × £1,000)	100
Bad debt	211
	4,111

4 **Cost of wall and construction**

Number of blocks used (762,000 − 765,000) = 6,000

Direct costs (see note)

		£	£
Labour	£11,000 × 1.1 × 6,000/770,000		94.29
Cement	£3,300 × 1.05 × 6,000/770,000		27.00
Aggregate	£2,200 × 6,000/770,000		17.14
			138.43
Fixed costs			
Plant expenses and production overheads			
£2,458 × 6,000/784,000)		18.81	
Depreciation of plant £150 × 6,000/784,000		1.15	
Depreciation of buildings £80 × 6,000/784,000		0.61	
			20.57
Cost of blocks used			159.00
carried forward			159.00

	£	£
brought forward		159.00

Cost of construction (see note)
  Labour
  £12,540 − £11,000 × 1.1 × 784,000/770,000   220.00
  Cement
  £3,590 − £3,300 × 1.05 × 784,000/770,000   62.00
  Aggregate
  £2,284 − £2,200 × 784,000/770,000   44.00
      326.00

Total cost of wall and construction   485.00

Note. Whilst it would be preferable to base the cost of blocks on the cost of production figures for the half year to 31 March 1983 this is not possible for the direct costs since they contain not only the cost of block production but also the cost of wall construction. The latter may be identified by comparing the actual profit and loss account charge with the actual cost of production by using figures for the half year to 30 September 1982 and updating for increased costs and production.

5 **Valuation of closing stocks**

The valuation of closing stock has been calculated on a total absorbtion costing basis:

£21,102 × 24,000/784,000 = £646

However, the total costs (£21,102) include the cost of wall construction, which must be eliminated. This amounts to:

£326 × 24,000/784,000 = £10

Thus the correct value of closing stocks is:

	£	£
Cement and aggregate		304
Blocks, per question	646	
Less: overvaluation	10	
		636
		940

5

(a) **Profit and loss account for the year ended 31 March 1983**

	Notes	£ thousands
Turnover		5,125
Cost of sales		4,081
Gross profit		1,044
Distribution costs		200
Administrative expenses		615
Operating profit	1	229
Income from other fixed-asset investments		10
Interest payable and similar charges	2	(42)
Profit on ordinary activities before taxation		197
Tax on profit on ordinary activities	3	30
Profit on ordinary activities after taxation		167
Extraordinary item	4	21
Profit for the financial year		188
Retained profit at 1 April 1982		1,523
Retained profit at 31 March 1983		1,711

(b) **Balance sheet as at 31 March 1983**

	Notes	£ thousands	£ thousands
Fixed assets			
Intangible asset: goodwill	7		140
Tangible assets	8		2,310
Investments	9		30
			2,480
Current assets			
Stocks	10	294	
Debtors	11	304	
Cash at bank and in hand		2	
		600	
Creditors: amounts falling due within one year	12	294	
Net current assets		—	306
Total assets less current liabilities			2,786
Creditors: amounts falling due after more than one year	13		375
			2,411

	Notes	£ thousands	£ thousands
Capital and reserves			
Called-up share capital	15		500
Share premium account	14		150
Other reserves: capital redemption			
reserve	14		50
Profit and loss account			1,711
			2,411

Mr A)
) Directors
Mr B)

These accounts were signed on the board's behalf on . . . .

(c) **Notes to the accounts**

1 Operating profit is stated after charging:

	£
Auditors' fees	5,000
Depreciation of fixed assets	72,500
Directors' emoluments: Fees	7,500
Remuneration	123,000

2 Interest payable and similar charges

	£
Bank loans and overdrafts	12,000
Other loans repayable after more than five years	30,000
	42,000

3 Tax on profit on ordinary activities

	£
UK corporation tax at 52% on the year's income	25,000
Previous year's underprovision	2,000
Tax credit on dividend income	3,000
	30,000

4 Extraordinary item

	£
Surplus on disposal of fixed-asset investments	30,000
Attributable tax	9,000
Net surplus	21,000

5 Directors' emoluments

	£
The emoluments of the chairman were	36,500
The emoluments of the highest paid director were	42,500

The emoluments of the other directors working wholly
or substantially in the UK fell within the following ranges

Up to £5,000	One
£20,000 to £25,000	One

6 The average number of employees working for the company was:

Manufacturing	120
Distribution	10
Administrative	35
Total	165

The aggregate emoluments paid to employees amounted to £1,764,500, including one employee who received between £30,000 and £35,000.

7 Intangible fixed assets: goodwill

	£ thousands
Cost	
At 31 March 1983 and 1 April 1982	150
Depreciation	
At 1 April 1982	2.5
Year's amortisation	7.5
At 31 March 1983	10
Net book value	
At 1 April 1982	147.5
At 31 March 1983	140

8 Tangible fixed assets

	Land and buildings £ thousands	Plant and machinery £ thousands	Motor vehicles £ thousands	Total £ thousands
Cost				
At 1 April 1982	1,010	480	120	1,610
Additions	1,000	20	–	1,020
At 31 March 1983	2,010	500	120	2,630
Depreciation				
At 1 April 1982	50	175	30	255
Year's charge	10	35	20	65
At 31 March 1983	60	210	50	320
Net book value				
At 1 April 1982	960	305	90	1,355
At 31 March 1983	1,950	290	70	2,310

9 Investments

	Listed investments £ thousands
Cost	
At 1 April 1982	30
Additions	42
Disposals	(42)
At 31 March 1983	30

10 Stocks

	£ thousands
Raw materials and consumables	45
Work in progress	79
Finished goods and goods for resale	170
	294

11 Debtors

	£ thousands
Trade debtors	300
Prepayments and accrued income	4
	304

12 Creditors: amounts falling due within one year

	£ thousands
Bank loans and overdrafts	42
Trade creditors	210
Other creditors including taxation and social security:	
Taxation	34
Accruals and deferred income	8
	294

13 Creditors: amounts falling due after more than one year

	£ thousands
Debenture loans: 10% loan stock, redeemable 1990 (secured by floating charge)	300
Bank loans and overdrafts	75
	375

The bank loan carries an interest rate of 2% above the base rate, and is repayable in 1986.

14 Movements on reserves

	Share premium £ thousands	Capital redemption £ thousands
At 1 April 1982	–	50
On issue of shares	150	–
At 31 March 1983	150	50

15 Called-up share capital

	£ thousands
At 1 April 1982	350
Issued during year	150
At 31 March 1983	500

During the year shares of a nominal value of £150,000 were issued for £300,000 in order to part fund the acquisition of freehold land and buildings.

Accounting policies

1 Basis of accounting. The accounts have been prepared under the historical cost convention.

2 Depreciation. Depreciation has been provided on all fixed assets with a limited useful life to write off their cost over their estimated useful lives.

These lives are:

Goodwill	20 years
Building	50 years
Plant and machinery	20 years
Motor vehicles	5 years

3 Stocks. Stocks have been valued at the lower of cost and net realisable value. Cost includes overheads attributable to their stage of manufacture, and is computed on the first in, first out method of valuation.

4 Turnover. Turnover comprises the amount received and receivable for goods manufactured during the year, excluding value added tax.

(d) **Report of the directors to the members of Serpell plc**

The directors present their report and accounts for the year ended 31 March 1983.

Principal activities and business review

The principal activity of the company continued to be that of engineering. The business developed satisfactorily throughout the year, and was in a strong position at the end of the year.

Profits and dividends

The profit for the year after tax and extraordinary items amounted to £188,000, as set out on page x. The directors do not recommend the payment of a dividend.

Fixed assets

As part of the company's continuing policy of expansion, a freehold factory was purchased for £1,000,000 during the year.

The directors estimate the market value of the freehold land and buildings held at the end of the year to be £X.

Charitable and political contributions

A donation of £300 was made to the Social Democratic Party during the year.

Directors and their interests in shares

The directors of the company and their shareholdings throughout the year were:

	Beneficially held	Not beneficially held
Mr A	20,000 shares	10,000 shares
Mr B	20,000 shares	
Mr C	20,000 shares	
Mr D	20,000 shares	
Mr E	20,000 shares	

Employment of disabled people

Applications for employment by disabled persons are always fully considered, bearing in mind the respective aptitudes and abilities of the applicant concerned. In the event of employees becoming disabled every effort is made to ensure that their employment with the company continues and the appropriate training is arranged. It is the policy of the company that the training, career development and promotion of disabled persons should, as far as possible, be identical to that of a person who is fortunate enough not to suffer from a disability.

By order of the board

Mr F

Secretary
Date

11 Transfer of a business to a limited company, amalgamations and absorptions

INTRODUCTION

Examination questions involving the transfer of a business to a company appear quite frequently in professional examinations. Such questions may involve the conversion or transfer of a sole trader's business to a limited company or of a partnership to a limited company. Some questions involve an amalgamation of existing companies to form a new company which may or may not mean that the existing companies would go into liquidation depending upon whether the acquisiton is of shares or assets. Alternatively a larger company may absorb a smaller company by either a share purchase or a purchase of assets, the smaller company either continuing in existence (where the purchase is of shares) or going into liquidation (where the purchase is of assets). Although questions are many and varied the principles involved are very similar. If the question asks for the entries in the books of a business which is going into liquidation the main account required is the realisation account (sometimes referred to as liquidation account) which is prepared to calculate the profit or loss on realisation. If the question asks for the entries in the books of a business which is taking over the assets and liabilities of a business which is going into liquidation the main account is a purchase of business account, which reflects the assets and liabilities taken over and the purchase consideration, the balancing figure (if any) being the profit or loss on acquiring the other business.

Six questions appear in this chapter which attempt to cover some of the different aspects which could appear in examination papers. Question 4 deals with the problems of pre-incorporation profits.

QUESTIONS

1 It was agreed that with effect from 1 January 1983, Pooh Ltd would acquire the whole of the issued capital of Tiger Ltd and the fixed assets, stocks and goodwill of Kanga and Roo, a partnership, by the issue of ordinary shares of £1 each fully paid at their then market value of 125p per value.

In computing the number of shares to be issued for each business:

(1)   The fixed assets were to be taken at the value placed on them by an independent valuer.

(2)   Stocks were to be taken at book value subject to a deduction of £1,000 from the stocks of Kanga and Roo for obsolete stock.

(3)   In the case of Tiger Ltd, debtors, creditors and balance at bank were to be taken at book value less £1,500 in respect of a bad debt.

(4)   Goodwill was to be valued at two years' purchase of the average profits of the last three years subject only to the following adjustments:

   (i)   In the case of Tiger Ltd the directors' remuneration charged in each year was to be reduced by £2,500.
   (ii)   In the case of Tiger Ltd, the depreciation charged in each year on other fixed assets was to be substituted by depreciation on those assets calculated at 10% of cost on a straight-line basis.
   (iii) In the case of Kanga and Roo notional salaries of £5,000 p.a., in total, were to be charged for the partners.
   (iv)   In the case of Kanga and Roo £2,000, being an exceptional item of expense, was to be added back to the profits in the year to 31 December 1981.

The summarised balance sheets of the three businesses at 31 December 1982 were:

	Pooh Ltd £	Tiger Ltd £	Kanga and Roo £
Freehold premises at cost	50,000	18,000	12,000
Other fixed assets at cost less depreciation	158,000	37,000	20,000
Stocks at cost	135,000	18,000	11,000
Debtors	123,000	43,000	21,000
Balance at bank	21,000	12,000	5,500
	487,000	128,000	69,500
Ordinary shares £1 each fully paid	300,000	50,000	
Capital account Kanga			30,500
Capital account Roo			11,000
Profit and loss account	122,000	26,000	
Creditors	65,000	52,000	28,000
	487,000	128,000	69,500

You ascertain that:

		Pooh Ltd £	Tiger Ltd £	Kanga and Roo £
(1)	The depreciation deducted from the cost of other fixed assets at 31 December 1982 was	62,000	25,000	10,000
(2)	The independent valuations at 31 December 1982 were:			
	Freehold premises		60,000	25,000
	Other fixed assets		33,000	21,000
(3)	The profits for the last three years ending on 31 December:			
	1980		9,000	9,000
	1981		12,106	6,500
	1982		13,100	9,500
	after charging depreciation amounting to:			
	1980		5,250	
	1981		4,458	
	1982		4,536	
(4)	The other fixed assets at 31 December 1982, at cost were:			
	before 31 December 1979		52,000	
	purchased 1 January 1981		10,000	
(5)	Tiger Ltd had disposed of other fixed assets on 1 January 1982 which had cost £8,000 on 1 January 1980.			

You are required to prepare:

(a)   A statement showing the number of shares to be issued by Pooh Ltd to pay for the acquisitions.   *10 marks*

(b)   The balance sheet, as far as the required information is available, of Pooh Ltd on 1 January 1983, after giving effect to the issue of shares for the acquisitions.
                                                                              12 marks
                                                                        Total 22 marks

2   T, a sole trader, desiring to expand his business, decided to convert the business into a limited company as at 1 January 1983 and to obtain additional finance by issuing further shares for cash. His balance sheet at 31 December 1982 was as follows:

	£			£	£
Capital account	14,270	Fixed assets at cost			
Creditors	892	less depreciation:			
		Freehold buildings		6,660	
		Furniture and fixtures		2,900	9,560
		Current assets:			
		Stocks		2,920	
		Debtors		1,734	
		Cash at bank		948	5,602
	15,162				15,162

A new company, T Ltd, was formed with an authorised share capital of £40,000 in shares of £1 each on 1 January 1983. T received fully paid shares at par in satisfaction of the assets taken over, the balance of the share capital being issued at 125p per share for cash, of which 25p per share was payable on application, 50p per share on allotment (including the premium) and 50p per share on 1 April 1983.

The assets were transferred to the new company at the following values: goodwill, £10,000; freehold buildings, £12,000; furniture and fixtures, £3,600; stocks, £2,800; debtors, £1,600.

T retained the bank balance and paid off the creditors.

Applications for 36,000 shares were received on 6 January 1983, and the appropriate allotments were made on 15 January 1983. Pro rata allotments were made to all applicants for shares and by agreement with the applicants, all surpluses on application and allotment were to be carried forward against the call.

Costs of the transactions were borne by T personally.

You are required to prepare:

(a) Journal entries closing T's books.   *12 marks*
(b) The balance sheet of T Ltd as at 15 January 1983, assuming that no trading transactions took place between 31 December 1982 and 15 January 1983.
                                                            13 marks

Ignore taxation.

                                                        Total 25 marks

3   The following are the balance sheets of B Ltd and W Ltd as at 31 March 1983:

	B Ltd	W Ltd
	£	£
Ordinary shares of £1 each fully paid	10,000	
Ordinary shares of 50p each fully paid		5,000
Profit and loss account	6,000	3,000
Creditors	4,000	3,000
	20,000	11,000

| | B Ltd | W Ltd |
	£	£
Freehold buildings	4,000	2,000
Plant and machinery	5,000	3,000
1,000 ordinary shares in W Ltd at cost	1,000	–
Stock	2,700	1,500
Debtors	6,000	2,000
Balance at bank	1,300	2,500
	20,000	11,000

It was decided that on 1 April 1983 both companies should go into liquidation and that a new company N Ltd should be formed with an authorised capital of £50,000 divided into 100,000 ordinary shares of 50p each to take over all the assets and liabilities of both companies at book values subject to the following adjustments:

(1)   The freehold buildings of both companies are to be increased by 50%.

(2)   The stock of B Ltd is to be reduced by £200.

(3)   B Ltd is to receive £2,500 for goodwill and W Ltd £1,700.

(4)   The debtors of W Ltd are to be valued at £1,800.

(5)   A 5% discount is receivable from the creditors and suitable adjustment is to be made before liquidation.

You are to show:

(a)   The journal entries closing the books of B Ltd.   *10 marks*

(b)   A statement of the shares allotted to the shareholders of each company.
                                                                          9 marks

(c)   The balance sheet immediately after the amalgamation has been completed.
                                                                          6 marks
                                                                 Total 25 marks

4   Rowlock Ltd was incorporated on 1 October 1981 to acquire Rowlock's mail order business, with effect from 1 June 1981.

The purchase consideration was agreed at £35,000 to be satisfied by the issue on 1 December 1981 to Rowlock or his nominee of 20,000 ordinary shares of £1 each, fully paid; and £15,000 7% debentures.

The entries relating to the transfer were not made in the books which were carried on without a break until 31 May 1982.

On 31 May 1982 the trial balance extracted from the books showed the following:

	£	£
Sales		52,185
Purchases	38,829	
Wrapping	840	
Postage	441	
Warehouse rent and rates	921	
Packing expenses	1,890	
Office expenses	627	
Stock on 31 May 1981	5,261	
Director's salary	1,000	
Debenture interest (gross)	525	
Fixed assets	25,000	
Current assets (other than stock)	9,745	
Current liabilities		4,162
Formation expenses	218	
Capital account: Rowlock, 31 May 1981		29,450
Drawings account: Rowlock	500	
	85,797	85,797

You also ascertain the following:

(1) Stock on 31 May 1982 amounted to £4,946.

(2) The average monthly sales for June, July and August were one-half of those for the remaining months of the year. The gross profit margin was constant throughout the year.

(3) Wrapping, postage and packing expenses varied in direct proportion to sales, whilst office expenses were constant each month.

(4) Formation expenses are to be written off.

You are required to prepare the trading and profit and loss account for the year ended 31 May 1982 apportioned between the periods before and after incorporation, and the balance sheet as on that date. The accounts you prepare are for internal use only and thus need not conform with the 1981 Companies Act layout.

25 marks

5 Cotton and Silk decided to amalgamate on 1 July 1983, by selling their separate businesses to Modern Ltd, a new company formed for that purpose with an authorised capital of £40,000 in ordinary shares of £1 each. The following are the summarised balance sheets of the respective businesses as at 30 June 1983:

	Cotton £	Silk £		Cotton £	Silk £
Capital accounts	25,018	11,494	Freehold property	–	14,400
Loan		10,000	Plant and machinery	12,462	4,864
Creditors			Stocks	5,348	5,562
Loan interest			Debtors	13,750	4,014
accrued		300	Bank balance	9,640	10,774
Sundry other					
creditors	16,182	17,820			
	41,200	39,614		41,200	39,614

It was agreed that:

(1) The company should take over the assets and assume the liabilities of the two businesses except (i) bank balances and (ii) the loan and interest accrued thereon. The loan and accrued interest was settled by Silk who introduced the necessary additional cash for the purpose into his business.

(2) The sale values should be the book amounts after adjustment for (i) an agreed value of £18,000 for the freehold property, (ii) obsolete stock of Cotton included at £720*, (iii) a debt of £350 owed to Silk but agreed to be irrecoverable and (iv) an error of £440 in the accounts of Silk, being the omission of an invoice for goods supplied to him. Silk's stock figure is correct.

(3) The company should issue 16,000 ordinary shares at par to Cotton, and 15,000 ordinary shares at par to Silk in consideration for (i) the amounts due to them respectively for the net assets acquired as above and (ii) a cash payment from each vendor for the balance.

*This obsolete stock has zero value.

All the foregoing transactions were completed by the company as agreed on 1 July 1983.

You are required to prepare:

(a) (i) A statement showing the amount of cash to be paid by Cotton and Silk in respect of the shares allotted to them; and

    (ii) The balance sheet of Modern Ltd, as it would appear immediately after the completion of the acquisition, assuming that there were no other transactions, and ignoring taxation and any further costs. *12 marks*

(b) By way of ledger accounts, the closing of the books of Silk. *8 marks*
Total 20 marks

6 A new company, Sponge plc, was formed on 30 April 1983 to take over the business of each of the following companies, all of which went into voluntary liquidation on the following day. The new company was incorporated with a capital

of £300,000 divided into 200,000 ordinary £1 shares and 100,000 10% £1 cumulative preference shares. The three companies taken over had the following summary balance sheets as at 30 April 1983:

	Almond Ltd £ thousands	Battenby Ltd £ thousands	Cherry Ltd £ thousands
Debit balances			
Bank	15		
Investments	10		
Trade debtors	50	48	8
Stock	33	13	8
Plant and machinery	22	8	4
Land and buildings	20	6	
Goodwill	18		4
Preliminary expenses		1	
Profit and loss		12	
	168	88	24

	£ thousands	£ thousands	£ thousands
Credit balances			
Trade creditors	35	20	2
Bank overdraft		18	1
Issued and paid-up capital			
Ordinary £1 shares	100	50	10
10% cumulative preference	100	50	10	20
Profit and loss	—	13	—	1
Revenue reserve	20		
	168	88	24

The basis of absorption of the three companies was as follows:

Almond Ltd. All assets and liabilities to be taken over at book values and settlement to be by 5 fully paid ordinary shares in Sponge plc, to be issued for every 4 shares held in Almond Ltd.

Battenby Ltd. All assets and liabilities to be taken over at book values and settlement to be by 1 fully paid ordinary share and 3 cumulative preference shares paid £0.50 each in Sponge plc, to be issued for every 5 shares held in Battenby Ltd. Sponge plc was to provide for doubtful debts of £9,000 and revalue the stock in hand at £10,000.

Cherry Ltd. Sponge plc to purchase the assets and goodwill for £20,000 cash. Trade creditors to be paid by Cherry Ltd. Cherry Ltd also to pay liquidation expenses of £1,000 and to provide for and pay the outstanding current preference dividend. Sponge plc was to provide £2,000 for doubtful debts and to revalue stock at £7,000.

40,000 cumulative preference shares in Sponge plc are offered to and subscribed for by the public, 50p being called and all but £1,000 being received by 30 June 1983.

All Sponge plc shares are issued at par.

You are required to prepare:

(a)   The liquidation accounts and sundry shareholders accounts of the three vendor companies with the addition, in the case of Cherry Ltd, of its bank account showing the distribution of the available cash among the creditors and respective classes of shareholders. *14 marks*

(b)   The balance sheet of Sponge plc, as at 30 June 1983, there being no transactions other than those above between 30 April and 30 June 1983. *6 marks*

Workings must be submitted and should include the purchase of business account in the books of Sponge plc.

Taxation is to be ignored.

Total 20 marks

ANSWERS

1

(a) Statement of shares to be issued on acquisitions

	Tiger Ltd £	Kanga and Roo £
Net assets acquired at agreed values		
Freehold premises	60,000	25,000
Other fixed assets	33,000	21,000
Stocks	18,000	10,000
Debtors	41,500	
Balance at bank	12,000	
Goodwill (Workings)	24,500	8,000
	189,000	64,000
Less: Creditors assumed	52,000	
Purchase prices	137,000	64,000
Shares to be issued		
£1 ordinary shares at agreed issue price of 125 pence	109,600	51,200

(b) Balance sheet at 1 January 1983

	Cost or valuation £	Accumulated depreciation £	£
Fixed assets			
Intangible assets			
Goodwill			32,500
Tangible assets			
Freehold premises	135,000	–	135,000
Other fixed assets	274,000	62,000	212,000
			379,500
Current assets		£	
Stocks		163,000	
Debtors		164,500	
Balance at bank		33,000	
		360,500	
carried forward		360,500	379,500

	Cost of valuation £	Accumulated depreciation £	£
brought forward		360,500	379,500
Creditors: amounts falling due within one year			
Trade creditors		117,000	
Net current assets			243,500
			623,000
Capital and reserves			
Called-up share capital in £1 ordinary shares			460,800
Share premium account			40,200
Profit and loss account			122,000
			623,000

Note. It should be noted that Pooh Ltd has not complied with SSAP 12 in providing depreciation on freehold buildings.

Workings

1 Goodwill computation

	Tiger Ltd		Kanga and Roo	
	£ −	£ +	£ −	£ +
Profits as given: 1980		9,000		9,000
1981		12,106		6,500
1982		13,100		9,500
		34,206		25,000
Reduction of directors' remuneration (3 × £2,500)		7,500		
Depreciation adjustment (see below)	4,956			
Notional salaries (3 × £5,000)			15,000	
Exceptional item				2,000
	4,956	41,706	15,000	27,000
		4,956		15,000
Adjusted profit for three years		36,750		12,000

199

	Tiger Ltd	Kanga and Roo
	£	£
Annual average	12,250	4,000
Goodwill: two years' purchase of profit	24,500	8,000

2 Depreciation adjustment: Tiger Ltd

	£
Amount charged: 1980	5,250
1981	4,458
1982	4,536
	14,244

Amount to be charged for goodwill purposes

1980 (10% × £60,000)	6,000	
1981 (10% × £70,000)	7,000	
1982 (10% × £62,000)	6,200	
		19,200
Increase in charge		4,956

2

(a) Journal

		£Dr	£Cr
1983	Realisation account	14,214	
1 Jan	Freehold buildings		6,660
	Furniture and fittings		2,900
	Stocks		2,920
	Debtors		1,734
	Being assets transferred to company at book values		
	T Ltd	30,000	
	Realisation account		30,000
	Being consideration due from company for assets transferred		
	Realisation account	15,786	
	Capital account		15,786
	Being profit on realisation		
	Capital account	30,000	
	T Ltd		30,000
	Being discharge of purchase consideration		
	Creditors	892	
	Capital account	56	
	Bank		948
	Being application of cash retained by vendor		

(b) Balance sheet at 15 January 1983

	£	£
Fixed assets		
Intangible assets		
Goodwill		10,000
Tangible assets		
Freehold buildings		12,000
Furniture and fittings		3,600
		25,600
Current assets		
Stocks	2,800	
Debtors	1,600	
Bank	9,000	13,400
		39,000
Capital and reserves		
Called-up share capital (Note 1)		35,000
Share premium account		2,500
Calls in advance		1,500
		39,000

Notes

1 Authorised share capital: 40,000 ordinary shares of £1 each

	£
Issued share capital:	
30,000 ordinary £1 shares fully paid	30,000
10,000 ordinary £1 shares 50p called and paid	5,000
	35,000

3

(a) Journal: B Ltd

		£Dr	£Cr
1983	Realisation account	16,200	
1 Apr	Creditors	4,000	
	Freehold buildings		4,000
	Plant and machinery		5,000
	Shares in W Ltd		1,000
	Stock		2,700
	Debtors		6,000
	Bank		1,300

	£ Dr	£Cr
Discount receivable		200
Being assets and liabilities transferred to the company at book values		
N Ltd (see note to part (b))	20,565	
Realisation account		20,565
Being agreed purchase price		
Realisation account	4,365	
Shareholders account		4,365
Being profit on realisation transferred to shareholders		
Ordinary share capital account	10,000	
Profit and loss account	6,000	
Shareholders account		16,000
Being transfer of shares and reserves to shareholders account		
Discount receivable	200	
Shareholders account		200
Being 5% discount adjustment on creditors		
Shareholders account	20,565	
N Ltd		20,565
Being settlement of consideration from N Ltd		

(b)

	B Ltd £	W Ltd £
Assets at book values	20,000	11,000
Increase in asset values:		
Freehold buildings	2,000	1,000
Goodwill	2,500	1,700
	24,500	13,700
Reduction in asset values:		
Stocks	200	
Debtors		200
	24,300	13,500
Creditors taken over (after adjustment)	3,800	
Shares in W Ltd (to be settled by W Ltd)	1,000	2,850
Valuation of both companies by N Ltd	19,500	10,650

B Ltd	W Ltd
Satisfied by issue of 39,000 shares of 50p each by N Ltd	Satisfied by issue of 21,300 shares of 50p each by N Ltd.
Add shares transferred from W to B 21,300 × 1/10 = 2,130	Less shares transferred from W to B 21,300 × 1/10 = 2,130
Total shares received in new company = 41,130	Total shares received in new company = 19,170

Note

	£
Consideration due to B Ltd from N Ltd =	19,500 (direct)
1/10 interest in W Ltd £10,650 × 1/10 =	1,065 (indirect)
	20,565

(c) **Balance sheet at 1 April 1983**

	£	£
Fixed assets		
Intangible assets		
Goodwill		4,200
Tangible assets		
Freehold buildings		9,000
Plant and machinery		8,000
		21,200
Current assets		
Stocks	4,000	
Debtors	7,800	
Bank	3,800	
	15,600	
Creditors: amounts falling due within one year	6,650	
Net current assets		8,950
		30,150
Capital and reserves		
Called-up share capital (Note 1)		30,150
		30,150

Note

1   Authorised share capital: 100,000 ordinary shares of 50p each.
    Issued share capital: 60,300 ordinary shares of 50p each fully paid: £30,150.

Trading and profit and loss account for the year ended 31 May 1982

	£	£		£	£
Stock, 31 May 1981		5,261	Sales		52,185
Purchases		38,829			
		44,090			
Less: Stock, 31 May 1982		4,946			
		39,144			
Gross profit, carried down:					
1 June 1981 to					
30 September 1981	3,105				
1 October 1981 to					
31 May 1982	9,936				
		13,041			
		52,185			52,185

	1 June 1981 to 30 September 1981 £	1 October 1981 to 31 May 1982 £		1 June 1981 to 30 September 1981 £	1 October 1981 to 31 May 1982 £
Packing, postage and wrapping	755	2,416	Gross profit brought down	3,105	9,936
Warehouse rent and rates	307	614			
Office expenses	209	418			
Director's salary		1,000			
Debenture interest		525			
Formation expenses		218			
	1,271	5,191			
Pre-incorporation profit transferred to goodwill account	1,834				
Balance carried forward		4,745			
	3,105	9,936		3,105	9,936

Balance sheet as at 31 May 1982

	£		£
Issued share capital: 20,000 ordinary shares of £1 each, fully paid	20,000	Fixed assets	25,000
		Goodwill	3,716
Profit and loss account	4,745	Current assets (other than stock)	9,745
	24,745	Loan account: Rowlock	500
7 per cent debentures	15,000	Stock	4,946
Current liabilities	4,162		
	43,907		43,907

Workings

1 Calculation of ratio between pre and post-incorporation sales

	Pre-incorporation	Post-incorporation
1981		
June, July, August (one each)	3	
September to December (two each)	2	6
1982		
January to May (two each)		10
Ratio	5	16

The gross profit, wrapping, postage, and packing expenses have therefore been apportioned in this ratio (5 : 16). The other expenses are either wholly post-incorporation, or have been apportioned on a time basis (i.e., 1 : 2).

2 Goodwill

	£
Excess of purchase consideration over Rowlock's capital account £35,000 − £29,450	5,550
Deduct: Pre-incorporation profit	1,834
	3,716

Notes

1 It is assumed that Rowlock is the director of the company and that the salary in the trial balance is in respect of the period commencing 1 October 1981, and that there is no agreement that he was to receive remuneration at the same rate for the period from 1 June to 30 September 1981. If there was such an agreement then his drawings in the first period would be treated as a payment on account of such remuneration and charged against the profits for the first four months,

with the result that goodwill would appear in the balance sheet at £500 more, i.e., £4,216.

2 Goodwill should be written off immediately or on a systematic basis over a period not exceeding 20 years as per ED 30.

5

(a) (i) **Statement showing cash to be paid by Cotton and Silk in respect of shares alloted.**

	Cotton		Silk	
	£	£	£	£
Freehold property		–		18,000
Plant and machinery		12,462		4,864
Stocks	5,348		5,562	
Less: Obsolete	720		–	
		4,628		5,562
Debtors	13,750		4,014	
Less: Bad debt	–		350	
		13,750		3,664
		30,840		32,090
Less: Liabilities	16,182		17,820	
Additional liability	–		440	
		16,182		18,260
		14,658		13,830
Cash introduced		1,342		1,170
		16,000		15,000

(ii) **Balance sheet of Modern Ltd at 1 July 1983**

	£	£
Fixed assets		
Tangible assets		
Freehold property		18,000
Plant and machinery		17,326
		35,326
Current assets		
Stocks	10,190	
Debtors	17,414	
Bank	2,512	
	30,116	
carried forward	30,116	35,326

	£	£
brought forward	30,116	35,326
Creditors: amounts falling due within one year		
Trade creditors	34,442	
Net current assets		(4,326)
		31,000
Capital and reserves		31,000
Called-up share capital (Note 1)		

Note

1 Authorised share capital: 40,000 ordinary shares of £1 each.
   Issued and fully paid share capital: 31,000 ordinary shares of £1 each.

(b) **Books of Silk: closing entries**

Capital account Silk

	£		£
Modern Ltd	15,000	Balance	11,494
		Realisation account	2,810
		Bank	696
	15,000		15,000

Loan account

	£		£
Bank	10,300	Balance	10,000
		Loan interest	300
	10,300		10,300

Realisation account

	£		£
Freehold property	14,400	Sundry creditors	17,820
Plant and machinery	4,864	Modern Ltd	13,830
Stocks	5,562		
Debtors	4,014		
Capital account:			
surplus on realisation	2,810		
	31,650		31,650

Modern Ltd

	£		£
Realisation account purchase price	13,830	Capital account Silk: shares	15,000
Bank	1,170		
	15,000		15,000

Bank

	£		£
Balance	10,774	Modern Ltd	1,170
Capital account, Silk	696	Loan account	10,300
	11,470		11,470

6

(a) **Books of Almond Ltd**

Liquidation account

	£ thousands		£ thousands
Sundry asset accounts	168	Sponge plc	125
		Sundry creditor accounts	35
		Sundry shareholders, loss	8
	168		168

Sundry shareholders account

	£ thousands		£ thousands
Liquidation account loss	8	Share capital account	100
Sponge plc	125	Profit and loss account	13
		Revenue reserve account	20
	133		133

Books of Battenby Ltd

Liquidation account

	£ thousands		£ thousands
Sundry asset accounts	75	Sundry liability accounts	38
		Sponge plc	25
		Sundry shareholders, loss	12
	75		75

Sundry shareholders account

	£ thousands		£ thousands
Preliminary expenses	1	Share capital account	50
Liquidation account loss	12		
Profit and loss account	12		
Sponge plc	25		
	50		50

Books of Cherry Ltd

Liquidation account

	£ thousands		£ thousands
Sundry asset accounts	24	Sponge plc	20
Bank, liquidation expenses	1	Sundry ordinary shareholders, loss	5
	25		25

Sundry ordinary shareholders account

	£ thousands		£ thousands
Liquidation account loss	5	Share capital account	10
Bank	5	Profit and loss account (after providing preference dividend)	Nil
	—		—
	10		10
	=		=

Sundry preference shareholders account

	£ thousands		£ thousands
Bank	11	Share capital account	10
		Profit and loss, dividend	1
	—		—
	11		11
	=		=

Bank account

	£ thousands		£ thousands
Sponge plc	20	Balance, overdraft	1
		Liquidation account expenses	1
		Trade creditors	2
		Sundry preference shareholders	11
		Sundry ordinary shareholders	5
	—		—
	20		20
	=		=

Books of Sponge plc

Purchase of business account

	£ thousands		Almond £ thousands	Battenby £ thousands	Cherry £ thousands	Total £ thousands
Sundry liabilities			Sundry assets			
A Ltd, creditors	35		Bank	15			15
B Ltd, creditors	20		Investments	10			10
B Ltd, overdraft	18		Debtors	50	48	8	106
B Ltd, provision for doubtful debts	9		Stock	33	10	7	50
C Ltd, provision for doubtful debts	2		Plant and machinery	22	8	4	34
		11	Land and buildings	20	6		26
		84		150	72	19	241
			Goodwill				13
Purchase price							
Almond Ltd account		125					
Battenby Ltd account		25					
Cherry Ltd account		20					
		254					254

Bank accounts

	£ thousands		£ thousands
Almond Ltd balance	15	Battenby Ltd balance	18
Cumulative preference		Cherry Ltd account	20
shareholders account	19		—
	—		38
	34	Balance c/d	14
Balance c/d	18		—
	—		
	52		52
	—		—
Balance b/d	14	Balance b/d	18

Almond Ltd account

	£ thousands		£ thousands
Ordinary share capital account 125,000 £1 shares	125	Purchase of business account	125

Battenby account

	£ thousands		£ thousands
Ordinary share capital account 10,000 £1 shares	10	Purchase of business account	25
10% cumulative preference shares account 30,000 × 50p	15		
	25		25

Cherry Ltd account

	£ thousands		£ thousands
Bank	20	Purchase of business account	20

(b) **Sponge plc: balance sheet at 30 June 1983**

	£ thousands	£ thousands	£ thousands
Fixed assets			
Intangible assets			
Goodwill			13
Tangible assets			
Land and buildings			26
Plant and machinery			34
Investments			10
			83
Current assets			
Stocks		50	
Trade debtors		95	
Calls in arrear		1	
Bank balance		14	
		160	
Creditors: amounts falling due within one year			
Trade creditors	55		
Bank overdraft	18	73	
Net current assets	—	—	87
			170
Capital and reserves			
Called-up share capital (Note 1)			170

	£ thousands
Note	
1 Authorised share capital	
100,000 10% cumulative preference £1 shares	100
200,000 ordinary £1 shares	200
	300
Issued share capital	
70,000 10% cumulative preference £1 shares 50p called	35
135,000 ordinary £1 fully paid shares	135
	170

12 Reorganisations, reconstructions and capital reductions

INTRODUCTION

Examination questions involving capital reconstruction and reduction problems normally fall into two different categories. The first type of problem which may be encountered is one where all the necessary information in respect of the proposed scheme is given and all that is necessary is for the student to make the necessary entries in the books of the company concerned. There should not be too much difficulty with this type of question which is a matter of fairly routine book-keeping. The second type of problem which may be asked in examinations is one where a student is required to devise a suggested scheme of capital reconstruction or reduction from information provided. This type of question is much more demanding and there is no best solution. It is important when devising a scheme for students to apply their knowledge of the law and accounting principles, to bear in mind the needs of all the interested parties and to state clearly any assumptions made and the reasons for any proposals which are made. If these matters are taken into account a student should be able to provide a credible solution.

Six questions appear in this chapter, the first two of which are of a fairly routine nature and the remainder are more demanding as they require students to devise a scheme of reconstruction. It must be remembered that the answers provided are possible solutions to the problems, but there are a number of other approaches which would be perfectly feasible.

QUESTIONS

1

(a) You are required to state, briefly, what object is served by a scheme for reduction of capital where a company has incurred heavy losses. By whom should such losses be borne and why? *10 marks*

(b) Ayling Ltd has been operating unprofitably for several years and a balance sheet produced at 31 May 1983 revealed the following positions:

	Cost £	Aggregate depreciation £	£
Fixed assets			
Intangible assets			
Goodwill	50,000		50,000
Tangible assets			
Freehold land and buildings	75,000		75,000
Plant and machinery	98,500	15,000	83,500
Motor vehicles	35,000	12,500	22,500
	258,500	27,500	231,000
Current assets			
Stocks		75,000	
Debtors		68,050	
Cash in hand		1,050	
		144,100	
Creditors: amounts falling due within one year			
Trade creditors		165,000	
Bank overdraft		50,100	
		215,100	
Net current assets			(71,000)
			160,000
Capital and reserves			
Called-up share capital (Note 1)			300,000
Profit and loss account			(140,000)
			160,000

216

Notes

1   Authorised share capital: 250,000 £1 ordinary shares
                                 250,000 £1 8% cumulative preference shares
    Issued share capital: 200,000 £1 ordinary shares, fully paid
                                 100,000 £1 8% cumulative preference shares,
                                 fully paid.

2   The dividend on the 8% cumulative preference shares is in arrear for the
    past five years.

The board of directors has recently been reconstituted and the court has
approved a scheme of reconstruction, agreed by all interested parties, on the
following terms:

(1)   The ordinary shares to be written down to 25p each and then converted
      into fully paid £1 shares.

(2)   The preference shareholders have agreed to accept 60,000 ordinary £1
      shares fully paid at par in place of their preference shares, and have
      waived their rights to the arrears of dividend by agreeing to accept
      10,000 ordinary shares of £1 each, fully paid at par in full settlement.

(3)   The property to be revalued to £130,000; the plant and machinery to
      £60,000; the motor vehicles to £17,500; the stocks to £65,000.

(4)   A provision to be created in respect of doubtful debts amounting to
      6% of debtors.

(5)   The creditors have agreed to take 100,000 ordinary shares of £1 each,
      fully paid at par in part settlement of their claim; and to provide
      £100,000 in cash against the issue to them of £100,000 10% debentures,
      secured on a floating charge.

(6)   Goodwill to be written off.

From the information given, you are required to prepare:

(i)   The reconstruction account.   *10 marks*
(ii)   The balance sheet of the reconstructed company, assuming all the
       transactions to have been completed by 1 June 1983.   *12 marks*
                                                               Total 22 marks

2   Roberts Ltd had incurred exceptional losses, and a scheme of reconstruction,
involving a creditors' voluntary liquidation was approved by all parties. The
summarised balance sheet on 30 June 1983 was as follows:

	£	£	£
Fixed assets at cost less depreciation			300,000
Current assets			
Stocks		120,000	
Trade debtors		160,000	
		280,000	
Creditors: amounts falling due within one year			
Trade creditors*	250,000		
Bank overdraft (secured)	200,000	450,000	(170,000)
			130,000
Capital and reserves			
Called-up share capital (Note 1)			280,000
Profit and loss account			(150,000)
			130,000

*£10,000 of the trade creditors are preferential.

Note

1 Authorised, issued and fully paid share capital

	£
200,000 ordinary shares of £1 each	200,000
80,000 6% cumulative preference shares of £1 each	80,000
	280,000

The scheme of reconstruction provided for:

(1) A new company, Grove Ltd, which was incorporated with an authorised capital of £500,000 divided into 250,000 7% cumulative preference shares and 250,000 ordinary shares, all of £1 each, to take over on 30 June 1983 the assets and liabilities of Roberts Ltd.

(2) 40,000 ordinary shares of £1 each in Grove Ltd credited as 50p per share paid up, to be issued to the liquidator of Roberts Ltd for the benefit of that company's ordinary shareholders, who had agreed to pay up the balance of 50p per share immediately.

(3) 80,000 preference shares of £1 each in Grove Ltd credited as 75p per share paid up, to be issued to the liquidator of Roberts Ltd for the benefit of that company's preference shareholders, who had agreed to pay the balance of 25p per share immediately. In addition, £9,600 in 10% unsecured loan notes 1989/90 to be issued as compensation for arrears of preference dividends.

(4) Grove Ltd to pay the liquidation expenses of Roberts Ltd of £2,000.

(5) Grove Ltd adopted the following values for the tangible assets acquired: £280,000 for the fixed assets, £100,000 for stock and £160,000 for trade debtors.

218

(6) £40,000 to be paid off the bank overdraft out of the proceeds of the share issues and the balance to be secured on the fixed assets of Grove Ltd.

(7) Grove Ltd immediately to discharge the preferential creditors in cash. Liabilities to ordinary creditors to be fully satisfied by cash payments of 50p in the £ and the issue of 10% unsecured loan notes 1989/90 for the balance.

(8) The directors of Grove Ltd to introduce £140,000 in cash on loan on 1 July 1983 for £140,000 unsecured loan notes 1989/90.

You are required:

(a) To show the closing entries in the books of Roberts Ltd as recorded in (i) the realisation account* and (ii) the sundry members account having separate columns for preference and ordinary shareholders. *8 marks*

*The purchase consideration should be included in the realisation account as one figure and its detailed make-up shown by way of a note.

(b) To show (i) the journal entries (including cash items) in the books of Grove Ltd and (ii) the opening balance sheet of that company as it would appear assuming that the only transactions were those referred to above. *17 marks*
Total 25 marks

3 D. Whittington (London) plc had traded profitably for countless years selling the services of cats to rat-infested cities. However, since the last change in government the company's major overseas market has fallen foul of European competition, especially the French, and caused the company to accumulate losses of £12,000.

The managing director, Mr Fitzwarren, has called you in to suggest a capital reduction scheme which is likely to be acceptable to both classes of shareholders. He provides you with the following information:

Balance sheet at 31 March 1983

	£	£	£
Fixed assets			
Intangible assets			
Patent and trade mark			650
Goodwill			7,200
Tangible assets			
Land and buildings			6,300
Plant and machinery			2,900
			17,050
Current assets			
Stock		6,200	
Trade debtors		2,750	
		8,950	
carried forward		8,950	17,050

	£	£	£
brought forward		8,950	17,050
Creditors: amounts falling due within one year			
Trade creditors	2,500		
Bank overdraft	5,500	8,000	
Net current assets			950
			18,000
Capital and reserves			
Called-up share capital (Note 1)			30,000
Profit and loss account			(12,000)
			18,000

Notes

1 Authorised and issued share capital: 20,000 £1 ordinary shares, 10,000 £1 9% preference shares.

2 Land and buildings are considered to be worth £5,700, and plant and machinery £500.

3 The realisable value of stock is £6,000 and debtors are good to the extent of £2,000.

4 The preference dividend is £1,800 in arrears at 31 March 1983 (preference shares are entitled on liquidation to repayment before ordinary shareholders).

5 The current yield on preference shares is 10%.

6 If the company was liquidated at this point the expenses of such liquidation would be about £1,000.

7 The existing shareholders are prepared to subscribe £5,000 as additional capital if the reduction scheme is acceptable to them.

8 The bank is prepared to grant overdraft facilities of £5,000 with a fixed charge on the buildings as security.

9 The company expects that the future activity, sale of high technology rat suppression devices, developed jointly with P. Piper of Hamelin, will generate a pre-tax profit of £1,500 in 1984 and £2,000 in 1985, and that there will be a continuing improvement in subsequent years.

25 marks

4   The balance sheet of Rollers plc as at 30 September 1983 is as follows:

	£	£	£
Fixed assets			
Intangible assets			
Patents			80,000
Goodwill			100,000
Tangible assets			
Freehold land and buildings			135,000
Plant and machinery			85,000
			400,000
Current assets			
Stocks		79,900	
Debtors		110,000	
Cash in hand		100	
		190,000	
Creditors: amounts falling due within one year			
Bank overdraft	24,000		
Trade creditors	64,000		
Accruals	12,000	100,000	
Net current assets			90,000
Total assets less current liabilities			490,000
Creditors: amounts falling due after more than one year			
6% debenture loans			100,000
			390,000
Capital and reserves			
Called-up share capital (Note 1)			500,000
Profit and loss account			(110,000)
			390,000

Note

	£
1 Authorised, issued and fully paid share capital	
250,000 6% £1 cumulative preference shares	250,000
250,000 £1 ordinary shares	250,000
	500,000

Dividends on the preference shares are five years in arrears, and accruals represent two years' arrears of debenture interest. Current trading results show marked improvement and the anticipated profit next year is £24,000, after debenture interest of £6,000 has been charged. It is expected that profits after that will show substantial improvements year by year (present estimates are 10% increase per annum).

The resumption in the payment of dividends as soon as possible is desired and accordingly the directors are considering the reduction of the company's capital. The debenture holders have expressed their willingness to exchange their arrears of interest for equity in the business equal to half the nominal value of the arrears and to provide £25,000 (on floating charge) to repay the bank overdraft and to provide working capital of £1,000. The preference shareholders have expressed their willingness to a reduction in the rate of dividend to 5% and to forgo two-thirds of their arrears, provided they receive an interest in the equity equal in nominal value to the remaining one-third.

You are required:

(a)   To draft a suggested scheme for the reduction in capital which should include the elimination of goodwill and the profit and loss account balance, the reduction of the value of patents by £50,000, and the provision of a capital reserve through which any adjustments arising out of the capital rearrangements etc. may be dealt. After reduction the ordinary shares to be converted into 10p shares.   *18 marks*

(b)   To redraft the balance sheet giving effect to the scheme you suggest.   *7 marks*
                                                                      Total 25 marks

5   Material Handling plc is an old-established listed company engaged in general engineering steel fabrication and erection work. Until 1979 the directors had relied on obtaining each year a major contract for mining equipment to keep the workforce fully employed. In 1980 and 1981 no such contracts were obtained and Material Handling plc incurred trading losses.

In 1982 a new managing director was appointed who has succeeded in building up a good order book at acceptable profit margins. However, because of the previous trading losses and the need for working capital to finance production of the orders on hand, Material Handling plc is facing a cash crisis.

It has been suggested to the directors that a suitable means of reorganising the affairs of the company and providing additional working capital would be a scheme for reduction and reconstruction of capital, and as financial adviser you have been asked to assist in the matter.

The summarised balance sheet of Material Handling plc as at 31 December 1982 is as follows:

	£ thousands	£ thousands	£ thousands
Fixed assets			
Intangible assets			
Trade marks			5
Goodwill			25
Tangible assets			
Land and buildings			375
Plant and equipment			65
carried forward			470

	£ thousands	£ thousands	£ thousands
brought forward			470
Current assets			
Stocks		145	
Debtors		193	
		338	
Creditors: amounts falling due within one year			
Trade creditors	230		
Bank overdraft	203	433	
Net current assets			(95)
Total assets less current liabilities			375
Creditors: amounts falling due after more than one year			
Long-term loan			125
			250
Capital and reserves			
Called-up share capital (Note)			225
Share premium account			100
Profit and loss account			(75)
			250

Note

	£ thousands
Issued share capital	
125,000 £1 ordinary shares	125
100,000 7% preference shares of £1 each	100
	225

During the course of your investigation, you obtain the following information:

(1) Preference shareholders do not have priority for the repayment of capital in a winding up but do have priority for arrears of dividend. The preference dividend is three years in arrears and in the terms of the articles of association preference shareholders have one vote per share when the dividend is in arrears.

(2) The company had an audited pre-tax loss of £100,000 for the year ended 31 December 1982 but is forecasting a profit before tax of £25,000 for the year ending 31 December 1983 and substantially increased profitability thereafter.

(3) A firm of professional valuers has valued the land and buildings at £275,000 on a going-concern basis and £250,000 on a break-up basis. Plant and equipment has been valued on a going-concern basis at £70,000 by the directors but may only realise written-down book value on a forced sale.

(4) It is estimated that in the event of liquidation, stock and debtors with a book value of £338,000 would realise only £268,000 before expenses of realisation and liquidation, estimated at £20,000.

(5) The bank overdraft facility is £175,000 and is secured by a floating charge.

(6) The long-term loan from Merchant Bank plc comprises £125,000 10% debentures 1993 secured over the land and buildings. Included in current liabilities are arrears of interest amounting to £12,500. Merchant Bank plc does not wish to gain control of Material Handling plc but would consider:
  (i) Cancellation of the arrears of interest in exchange for an interest in the equity; and
  (ii) Subscribing up to £100,000 for further ordinary shares.

(7) The directors wish consideration to be given to the conversion of the preference shares to unsecured loan stock.

You are required:

(a) To draft a scheme for reduction and reconstruction of capital, giving reasons for the method you suggest.   *18 marks*

(b) To redraft the balance sheet of Material Handling Ltd at 31 December 1982 after implementation of the proposed scheme and show the effect of the scheme on forecast future earnings.   *7 marks*
                    Total 25 marks

6 Munster Ltd are considering a capital reduction and reconstruction scheme. A balance sheet was prepared on 31 March 1983 as follows:

	£	£	£ Current value
Fixed assets			
Intangible assets, Goodwill		34,000	
Tangible assets			
Land and buildings (Note 1)	45,000		75,000
Plant and machinery	10,000		8,000
Fixtures and fittings	10,000	65,000	7,000
		99,000	
Current assets			
Stocks	44,000		44,000
Debtors	55,000		55,000
	99,000		
Creditors: amounts falling due within one year (Note 2)	88,000		
Net current assets		11,000	
Total assets less current liabilities		110,000	
carried forward		110,000	

224

	£	£	£
			Current value
brought forward		110,000	
Creditors: amounts falling due after			
more than one year			
12% debentures		(20,000)	
		90,000	
Capital and reserves			
Called-up share capital			
Ordinary shares of £1 fully paid		100,000	
15% preference shares of £1 fully paid		30,000	
		130,000	
Profit and loss account		(40,000)	
		90,000	

Notes

1 There are three sets of premises with a book value of £15,000 each. The current value of each is £25,000.

2 Amounts falling due within one year:

	£
Bank overdraft	60,000
Trade creditors	20,000
PAYE due	3,200
Accrued interest on debentures	4,800
	88,000

Having consulted interested parties, the following seven conditions were specified:

(1) Sufficient profits must be earned to ensure the payment of ordinary dividends of at least £10,000 p.a. This will cover the existing and new ordinary shares.

(2) Preference share capital is to be reduced by 10%. In lieu of arrears of dividend, 9,000 new £1 ordinary shares fully paid are to be issued.

(3) £40,000 is to be paid off the bank overdraft. The balance is to be converted into a term loan. Annual repayments will be £5,000 (£4,000 in capital; £1,000 in interest).

(4) Debenture interest and PAYE due are to be paid immediately.

(5) Future profits (including interest received) are to be £20,000 in excess of all dividends and interest payable.

(6)   A cash balance of £10,000 is to be available when the reconstruction has been completed.

(7)   Intangible balances are to be written off.

The following information is relevant.

Two of the three sets of premises are surplus to requirements. They can be sold at £25,000 each, or one set can be sold and the other let for an annual rent of £4,000.

Ordinary shareholders will subscribe for 20,000 new ordinary shares of £1 each.

Projected profits, excluding interest payable or receivable, will be in the range £35,000 to £40,000.

All money surplus to requirements can be invested at 15% p.a.

All shares which are reduced are to be consolidated into £1 shares fully paid.

You are required:

(a)   To write a short note outlining the formalities necessary for the proposed scheme to proceed.   *4 marks*

(b)   To calculate the minimum profit required to meet the above conditions.
                                                                        6 marks

(c)   To prepare the revised balance sheet as it will appear after the reconstruction.
                                                                        10 marks

Ignore taxation.
                                                                Total 20 marks

ANSWERS

1

(a) The main object of a scheme for capital reduction is the resumption of the payment of dividends out of expected future profits without the necessity for using such profits to write back the deficit on the profit and loss account. There is no point in such a scheme being introduced unless recovery of profitability prospects are favourable.

Paid-up capital which is lost or unrepresented by assets is written down. Losses are written off and all overvalued assets are written down to their current valuation. Fictitious assets such as goodwill would normally be eliminated.

The main burden of the losses should be borne primarily by the ordinary shareholders. Preference shares are normally entitled to preference in repayment of capital as well as preferential payment of dividends, and if a liquidation ensues it is the ordinary shareholders who would suffer the greatest loss.

The preference shareholders may agree to forgo arrears of preference dividend in anticipation that the scheme would lead to a resumption of their dividends, but any reduction in their capital may require an increase in the rate of their dividend so that they receive the same amount of dividend as they did previously.

Creditors, including debenture holders, may agree to reduce their claims if they see this as more favourable than the return they may receive on the enforced liquidation of the company, but each case must be considered on its merits.

It is inevitable, however, that it is the ordinary shareholders who would normally carry the heaviest burden of the capital reduction. The write-down of the equity is merely a recognition of events which have already happened. As far as their participation in future profits is concerned they will still enjoy the residue after providing for the preference dividend, even though the nominal value of their shares may have been reduced.

(b)

Reconstruction account

	£		£
Ordinary share capital		Ordinary share capital	150,000
In lieu of dividend	10,000	Preference share capital	100,000
In lieu of preference		Freehold land and	
shares	60,000	buildings	55,000
Plant and machinery	38,500	Aggregate depreciation	
Motor vehicles	17,500	Plant	15,000
Stocks	10,000	Motor vehicles	12,500
carried forward	136,000	carried forward	332,500

	£		£
brought forward	136,000	brought forward	332,500
Provision for doubtful debts	4,083		
Goodwill	50,000		
Profit and loss account	140,000		
Capital reserve, profit on reconstruction	2,417		
	332,500		332,500

Balance sheet at 1 June 1983 (as reconstructed)

	£	£
Fixed assets		
Tangible assets		
Freehold land and buildings		130,000
Plant and machinery		60,000
Motor vehicles		17,500
		207,500
Current assets		
Stocks	65,000	
Debtors	63,967	
Cash at bank and in hand	50,950	
	179,917	
Creditors: amounts falling due within one year		
Trade creditors	65,000	
Net current assets		114,917
Total assets less current liabilities		322,417
Creditors: amounts falling due after more than one year		
10% debentures (secured)		100,000
		222,417
Capital and reserves		
Called-up share capital (Note 1)		220,000
Reserves: profits on reconstruction		2,417
		222,417

Note

1 Authorised share capital: 250,000 £1 ordinary shares
   250,000 £1 8% cumulative preference shares
   Issued share capital: 220,000 £1 ordinary shares fully paid

(a)

Realisation account

	£		£
1983		**1983**	
30 June		**30 June**	
Sundry assets transferred		Grove Ltd: purchase	
Fixed assets	300,000	consideration	91,600*
Stock	120,000	Sundry members account:	
Debtors	160,000	loss on realisation	50,000
Creditors: liquidation		(preference shareholders	
expenses	2,000	£20,000)	
Preference shareholders:		(ordinary shareholders	
compensation for		£30,000)	
dividend arrears	9,600	Sundry creditors transferred	
		Trade creditors	250,000
		Bank overdraft	200,000
	591,600		591,600

*Purchase consideration

	£
Ordinary shares	20,000
Preference shares	60,000
10% unsecured loan notes	9,600
Liability for liquidation expenses	2,000
	91,600

Sundry members account

	£ Preference	£ Ordinary		£ Preference	£ Ordinary
1983			**1983**		
30 June			**30 June**		
P & L account	–	150,000	Share capital		
Grove Ltd account			account	80,000	200,000
10% unsecured			Realisation		
loan notes	9,600		account:		
80,000 £1			compensation for		
preference shares			dividend arrears	9,600	
75p paid	60,000				
40,000 £1 ordinary					
shares 50p paid		20,000			
Balances: loss on					
realisation	20,000	30,000			
	89,600	200,000		89,600	200,000

(b)

1983 30 June	Discharge of formation expenses	Dr £	Cr £
	Sundry assets		
	Fixed assets	280,000	
	Stock	100,000	
	Trade debtors	160,000	
	Goodwill (balance)	1,600	
	Trade creditors		250,000
	Bank overdraft		200,000
	Liquidator of Roberts Ltd: consideration		91,600
	Assets and liabilities taken over on reconstruction and goodwill arising		

	Liquidator of Roberts Ltd	91,600	
	Creditors: liquidation expenses		2,000
	10% unsecured loan notes 1989/90		9,600
	Share capital:		
	80,000 £1 preference shares 75p paid		60,000
	40,000 £1 ordinary shares 50p paid		20,000
	Purchase consideration discharged		

	Application and allotment account		
	Preference shares 25p for each of the		
	80,000 shares called	20,000	
	Ordinary shares 50p for each of the		
	40,000 shares called	20,000	
	Preference share capital account		20,000
	Ordinary share capital account		20,000
	Cash	40,000	
	Application and allotment account		
	Preference shares		20,000
	Ordinary shares		20,000
	Allotments called and received as agreed		

	Cash	140,000	
	10% unsecured loan notes 1989/90		140,000
	Loans by directors as agreed		

	Creditors		
	Preferential	10,000	
	Ordinary	240,000	
	Liquidation expenses	2,000	
	Bank overdraft	40,000	
	Cash		172,000
	10% unsecured loan notes 1989/90		120,000
	Discharge of creditors and reduction of bank overdraft as per scheme.		

Grove Ltd balance sheet at 1 July 1983 (reconstructed)

	£	£
Fixed assets		
Intangible assets		
Goodwill at cost		1,600
Tangible assets		
Sundry fixed assets at cost (details not given)		280,000
		281,600
Current assets		
Stocks	100,000	
Trade debtors	160,000	
Cash at bank and in hand (W1)	8,000	
	268,000	
Creditors: amounts falling due within one year		
Bank overdraft (secured)	160,000	
Net current assets		108,000
Total assets less current liabilities		389,600
Creditors: amounts falling due after more than one year		
10% unsecured loan notes 1989/90		269,600
		120,000
Capital and reserves		
Called-up share capital (Note1)		120,000

Note		£
1 Authorised share capital		
250,000 £1 ordinary shares		250,000
250,000 £1 7% cumulative preference shares		250,000
		500,000
Issued and fully paid share capital		
40,000 £1 ordinary shares		40,000
80,000 £1 7% cumulative preference shares		80,000
		120,000

Workings

	£	£
1 **Cash at bank and in hand**		
Receipts		
Cash from preference shareholders		20,000
Cash from ordinary shareholders		20,000
10% loan notes (directors)		140,000
carried forward		180,000

		£	£
brought forward			180,000
Payments			
Preferential creditors		10,000	
Ordinary creditors		120,000	
Liquidation expenses		2,000	
Bank overdraft		40,000	
			172,000
Balance			8,000

3 If the company was to go into liquidation the situation would be as follows:

	£	£
Sale price of assets		
Land and buildings		5,700
Plant and machinery		500
Stock		6,000
Debtors		2,000
		14,200
Payments due out of proceeds of sale		
Trade creditors	2,500	
Bank overdraft	5,500	
Liquidation costs	1,000	
		9,000
All paid to preference shareholders who have prior rights to repayment		5,200
Loss suffered by shareholders		
Preference share capital	10,000	
Arrears of dividend	1,800	
	11,800	
Less: Amount of repayment	5,200	6,600
Ordinary share capital		20,000
		26,600

To ensure that any capital reduction scheme would be acceptable to preference shareholders they would require an income from the reconstructed company which would at least equal the income which they would receive from the proceeds of liquidation, i.e. income of £520 (£5,200 at 10%). They would also require some security of capital. As can be seen the ordinary shareholder will receive no repayment of capital.

Before suggesting a proposed scheme it is necessary to calculate the total amount which has to be written off the assets, as this loss must then be borne by the shareholders.

	£
Schedule of losses	
Intangible assets	
Goodwill	7,200
Patent and trade mark	650
Tangible assets	
Land and buildings	600
Plant and machinery	2,400
Current assets	
Stock	200
Debtors	750
	11,800
Losses already included in balance sheet	12,000
	23,800
Provision for costs of scheme (estimated)	2,000
	25,800

It is suggested that the total loss of £25,800 could be written off the share capital as follows:

	Amount of write down £
20,000 £1 ordinary shares reduced to 1p shares	19,800
10,000 £1 9% preference shares reduced to 40p shares	6,000
	25,800

The 10,000 9% preference shares of 40p each could be consolidated into 4,000 10% preference shares of £1 each fully paid and the 20,000 1p ordinary shares could be consolidated into 2,000 ordinary shares of 10p each fully paid. The yield on preference shares has been raised to what is deemed to be a reasonable current yield and all shares have been converted into marketable denominations. In addition, to compensate the preference shareholders for loss of two years' dividend plus loss of capital each preference shareholder may be given the option to convert one half of his preference holding into ordinary shares at the rate of 10 ordinary shares for each preference share.

Assuming the above scheme is successful, and that all the legal formalities have been carried out, and all the preference holders take up the conversion offer then the ordinary shareholders (excluding the preference shareholders who converted) would immediately subscribe £5,000 in respect of 50,000 ordinary shares of 10p each.

The reconstructed balance sheet would be as follows:

	£	£	£
Fixed assets			
Tangible assets			
Land and buildings			5,700
Plant and machinery			500
Current assets			
Stocks		6,000	
Debtors		2,000	
		8,000	
Creditors: amounts falling due within one year			
Trade creditors	2,500		
Other creditors*	2,000		
Bank overdraft	500	5,000	
Net current assets			3,000
			9,200
Capital and reserves			
Called-up share capital			9,200

Authorised share capital: this should be restored to its original value of £30,000 in order to avoid stamp duties on subsequent issues and to allow further capital to be issued as required.

	£
Issued and fully paid share capital	
2,000 10% £1 preference shares	2,000
72,000 ordinary 10p shares	7,200
	9,200

*Provision for costs of scheme not yet paid.

1984 income allocation	£	Original preference shareholders	£	Original ordinary shareholders	£
Pre-tax profit	1,500				
Taxation	–				
	1,500				
Preference dividend	200		200		–
Available for ordinary shareholders	1,300	£1,300 × 20,000/72,000 =	361	£1,300 × 52,000/72,000 =	939
			561		939

1985 income allocation	£	Original preference shareholders	£	Original ordinary shareholders	£
Pre-tax profit	2,000				
Taxation*	–				
	2,000				
Preference dividend	200		200		–
Available for ordinary shareholders	1,800	£1,800 × 20,000/72,000 =	500	£1,800 × 52,000/72,000 =	1,300

*Tax losses brought forward negate the requirement to provide for taxation. Also it is assumed that there will be long-term capital investment in high-technology plant and deferred tax will not need to be provided for as no reversing of timing differences is expected.

The suggested scheme would mean that the income to preference shareholders would not be less than they would receive if the company were to go into liquidation, and it appears that future results will give them reasonable security. Also it appears that ordinary shareholders should receive reasonable dividends in the future.

4

(a) The first step in devising a scheme of capital reduction is to calculate the amount of the losses, including reduction in asset values which have to be written off.

The amount to be written off is calculated as follows.

	£
Patents	50,000
Goodwill	100,000
Profit and loss account, aggregate losses	110,000
Arrears of preference dividend (one-third)	25,000
	285,000
Less: Debenture interest forgone	6,000
	279,000

The next step is to describe how the amount to be written off should be apportioned between the ordinary and preference shareholders. Bearing in mind that the ordinary shareholders should suffer the major part of the loss it is suggested that the ordinary shares be reduced from £1 to 10p shares. 250,000 ordinary £1 shares reduced to 10p shares will write off £225,000.

It is suggested that the preference shares be reduced from £1 to 78p shares. 250,000 preference £1 shares reduced to 78p shares will write off £55,000.

The total amount by which the share capital is reduced is therefore £225,000 + £55,000 = £280,000.

The surplus of £1,000 (i.e. £280,000 − £279,000) can be transferred to a capital reserve account.

The present ordinary shareholders will have 250,000 ordinary £1 shares reduced to 10p shares. Their new ordinary shareholding will be 250,000 ordinary shares of 10p each = £25,000.

The present debenture holders will require ordinary shares which have a value of half their arrears of interest, i.e. £6,000. So their ordinary shareholding will be 60,000 ordinary shares of 10p each = £6,000.

To compensate for arrears of dividend the present preference shareholders will require ordinary shares which will have a value of one-third of their arrears of dividend, i.e. £25,000. So their ordinary shareholding will be 250,000 ordinary shares of 10p each = £25,000.

The present preference shareholders will also have 250,000 £1 preference shares reduced to 78p shares = £195,000. Some of these shares could then be converted into ordinary shares to compensate the preference shareholders for their loss of capital, to give them control in the reconstructed company, to give the company some gearing and to maintain a reasonable allocation of dividends. It is suggested that the conversion should be such that their new preference shareholding would be 250,000 preference shares of 50p each = £125,000 and 700,000 ordinary shares of 10p each = £70,000.

		Original debenture holders	Original preference shareholders	Original ordinary shareholders
Income allocation next year	£	£	£	£
Expected profits (before interest)	30,000			
Debenture interest (after new issue)	7,500	7,500		
	22,500			
Taxation*	—			
Preference dividend	6,250		6,250	
Available for ordinary shareholders		£16,250 × 60/1,260 =	£16,250 × 950/1,260 =	£16,250 × 250/1,260 =
	16,250	774	12,252	3,224

*Tax losses brought forward negate the requirements to provide for taxation in the next few years.

If the projected increases in profits materialise even when all the tax losses have been utilised and tax becomes payable on the profits there should still be at least the amount shown above available for the ordinary shareholders.

Summary

(i)   The company is relatively highly geared but this is necessary because there are a large number of debentures in issue and also the preference shareholders will wish to retain a reasonable number of preference shares to provide them with security of income. However, despite the high gearing the company should not have any problems in meeting the preference dividends and debenture interest on the projections which are available.

(ii)   It does not seem that the company should have problems meeting the debenture interest commitments which seem reasonably secure. Also the debenture holders have received some compensation in ordinary shares for interest forgone and it appears that the ordinary dividend is reasonably secure and that the rate payable should be reasonable on the results expected (the rate being higher than that obtained on the debentures).

(iii)   The preference shareholders have forgone £50,000 arrears of dividend, reduced the rate on the shares from 6% to 5% and received a reduction of 22p in the £ on the nominal value of their shares. It seems reasonable that substantial compensation should be received in return. It can be seen that these shareholders, as a result of the issue to them of ordinary shares, now have a large control over the company. They have good cover for their preference dividend which should improve even further in later years. In addition if results do improve as expected they will be the ones who gain most as a result of their large holding of ordinary shares.

(iv)   The ordinary shareholders are the risk-bearers of the company and therefore it seems reasonable that they should suffer the major part of the loss which they in fact have done. They have received a reduction of 90p in the £ on the nominal value of their shares, in addition to having control of the company transferred from them to the preference shareholders. However, in respect of the shares which they still hold it does appear that dividends should be reasonable and should improve over the next few years. The company appears now to be under a sounder footing and although they no longer have control they should be able to make a reasonable return on their investment in the future.

Note

An alternative approach could be to issue the preference shareholders with fewer ordinary shares than suggested and more new preference shares. This would mean that control could remain with the present ordinary shareholders. However, there would be a problem in that the company would be more highly geared than under the proposal put forward and this would reduce the cover for the preference dividend. In addition this would leave less available for ordinary shareholders, perhaps even a negligible amount if expectations did not materialise.

(b)   The reconstructed balance sheet is as follows:

	£	£
Fixed assets		
Intangible assets		
Patents		30,000
Tangible assets		
Freehold land and buildings		135,000
Plant and machinery		85,000
carried forward		250,000

	£	£
brought forward		250,000

Current assets

Stocks	79,900	
Debtors	110,000	
Cash in hand and at bank*	1,100	
	191,000	

Creditors: amounts falling due within one year

Trade creditors	64,000	
Net current assets		127,000
Total assets less current liabilities		377,000

Creditors: amounts falling due after more than one year

6% debenture loans (secured)		125,000
		252,000

Capital and reserves

Called-up share capital (Note 1)		251,000
Capital reserve		1,000
		252,000

*Includes £25,000 from new debenture issue.

Note

1 Authorised share capital:
   This should be restored to its original value of £500,000 in order to allow
   further capital to be issued as required.

	£
Issued share capital:	
250,000 5% preference shares of 50p each	125,000
1,260,000 ordinary shares of 10p each	126,000
	251,000

5

(a) The first step in drafting a suitable scheme for reduction and reconstruction
     of capital is to look at the position of the various parties if the company were
     to be liquidated.

Valuation on a break-up basis

	£ thousands
Land and buildings	250
Plant and equipment	65
Trade marks	—
Goodwill	—
carried forward	315

	£ thousands
brought forward	315
Stocks and debtors	268
	583
Less: Expenses of realisation and liquidation	(20)
Estimated proceeds of realisation	563

The estimated proceeds would be distributed as follows:

Total available	563
To repay secured long-term loan	(125)
	438
To repay secured element of bank overdraft	(175)
Balance for unsecured creditors	263
Creditors (including interest arrears)	(230)
Unsecured element of bank overdraft	(28)
Balance to pay part of arrears of preference dividend	5

Proposed scheme of reduction and reconstruction

Since the ordinary and preference shareholders stand to receive virtually nothing if the company is liquidated, then they must be made to suffer the major loss in the proposed scheme. In addition the majority of the cash required to reduce the overdraft to an acceptable level must come from the existing ordinary shareholders, since they are the people who stand to gain most if the scheme is successful.

A possible scheme is therefore:

(i) The existing ordinary shares of £1 to be cancelled and reissued as ordinary shares of 25p fully paid (W3). The balance on share premium account to be written off.

(ii) The ordinary shareholders to subscribe for three new ordinary shares of 25p for each share currently held (W4).

(iii) Goodwill and trade marks to be written off, together with 10% of the book value of the stock (latter estimated).

(iv) Merchant Bank plc to accept ordinary shares of 25p at par in exchange for the arrears of interest, and in addition to subscribe cash for 225,000 ordinary shares of 25p (W4).

(v) Land and buildings and plant and equipment to be revalued at their going-concern valuation.

(vi) The preference shares to be written down by the balance of the loss on the scheme, and then converted into 10% unsecured loan stock (W3).

(b)   Redrafted balance sheet at 31 December 1982

	£	£	£
Fixed assets			
Tangible assets			
Land and buildings			275,000
Plant and equipment			70,000
			345,000
Current assets:			
Stock and work in progress (W1)		130,500	
Debtors		193,000	
		323,500	
Creditors: amounts falling due within			
one year			
Creditors (W2)	217,500		
Bank overdraft (W4)	53,000		
		(270,500)	
			53,000
Total assets less current liabilities			398,000
Creditors: amounts falling due after			
more than one year			
Long-term loan		125,000	
10% unsecured loan stock (W3)		79,250	
			204,250
			193,750
Capital and reserves			
Called-up share capital			
(775,000 ordinary shares of 25p each)			193,750

Effect of scheme on forecast future earnings

	£
Forecast profit before taxation	25,000
Less: Interest on unsecured loan stock (10% × 79,250)	7,925
Balance available for distribution	17,075

Notes

1   It is assumed that no tax will be payable on these profits due to tax losses brought forward.

2   No account has been taken of the likely savings in bank overdraft interest. If interest on the overdraft is at 10% then this will increase earnings by approximately (£203,000 − £53,000) × 10% = £15,000

Workings

		£
1	Stock per balance sheet	145,000
	Less: 10% written down (estimated)	14,500
	Stock per redrafted balance sheet	130,500
2	Creditors	230,000
	Less: Interest converted into ordinary shares	(12,500)
	Per redrafted balance sheet	217,500

3 Amounts available for ordinary and preference shareholders, stating assets on a going-concern basis

	£	£
Fixed assets		
Land and buildings		275,000
Plant and equipment		70,000
		345,000
Current assets		
Stocks and work in progress (W1)	130,500	
Debtors	193,000	
	323,500	
Current liabilities		
Creditors	230,000	
		93,500
		438,500
Other liabilities		
Bank overdraft	203,000	
Long-term loan	125,000	
		328,000
Available for ordinary and preference shareholders		110,500
Preference capital	100,000	
Arrears of dividend	21,000	
		121,000
Ordinary capital		125,000
Total liabilities		246,000

The arrears of preference have priority in a winding up and any balance would be shared proportionately between ordinary and preference shareholders. A *reasonable* split of the £110,500 would be to give £79,250 in total to the preference shareholders and £31,250 to the ordinary shareholders. (This split is harsher on the ordinary shareholders than the preference shareholders as, if the preference shareholders are given unsecured loan stock in exchange for their shares, they will have no right to participate in the future growth of the company as have ordinary shareholders and if the company is successful their income will be less than that on ordinary shares.)

The ordinary shares are reduced to 125,000 shares of 25p each fully paid.

The preference shares are cancelled and, together with the arrears of dividend, are replaced by £79,250 10% unsecured loan stock.

4 Shares issued

The ordinary shares are reduced to £31,250 (125,000 at 25p) (W3).

It will be necessary to reduce the bank overdraft to an acceptable level (preferably well below the available facility) and this will be done by issuing shares to Merchant Bank plc and to the ordinary shareholders. Care must be taken to ensure that Merchant Bank plc does not obtain control of the company.

An acceptable arrangement would be:

(i)   To issue 50,000 ordinary shares of 25p each in cancellation of the arrears of interest of £12,500.
(ii) To issue 375,000 shares at 25p each to the ordinary shareholders (3 for 1) for cash.
(iii) To issue 225,000 shares at 25p each to Merchant Bank plc for cash.

Merchant Bank plc would then hold 275,000 shares out of a total of 775,000 (i.e. 35.5%) and cash of £150,000 would be raised. This cash can be used to reduce the bank overdraft to £53,000. It seems most sensible to reduce the bank overdraft by as much as possible in order to decrease the interest payable and then for the company to draw against the overdraft facility as and when cash is required.

5 Reconstruction and reorganisation account

	£		£
Profit and loss balance written off	75,000	Reduction in share capital (75p × 125,000)	93,750
Land and buildings written down	100,000	Share premium written off	100,000
Trade marks written off	5,000	Revaluation of plant and equipment	5,000
Goodwill written off	25,000	Balance, written off	
Stock written down	14,500	preference share capital	20,750
	219,500		219,500

It is possible to raise up to £100,000 in cash from issuing ordinary shares to Merchant Bank plc but it has been decided to issue less in order to restrict the control which they have in the company. However, it is possible to issue more shares to them and still leave them with less than a 50% interest.

6

(a) In order to effect the reduction of the share capital, the following formalities must be completed in accordance with the Companies Act 1948, ss. 66 to 69:

   (i)   The company must be authorised by its articles of association to reduce the share capital. If it is not then it must pass a special resolution to alter its articles of association.
   (ii) The company must pass a special resolution to reduce the share capital.
   (iii) The company must apply to the court for an order confirming the reduction.
   (iv) The court order must be presented to the Registrar of Companies, together with an office copy of the order for retention by him and a minute approved by the court showing the amount of the reduced share capital, i.e. £27,000 consisting of 27,000 15% preference shares of £1 each fully paid, and £74,000 consisting of 74,000 ordinary shares of £1 each fully paid.
   (v)   The registrar will then register the order and the minute.
   (vi) After registration of these, the resolution to reduce the share capital shall take effect.

(b) Calculation of cash required for implementation of scheme:

	£
Debenture interest	4,800
PAYE	3,200
Reduction of bank overdraft	40,000
Cash balance required	10,000
	58,000
Proceeds of share issue	20,000
Cash required	38,000

The company must thus sell two sets of premises for £25,000 each, and this will leave surplus cash of £50,000 − £38,000 = £12,000 available for investment.

Calculation of minimum profit required

	£
Preference dividend: £27,000 × 15%	4,050
Ordinary dividend	10,000
Interest on bank loan	1,000
Debenture interest: £20,000 × 12%	2,400
carried forward	17,450

		£
brought forward		17,450
Excess required (condition 5)		20,000
		37,450
Interest receivable £12,000 × 15%		1,800
Minimum profit required		35,650

(c) **Balance sheet at 31 March 1983 following reconstruction**

	£	£	£
Fixed assets			
Tangible assets			
Land and buildings			25,000
Plant and machinery			8,000
Fixtures and fittings			7,000
			40,000
Current assets			
Stocks		44,000	
Debtors		55,000	
Cash at bank and in hand (W3)		22,000	
		121,000	
Creditors: amounts falling due within			
one year			
Bank loans	4,000		
Trade creditors	20,000		
		24,000	
Net current assets			97,000
Total assets less current liabilities			137,000
Creditors: amounts falling due after			
more than one year (Note 1)			36,000
			101,000
Capital and reserves			
Called-up share capital			£
Ordinary shares of £1 each fully paid (W1)			74,000
15% preference shares of £1 each fully paid			27,000
			101,000

Note

	£
1 Amounts due after more than one year	
12% debentures	20,000
Medium-term bank loan (20,000 − 4,000 included as	
payable within one year)	16,000
	36,000

Workings

1 Calculation of ordinary share capital

	£
Balance before reconstruction	100,000
Issue of 20,000 £1 ordinary shares at par	20,000
Shares issued in lieu of preference dividend arrears	9,000
	129,000
Capital reduction account (W2)	55,000
	74,000

2 Capital reduction account

	£		£
Debit balance on profit and loss account	40,000	10% reduction in preference shares	3,000
Goodwill	34,000	Profit on sale of premises	20,000
Plant and machinery written down	2,000	Revaluation of premises	10,000
Fixtures and fittings written down	3,000	Balance, written off ordinary share capital	55,000
Issue of shares in lieu of arrears of preference dividend	9,000		
	88,000		88,000

3 Cash at bank and in hand

	£	£
Cash from sale of two premises		50,000
Cash from share issue		20,000
		70,000
Repayment of overdraft	40,000	
PAYE	3,200	
Debenture interest	4,800	
		48,000
		22,000

£12,000 of this balance can be invested at 15% p.a.

13 Income, capital and value measurement

INTRODUCTION

The topics covered in this chapter have to be studied for paper 2.8, 'The regulatory framework of accounting' in the Level 2 examination of the Association of Certified Accountants.

QUESTIONS

1 'The determination of what is business income has become one of the most controversial and thorny areas in accounting and economic circles; the debate is likely to continue for some time into the future.'

You are required:

(a) Briefly to contrast accounting and economic income.   *4 marks*

(b) To outline what you understand by the 'transactions basis'.   *4 marks*

(c) To describe four areas of importance in measuring income for a corporate entity.   *12 marks*
                                                                      Total 20 marks

2

(a) Explain how far the measurement of income may be considered to be related to the measurement of capital.   *10 marks*

(b) What do you understand by the entity and proprietary concepts of capital, and what are their implications for capital maintenance?   *10 marks*
                                                                      Total 20 marks

3 In recent years some accounting theorists have lost faith in (i) historical costs (HC) accounting, and now propound, in particular, three alternative accounting systems, based on (ii) current purchasing power (CPP), (iii) replacement cost (RC), and (iv) net realisable value (NRV).

You are required to compare and contrast the four systems, with regard to their usefulness and reliability, in an inflationary period, for:

(a) Income measurement.   *8 marks*

(b) Capital maintenance.   *8 marks*
                                                                      Total 16 marks

4

(a) Contrast Fisher's and Hicks's economic models with the traditional accounting models.   *12 marks*

(b) J. Brown purchases 5,000 ordinary shares in XY Ltd at the beginning of year 1 for £5,265. He received at annual intervals the following dividends: at the end of year 1 £500; end of year 2 £1,250; end of year 3 £1,850. He realises the shares at the end of year 4 for £3,500.

You are required:

(i) To compute economic income ideal under certainty.

(ii)   To show the amount of annual reinvestment in order to maintain capital and income.

The discount rate to be used is 10% being the next best rate of return which J. Brown could receive in an alternative investment. The present value of £1 receivable at the end of a period discounted at 10% p.a. is as follows:

End of year 1 0.909
End of year 2 0.826
End of year 3 0.751
End of year 4 0.683

Work to the nearest whole pound.

8 marks
Total 20 marks

ANSWERS

1

(a)   Accounting income is traditionally prepared on the matching principle, the periodic matching of revenues from sales with relevant costs. It is based on actualities and is measured after the event. The development of the accounting income statement was consequent upon the need for accounting information relevant for investor protection and decision-making: the first mandatory requirement for the publication of an income statement was in the Companies Act 1929.

Economic income is viewed from the personal rather than the entity concept; it is based on an individual's expectations and is measured in terms of the present value of a future stream of income. Its usefulness, to the economist, is as a theoretical tool for analysing the economic behaviour of the individual.

(b)   Traditional accounting income is firmly based upon recorded transactions which may be evidenced and verified. The same can be said of income models based upon current values for they utilise the historical cost transactions base before updating the data concerned into contemporary-value terms. All income models of the accountant can be said to be soundly based upon past transactions which may be evidenced as having taken place. Less directly the economic income models rely on past transactions as justification for the prediction of future cash flows stemming from the resources which were the subject of past transactions.

Transactions and the transactions basis are therefore relevant to both the accountant and the economist: the main difference between the two approaches is essentially a question of value.

(c)   The importance of measuring income for a corporate entity is:

(i)   As a guide in helping decide dividend and retention policies.
(ii)   To facilitate the assessment for taxation.
(iii) To measure the success or otherwise of the entity and to ensure the survival of the firm in a capitalistic economy.
(iv)   To provide a measure of management's stewardship of an entity's resources.
(v)   To provide investment criteria for present and potential investors and lenders of finance.
(vi)   As a managerial aid in a variety of decision areas both within and outside the entity, e.g., the review of pricing policies or the ascertainment of an entity's creditworthiness.

2

(a)   The theorists have put forward a number of concepts which aim at defining income and its relationship with capital. Two such concepts are those proposed by I. Fisher and J. R. Hicks. Fisher insists that income is simply consumption. Hicks, on the other hand, argues that income is consumption plus savings (the latter in the form of capital appreciation). However, he is careful to eliminate from his *income* measure those components of capital appreciation attributable to changing expectations and changing interest rates. The fundamental difference between the two refines itself to the question of how savings and dissavings are to be treated in the measurement of income. Fisher excludes savings but includes dissaving in his definition by insisting that income is measured by the money value of the goods and services actually consumed. Hicks, on the other hand, includes saving and excludes dissaving by focusing his attention on the amount that *could* be consumed while leaving capital intact. The value of capital is measured by the present value of the income stream and income is measured after adjustment for capital introduced and withdrawn. Fisher terms capital as a stock of wealth existing at a moment of time; income being the flow of benefits from wealth over the time. The value of capital depends upon the income that it produces: this can be measured as the present value of the flow of net benefits.

Hence it can be seen that the measurement of income and capital may be related.

(b)   The entity concept views capital as the physical assets of business and their operating capacity. Thus it perceives the business as a separate entity distinct from the providers of capital. The objective being to account for the interests of the enterprise and not the individual shareholder.

The proprietary concept views capital as the wealth subscribed by the shareholders. The company is perceived as being owned by a collection of shareholders and the objective is to account for their interest in the company.

The implications of these concepts for capital maintenance is that profit cannot be arrived at until capital in one of the above senses has been maintained. The impact of changing prices means that these two concepts would also have implications for the treatment of holding gains and changes in the purchasing power of money.

3

(a)   **Income measurement**

Historical cost (HC) matches revenues measured in current pounds with costs being measured in a mixture of historical and current pounds. The figure of money income produced is usually overstated as a measure of distributable earnings and is difficult to analyse and interpret. Fiscal laws require that historical cost profits are used as a basis for calculating taxation liabilities.

Current purchasing power (CPP) matches revenues and costs measured in terms of the period-end purchasing power. The CPP profit is distorted with the inclusion of the inflationary gain/loss on net monetary assets and liabilities for the period. With the use of a general price index there is normally very little relationship with the movements in actual prices of the fixed assets and stocks.

Replacement cost (RC), the basic principals of which were adopted into the current cost system, matches revenues measured in current pounds whilst costs are measured at the current cost of the assets consumed. Profits ascertained under this method exclude holding gains and so will give a more realistic figure of distributable earnings without any erosion of 'real' capital.

Net realisable value (NRV) calculates revenues as production or purchases at selling price, and matches them with the costs paid during the period plus depreciation calculated as the write-down of fixed assets from their cost (or opening net book value) to net realisable value at the period end. NRV anticipates profit on unsold goods and does not apply a consistent depreciation policy year by year. NRV contravenes SSAP 2 with respect to both the prudence and the consistency concepts.

(b)   **Capital maintenance**

HC capital is valued as an amalgam of the current value of the net monetary assets plus the unallocated historical costs of the non-monetary assets. HC aims to maintain the historical money capital contributed; any amount of equity in excess of this can be distributed. A full distribution of historical-cost retained earnings would cause the operating capability of the entity to be eroded in a period of inflation.

CPP capital (equity) is valued in current purchasing power terms for both the net monetary assets and the unallocated expenditure of the non-monetary assets. Capital is maintained at the current purchasing power of capital contributed. There is no relationship between the valuation of the non-monetary assets with their replacement or realisable values.

RC capital is valued as the current value of net monetary assets plus the net replacement cost of non-monetary assets. Its aim is to maintain the productive capital (operating capability) of the company. Holding gains are segregated from operating gains and only the latter may be distributed.

NRV capital is valued as the current net realisable value of all net assets. It aims to maintain the purchasing power of contributed capital; any distribution may be made out of any remaining surplus after the adjustments implied above.

4

(a)   In contrasting Fisher's and Hicks's economic models with the traditional accounting income model students would be expected to cover the following:

Fisher's concept of income

(i)   Restriction of economic income to actual personal consumption because he regarded it as the psychic enjoyment to be derived from consuming goods and services.

(ii)   Savings were not regarded as income until they were consumed – they were regarded as potential rather than actual income.

(iii)   The central factor in the determination of Fisher's income is whether or not the economic benefits from capital are consumed and enjoyed by the owner of the capital.
(iv)   Fisher's model is a personal rather than an entity based model.
(v)   Capital movements and savings are ignored and thus the owner's well being is not maintained.
(vi)   In view of (v) Fisher's model because of its psychological bases ignores economic reality and is in sharp contrast to Hicks's economic model in which income is based on capital.

Hicks's concept of income

(i)   Concerned with analysing the economic behaviour of individuals rather than their psychic experiences.
(ii)   Hicks's concept of 'welloffness'.
(iii)   The need to maintain capital.
(iv) $Ye = C + Kn - K_{n-1}$ shows that income is capital based and that economic income is based on the net increase in capital $Kn - K_{n-1}$ similar to the traditional accounting model.
(v)   It is a subjective model based on a personal concept rather than on an entity concept.
(vi)   The central problem is one of value since income is capital based.
(vii)   Value, the independent variable, in this economic model is based on the present value (PV) of net cash flows and therefore requires prediction of:

(1)   the magnitude and timing of the future cash flows;
(2)   an opportunity cost rate for discounting purposes which is subjective depending upon the individual's investment opportunities.

As far as accounting is concerned Hicks's model is too subjective and violates the concepts of objectivity, conservatism and realisation. Further it has little value in relation to stewardship accounting. It does however highlight the point that the true intrinsic value of an asset is its future earnings potential.

Traditional accounting model.

(i)   Like Hicks's model it is capital based though mainly ex-poste.
(ii)   Income is based on the matching of costs with revenues.
(iii)   It is regarded by its advocates as fulfilling the stewardship function and that accounting reports are objective and verifiable; but there are areas in which this is not true. Thus the valuation of stocks and the varying methods of calculating depreciation are subjective.
(iv)   It is based on the realisation concept; but there are areas which are ex-ante, for example, the estimation of residual value and the useful life of fixed assets.
(v)   A major difference between economic income and accounting income is that economic income recognises unrealised holding gains whereas accounting income, through the realisation concept does not.
(vi)   It can be shown that accounting income is a mixture of heterogeneous values which when aggregated is meaningless particularly in a period of inflation.

(b)

Period	Realised cash flows £	Capital at end of period £	Capital at beginning of period £	Economic income £	Periodic return on capital requiring reinvestment £
Year 1	500	5,293	5,267	528	(26)
Year 2	1,250	4,573	5,293	530	720
Year 3	1,850	3,182	4,573	459	1,391
Year 4	3,500	0	3,182	318	3,182
					5,267

Computation of economic capital:

Time	Anticipated flows discounted from end of year			
	1	2	3	4
Beginning of year 1	$(500 \times 0.909) + (1,250 \times 0.826) + (1,850 \times 0.751) + (3,500 \times 0.683)$ Capital = £5,267			
End of year 1	−	$(1,250 \times 0.909) + (1,850 \times 0.826) + (3,500 \times 0.751)$ Capital = £5,293		
End of year 2	−	−	$(1,850 \times 0.909) + (3,500 \times 0.826)$ Capital = £4,573	
End of year 3	−	−	−	$(3,500 \times 0.909)$ Capital = £3,182
End of year 4	−	−	−	− Capital = £ −

14   SSAP 16

INTRODUCTION

SSAP 16 including the Appendix runs to 20 pages and there will be no substitute for the reader but to refer to the original SSAP for analysis.

Suffice to say here that the basic objective of current cost accounts is to provide more useful information than is available from historical cost accounts alone for the guidance of the management of the business, the shareholders and others, on such matters as:

(a)   The financial viability of the business.
(b)   Return on investment.
(c)   Pricing policy, cost control and distribution decisions.
(d)   Gearing.

Basically, the objective is achieved by computing:

(a)   Cost of sales adjustment.
(b)   Depreciation adjustment.
(c)   Monetary working capital adjustment.
(d)   Gearing adjustment.

For a definition of these terms, the reader is referred to the statement; while the mechanical computations are dealt with in this chapter.

QUESTIONS

1 In relation to Statement of Standard Accounting Practice No. 16, 'Current cost accounting', explain the meaning and significance of the following:

(a)	Current cost operating adjustments.	*5 marks*
(b)	Gearing adjustment.	*5 marks*
(c)	Net borrowings.	*5 marks*
(d)	Current cost reserve.	*5 marks*

Total 20 marks

2 SSAP 16, 'Current cost accounting', requires plant and machinery to be included in the balance sheet at its value to the business.

(a) Provide a definition of value to the business. *8 marks*

(b) An extract from the plant register of Tresilion Engineering is produced below:

Date of purchase	1 January 1980
Description	Compressor
Cost	£10,000
Depreciation	25% p.a. straight-line
Location	Workshop B
Supplier	Compress Ltd

What additional information would you require about this asset before determining the amount to be included in a current cost balance sheet? *9 marks*

(c) What difficulties may arise as the result of rapid technological change when valuing plant and machinery under this valuation concept? *8 marks*

Total 25 marks

3 'The standard does not deal with the maintenance of financial capital in general purchasing power terms' (Statement of Standard Accounting Practice No. 16, paragraph 36).

(a) What is the underlying concept of capital in SSAP 16, 'Current cost accounting'? Define any terms you use in your explanation. *10 marks*

(b) What voluntary disclosure does SSAP 16, 'Current cost accounting', suggest for reporting the impact of changes in general purchasing power on shareholders' equity interest? Explain whether you consider this to be necessary. *10 marks*

Total 20 marks

4 You have been appointed to the corporate planning department of Anarchy plc. The chief planner has attended a meeting of senior executives called to discuss the possibility of introducing a system of current cost accounting for management accounting purposes. Anarchy plc has published only historical cost accounts in its annual reports so far, the chairman observing that 'We prefer to reserve judgment on these developments and to wait until the accountancy profession has fully considered the alternatives and come to a definite conclusion'.

As your first assignment the chief planner asks for your comments on five of the objections to the proposal which he noted down as having been made at the meeting. He stresses to you that he himself has a completely open mind about the proposal, and is not committed either way.

You are required to set out your observations on the following five objections to the introduction of a system of current cost accounting for management accounting purposes:

(a)   'If we use current costs we'll price ourselves out of the market.'   *5 marks*

(b)   'Just think of any fixed assets. Take that hydraulic press. I haven't a clue when we'll want to replace that, or even if we'll ever want to replace it, let alone what its replacement cost would be then. You can't seriously propose a system based on ideas like that.'   *5 marks*

(c)   'This idea of value to the business is just a muddle; it has no logical basis to it.'   *5 marks*

(d)   'You can't rely on measurements of current cost. They aren't objective, and you can't really verify them. It's all a guessing game.'   *5 marks*

(e)   'I know historical cost isn't ideal, but I can't see why it shouldn't be perfectly satisfactory as long as we use it consistently. Consistency is what really matters.'   *5 marks*
        Total 25 marks

5   You are the senior in charge of the audit of Jackson Pumps plc, which is preparing current cost accounts for the year ended 31 March 1983. Your manager has asked you to audit the cost of sales and monetary working capital adjustments.

The company has a new chief accountant who has asked you to show him the principles involved in calculating the cost of sales adjustment using the averaging method. To illustrate the method he has the following figures for finished goods stock of piston pumps. For both 1982 and 1983, finished goods stock represents two months' production, and materials were purchased one month prior to them being required for production. Manufacture of each pump takes one day and work in progress may be assumed to be nil for the purposes of the calculations. The other information relating to the pumps is as follows:

	1982	1983
Historical cost: materials	£2,435	£2,475
labour	£1,388	£1,374
Overhead (percentage of labour cost)	150%	150%
Indices		
Materials at 31 March	276	309
at 28 February	274	307

		1982	1983
Materials	at 31 January	272	304
	at 31 December	270	301
	average for year to 31 March	262	295
Labour	at 31 March	188	204
	at 28 February	187	202
	at 31 January	186	201
	at 31 December	185	200
	average for year to 31 March	182	197

The company calculates its own indices for labour costs, but uses Central Statistical Office indices for material costs. The major materials of the pumps are:

(i)   Steel, aluminium and cast iron castings.
(ii) Steel and aluminium for the parts.
(iii) Steel ball bearings and brass and white metal plain bearings.
(iv) Small electric motors to drive some of the pumps (these are purchased from outside suppliers).

You are required:

(a)   To briefly describe what you understand by the cost of sales adjustment.
        2 marks

(b)   To calculate, from the figures given above:

      (i)   The cost of sales adjustment for the pumps for the year ended 31 March 1983.
      (ii) The current cost of stock at 31 March 1982 and 31 March 1983.

      Answers should be calculated to the nearest pound.   *6 marks*

(c)   To describe how you would audit the cost of sales adjustment for the stock of Jackson Pumps plc for the year ended 31 March 1983.   *8 marks*

(d)   To describe how you would decide whether it was appropriate to use the stock index for calculating the monetary working capital adjustment. *4 marks*
        Total 20 marks

6   RS Ltd, a manufacturer of construction equipment, has decided to comply with the requirements of Statement of Standard Accounting Practice No. 16 in respect of the year ended 31 December 1980, by presenting its accounts on a historical cost basis supplemented by a current cost profit and loss account and balance sheet.

From the information given below you are required to prepare a current cost profit and loss account for the year ended 31 December 1980 and a current cost balance sheet as at that date.

Comparative figures are not required; all workings must be shown.

The historical cost accounts for the period were as follows:

Profit and loss account

	1980 £	1980 £	1979 £	1979 £
Turnover		6,633,000		5,559,000
Trading profit		594,980		618,600
Depreciation				
Freehold property	–		4,000	
Plant and machinery	64,670		53,650	
	64,670		57,650	
Auditors' remuneration	7,450		6,400	
Bank interest	8,160		2,950	
Directors' emoluments	92,400		84,400	
		172,680		151,400
Profit before taxation		422,300		467,200
Taxation		176,000		260,000
Profit after taxation		246,300		207,200
Dividends		78,000		70,000
Retained profit for year		168,300		137,200

Balance sheets at 31 December

	1980 £	1980 £	1979 £	1979 £
Fixed assets				
Freehold property, at valuation		300,000		180,000
Plant and machinery, at cost	770,600		651,600	
Less: Depreciation	228,600		181,600	
		542,000		470,000
		842,000		650,000
Current assets				
Stocks	1,286,000		1,025,600	
Work in progress	350,300		310,000	
Debtors	973,200		776,400	
	2,609,500		2,112,000	
Current liabilities				
Creditors	792,300		591,000	
Taxation	107,000		153,000	
Bank overdraft	148,200		6,300	
Proposed dividend	48,000		48,000	
	1,095,500		798,300	
		1,514,000		1,313,700
		2,356,000		1,963,700

	1980		1979	
	£	£	£	£
Share capital				
Ordinary shares of £1 each				
issued and fully paid		800,000		800,000
Capital reserves		120,000		–
Retained profits		726,000		557,700
Deferred taxation		710,000		606,000
		2,356,000		1,963,700

The freehold property was professionally valued at 31 December 1980 at £300,000 and no depreciation is to be provided in 1980.

On average, stocks and unallocated work in progress represent three months' purchases.

£152,400 of the work in progress was specifically allocated to customers at 31 December 1980. At 31 December 1979 the figure was £136,000.

For the purpose of calculating the gearing adjustment you may assume that the current cost reserve at 31 December 1979 would have been £226,200 made up as follows:

	£
Stocks (cost of sales)	5,200
Plant	221,000
	226,200

This is additional to the retained profits of £557,700 but in the absence of full information this notional figure of £226,200 is not required to be brought forward for incorporation into the balance sheet at 31 December 1980.

An analysis of the plant into years of acquisition gave the following figures:

	£
1975	223,400
1976	190,200
1977	111,000
1978	42,000
1979	85,000
1980	119,000
	770,600

Plant has been depreciated at 10% on a straight-line basis calculated from the date of acquisition or the date put into use whichever was the later. For current cost purposes, however, depreciation is to be calculated on the assumption that plant was acquired and put into use at the beginning of each financial year.

The relevant indices which are average or mid-period are set out below:

Plant and machinery		Stocks	
1975	962	Oct 1979	136.1
1976	1,179	Nov 1979	137.0
1977	1,354	Dec 1979	137.2
1978	1,557	Jan 1980	139.7
1979	1,758	Oct 1980	158.5
1980	1,970	Nov 1980	160.8
		Dec 1980	161.3
		Jan 1981	162.1

The actual index at 31 December 1980 for plant and machinery was 2,000.

45 marks

7   Dirigibles (UK) plc is a long-established manufacturing company. The following historical cost accounts have been prepared for the year ended on 31 March 1984.

Trading profit and loss account for the year ended 31 March 1984

	£ thousands	£ thousands
Sales		8,000
Less: cost of sales		6,200
		———
Gross profit		1,800
Less: Distribution costs	379	
Administration expenses	184	
	——	
		563
		———
		1,237
Less: Interest payable		75
		———
Profit on ordinary activities		1,162
Tax on ordinary activities		610
		———
Profit for the financial year		552
Less: Dividends		
Ordinary: Interim paid	100	
Final proposed	200	
	——	
		300
		———
Retained profit for the year		252
		═══

Balance sheet as at 31 March 1984

	1984 £ thousands	1984 £ thousands	1983 £ thousands	1983 £ thousands
Fixed assets				
Tangible assets		3,580		3,200
Current assets				
Stock	720		520	
Debtors	2,180		1,700	
Cash	15		180	
	2,915		2,400	
Creditors: amounts falling due within one year				
Trade creditors	1,228		985	
Dividend payable	200		150	
Corporation tax	510		260	
	1,938		1,395	
Net current assets		977		1,005
Total assets less current liabilities		4,557		4,205
Creditors: amounts falling due after more than one year				
Debenture stock	750		750	
Provisions for liabilities and charges				
Deferred taxation	250		150	
		1,000		900
		3,557		3,305
Capital and reserves				
Called-up share capital				
Ordinary shares of £1 each, authorised, issued and fully paid		1,500		1,500
Profit and loss account		2,057		1,805
		3,557		3,305

Additional information

	31 March 1984 £ thousands	31 March 1984 £ thousands
Fixed assets: Plant and machinery		
Cost	4,800	4,000
Accumulated depreciation	1,220	800
	3,580	3,200

There were no disposals during the year. Additional plant was acquired on 31 December 1983 for £800,000. The assets held at 31 March 1983 had been acquired on 1 April 1981.

Depreciation is calculated using the straight-line method at a rate of 10% p.a.

Depreciation is allocated within the profit and loss account, 80% within cost of sales and 20% within distribution costs.

Sales, purchases, distribution costs and administration costs have arisen evenly throughout the year.

Both opening and closing stocks represent two months' purchases.

Debtors and creditors at both balance sheet dates represent three months' sales and purchases.

The following (middle of the month) index numbers are considered appropriate:

	Plant and machinery	COSA and MWCA
1982 March	104.5	—
April	105.5	—
1983 January	—	173.3
February	—	175.4
March	114.5	177.4
April	115.5	179.6
November	121.4	193.6
December	121.8	195.6
1984 January	122.2	197.9
February	123.3	200.0
March	124.7	202.4
April	125.3	204.4
Average for year to 31 March 1984	120	190.8

You are required to prepare in accordance with SSAP 16:

(a) Current cost profit and loss account for the year to 31 March 1984. *10 marks*

(b) The current cost balance sheet as at that date.   *10 marks*

(c) The current cost revaluation account so far as is possible from the information available.   *5 marks*
                                                          Total 25 marks

8 Below are the historical cost profit and loss accounts of Achilles plc for the year ended 31 December 1981, and its balance sheet as at that date, with corresponding figures for the previous year.

Historical cost profit and loss account for the year ended 31 December 1981

	£ thousands	£ thousands
Turnover		6,000
Net trading profit, after charging		550
Depreciation		
Buildings	58	
Vehicles and equipment	575	
Losses (gains) on disposal of fixed assets		
Buildings	15	
Vehicles and equipment	(20)	
Investment income (gross of tax credits)		50
Net profit before interest		600
Debenture interest (gross)		150
Net profit before taxation		450
Taxation		225
Net profit for year		225
Dividends:		
Cumulative preference, paid	25	
Ordinary, paid	50	
Ordinary, proposed	75	150
Retained earnings for year		75

Historical cost balance sheet, 31 December 1981

	31 December 1980 Net £ thousands	Cost or valuation £ thousands	Net assets	Cost or valuation £ thousands	Depreciation £ thousands	Net £ thousands
			Fixed assets			
	300	300	Land	300	–	300
	700	1,000	Buildings	1,150	273	877
	1,150	2,000	Vehicles and equipment	2,300	1,125	1,175
	2,150	3,300		3,750	1,398	2,352
	400		Long-term investments at cost (market value £500,000; 1980, £450,000)			400
			Current assets			
	425		Stocks		650	
	475		Debtors and prepayments		700	
	4		Bank and cash balances		295	
	904				1,645	
			Less: current liabilities			
	350		Bank overdraft		–	
	250		Creditors and accruals		350	
	100		Corporation tax, 1981 (less ACT)		116	
	50		Proposed dividend		75	
	21		ACT on proposed dividend		32	
	771				573	
	133		Net current assets			1,072
	2,683					3,824

	£ thousands	£ thousands		£ thousands	£ thousands
Financed by					
Share capital: authorised, issued and fully paid 10% cumulative preference (£1 shares)	250			250	
Ordinary shares (£1 each)	1,000			1,000	
		1,250			1,250
Reserves					
Share premium account	300			300	
Fixed assets revaluation reserve	232			232	
Retained earnings	751			826	
	1,283			1,358	
		2,533			2,608
15% debentures	—			1,000	
Deferred taxation	150			216	
		2,683			3,824

Land was revalued in the books of account at £300,000 as at 1 January 1979.

Buildings (original cost £800,000, accumulated depreciation £160,000) were also revalued in the books at the same date, on the basis of £1,000,000 replacement cost as new. Depreciation is at the rate of 5% p.a. on gross book value, with a full year's charge in the year of acquisition and none in the year of disposal.

Professional valuations for current cost accounting purposes were:

Land (market value): 31 December 1980, £360,000; 31 December 1981, £400,000.

Buildings (gross replacement cost as new): 31 December 1980, £1,250,000; 31 December 1981, £1,600,000 (including 1981 additions, valued at £275,000). During 1981 some buildings were demolished, their valuations being: 1 January 1979 (for historical cost purposes), £100,000 gross, £25,000 net; 31 December 1980 (for current cost purposes), £120,000 gross, £18,000 net.

The vehicles and equipment on hand at 31 December 1980 were acquired as follows, on average at the middle of each year:

	Cost £	Accumulated depreciation £
1978	400,000	300,000
1979	600,000	300,000
1980	1,000,000	250,000
	2,000,000	850,000

In 1981 all the 1978 items were sold for £120,000, and new items were bought for £700,000. The company's policy is to charge depreciation at 25% p.a. on gross book value, with a full year's charge in the year of acquisition and none in the year of disposal. Of the 1979 equipment, £200,000 (at cost) was by 31 December 1981 deemed to be obsolescent. The directors of Achilles plc had contracted to replace it in 1982 with modern equipment costing £350,000, and having a service capacity 40% greater than that of the old equipment.

For CCA purposes, the relevant price index numbers for vehicles and equipment (taken as at the month end) were as follows:

1978	June	100
1979	June	115
1980	June	135
1980	December	150
1981	June	175
1981	December	200

The stocks were on average one month old as at 31 December in both years. The relevant price index numbers were:

1980	November	99
1980	December	100
1981	November	123
1981	December	125

The 15% debentures were issued at par on 1 January 1981.

For current cost accounting purposes, the profit and loss account adjustments were:

	£
Depreciation adjustment (including allowance for gains and losses on disposal of fixed assets)	208,000
Cost of sales/monetary working capital adjustment	177,000
Gearing adjustment	68,000

You are required to prepare the current cost balance sheet of Achilles plc as at 31 December 1981, with corresponding figures, on the same basis, for 31 December 1980 (without a general inflation adjustment).

Current cost reserve balances are to be inserted as balancing figures, and no extra marks will be given for computing them directly.

30 marks

ANSWERS

1

(a)   Three adjustments together make up the current cost operating adjustments. They are:

    (i)   Depreciation adjustment.
    (ii)   Cost of sales adjustment.
    (iii)   Monetary working capital adjustment.

In total they are deducted from the profit before interest and taxation on the historical cost basis to give the current cost operating profit.

Depreciation adjustment allows for the impact of price changes when determining the charge against revenue for the part of fixed assets consumed in the period. It is the difference between the 'value to the business' of the part of fixed assets consumed during the accounting period and the amount of depreciation charged on a historical cost basis.

Cost of sales adjustment (COSA) allows for the impact of price changes when determining the charge against revenue for stock consumed in the period. It is the difference between the value to the business of stock consumed and the cost of stock charged on a historical cost basis.

Monetary working capital adjustment (MWCA). As most businesses have other working capital besides stock involved in their day-to-day operating activities the standard provides for an adjustment in respect of the monetary working capital. This adjustment should represent the amount of additional (or reduced) finance needed for monetary working capital as a result of changes in input prices of goods and services used and financed by the business.

In a business which holds stocks, the MWCA complements the COSA and together they allow for the impact of price changes on the total amount of working capital used by the business in its day-to-day operations.

Monetary working capital consists of:

(1)   Trade debtors, prepayments and trade bills receivable; plus
(2)   Stocks not subject to COSA; less
(3)   Trade creditors, accruals and trade bills payable in so far as they arise from the day-to-day operating activities of the business as distinct from transactions of a capital nature.

Bank balances or overdrafts may fluctuate with the volume of stock or the items in (1), (2) or (3) above. The part of bank balances or overdrafts arising from such fluctuations should be included in the monetary working capital, together with any cash floats required to support day-to-day operations of the business, if to do so has a material effect on the current cost operating profit.

(b) The current cost operating profit is after the impact of price changes calculated as current cost operating adjustment, without taking into consideration the financing of the business. Where the business has raised finance whose repayment rights are fixed in money terms, it is necessary to determine what proportion of the net assets is financed by such borrowings.

The gearing adjustment therefore abates the operating adjustments in the gearing proportion in deriving the current cost profit attributable to shareholders.

The gearing adjustment, subject to interest on borrowing, indicates the benefit or cost to the shareholders which is realised in the period, measured by the extent to which a proportion of the net operating assets is financed by borrowings.

The gearing proportion mentioned above is the borrowings as a proportion of the net assets employed at current cost values.

(c) Net borrowings is the excess of:

(i) The aggregate of all liabilities fixed in monetary terms (including convertible debentures and deferred taxation but excluding proposed dividends) other than those included within monetary working capital and other than those which are, in substance, equity capital; over

(ii) The aggregate of all current assets other than those subject to a cost of sales adjustment and those included within monetary working capital.

(d) The current cost reserve is an additional reserve over those shown in the historical cost accounts. The balance of this reserve will be made up of:

(i) Unrealised revaluation surpluses on fixed assets, stock and investments;
(ii) The cumulative net total of the current cost operating adjustments;
(iii) The gearing adjustment; and
(iv) Translation differences arising on consolidation through changes in the rates used to translate the assets and liabilities of subsidiaries whose accounts are denominated in foreign currencies. In most cases these differences are, in effect, price changes which do not affect the operating capability of the group and in these cases they are not included in current cost profits but are reflected directly within this reserve.

2

(a) To estimate the operating capability of a business, and the costs which must be charged against profits to maintain this capability, assets in current cost accounts should be valued, not at historical costs, but at 'value to the business'. This has been defined as:

(i) The loss which a company would suffer if it were deprived of the asset — 'deprival value'.

270

(ii)   The extra funds which would be required to maintain the operating capability of the company if it suddenly 'lost' the asset.

SSAP 16 defines 'value to the business' as:

(i)   Net current replacement cost;

or, if a permanent diminution to below net current replacement cost has been recognised,

(ii)   Recoverable amount, which is the greater of the net realisable value of an asset and, where applicable, the amount recoverable from its further use.

If an asset is worth replacing its deprival value will always be net replacement cost. If the asset is not worth replacing, it might be disposed of straight away, or else it might be kept in operation until the end of its useful life.

(b)   The information required needs to be related to the basis of valuation as defined in (a), i.e.:

(i)   Net current replacement cost:
— Suppliers' price list.
— Government index (PINCCA)/private sector index.

(ii)   Net realisable value:
— Is it surplus to requirements?
— Is the asset to be sold in the near future?
— What is the market for that type of asset?
— What is the current equivalent second-hand price for this type of asset?

(iii)   Amount recoverable from its future use:
— Future 'useful life'.
— Future expected cash flows, including residual value.
— Estimate of future interest rates relevant.

Whichever valuation base is used it will be necessary to determine the remaining 'useful life' in order to write off the CCA value.

The same overall 'asset life' should be used for both historical and current cost accounting.

(c)   With technology changing rapidly the modern asset will have a substantially different purchase cost, operating costs, estimated life, output capacity and service potential. In these circumstances it would be unrealistic to take the cost of the modern asset and use it without adjustment as the current cost of the existing asset, because the capital cost of the modern equivalent asset includes the cost of the (operating) improvements so that like is not being compared with like.

3

(a) The current cost accounting system is based upon a concept of capital which is represented by the net operating assets of a business. These net operating assets (fixed assets, stock and monetary working capital) are the same as those included in the historical cost accounts, but in the current cost accounts the fixed assets and stock are normally expressed at current cost. The net operating assets can be said to represent, in accounting terms, the operating capability of the business and usually will have been financed both by shareholders' capital and borrowings.

(b) In part 1, 'Explanatory Note', of SSAP 16 (paragraph 36) it is recognised that some users may be interested in a statement of the change in the shareholders' equity interest after allowing for the change in the general purchasing power of money. A statement may be prepared voluntarily to reflect this. An example of such a statement is:

Statement of changes in shareholders' equity interest after allowing for changes in the general purchasing power of money for the year ended 31 March 1984

	£ thousands
Equity interest at the beginning of the year as shown in the current cost accounts	XX
Share capital issued during the year (date)	X
	XX
Amount required to compensate for the change in the general purchasing power of money during the year (see note)	XX(a)
Equity interest before dividends at the end of the year as shown in the current cost accounts	X
Excess (deficit)	XX

The excess can be analysed as follows:

	£ thousands
Current cost profit attributable to shareholders	X
Effect on equity interest of price changes experienced by the company being greater than the general rate of UK inflation	X
	XX

Note. The price index used to calculate the £XX(a) in the above calculation is the general index of changes in retail price, as follows:

31 March 1983	XX
30 September 1983	XX
31 March 1984	XX
Percentage change in the year	XX%

Current cost accounting takes the 'entity' view of the firm in that only the price changes that affect the operating capability of the firm are relevant. As the financing of the firm's operating capability comes from a mixture of individual share and loan stockholders, it would be useful to provide a 'proprietary' view of the operations of the company showing how it has affected the shareholders' money capital in relation to inflation in general.

The SSAP gives two areas for which it is considered that such a statement would be relevant:

(i) Where there are excess monetary assets; any excess of these assets over the borrowing is not covered by the current cost accounting framework, being more in the nature of assets held for investment.

(ii) Where part of the group has activities exempt under paragraph 46(c) of the SSAP.

4 Observations on the objections to the introduction of a CCA system for management accounting purposes:

(a) Unless Anarchy plc is in a monopoly or oligopoly situation, it is unlikely that it can influence market prices. Market forces probably determine the price at which Anarchy is able to sell the goods or services which it can offer, rather than a cost-plus pricing policy.

Current cost accounting (CCA) will give a more relevant and meaningful measure of profit than historical cost accounting (HCA) as it provides for the maintenance of the operating capacity of the business. It is therefore valid to use CCA for management accounting purposes, even if current costs are not used in the pricing decision because market forces prevail. However, a good costing system should incorporate current costs as the concept of deprival value is more relevant than historical costs in deciding whether to use assets on particular contracts, or whether to accept contracts at special prices.

(b) The problem of uncertainty about *when* assets are to be replaced also arises using an HCA system. In order to calculate both historical cost and current cost depreciation charges it is necessary to estimate the remaining useful lives of assets.

CCA does not attempt to set aside amounts for the replacement of particular assets, but it does provide a more accurate measure of the opportunity cost of using assets within the business, as annual depreciation charges are based on current values. Therefore, a CCA system is applicable even if there is no intention to replace the hydraulic press.

Anarchy does not need to know what the replacement cost of the press will be in the future; CCA is concerned with its net current replacement cost *now*.

(c) The idea of value to the business is not a muddle, but is based on the concept of deprival value. Deprival value is:

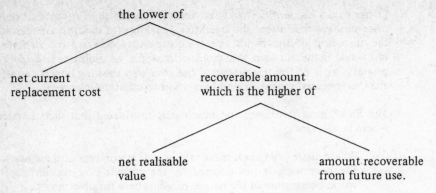

the lower of

net current
replacement cost

recoverable amount
which is the higher of

net realisable
value

amount recoverable
from future use.

By applying the concept of deprival value to the consumption of an asset, one is asking 'What sum of money would compensate us for the loss of the asset?' If the recoverable amount is higher than replacement cost, the business will replace the asset, and therefore replacement cost would compensate for the loss of the asset. Where replacement cost exceeds the recoverable amount, management would decide not to replace the asset, in which case the cost of losing the asset would be viewed as the higher of net realisable value and the amount recoverable from future use.

Of course, if net realisable value exceeds the amount recoverable from future use, management would be considering disposing of the asset, since this would be a more profitable course than keeping it in use.

Thus the concept of value to the business is logical, as it follows the principals on which management decisions are made.

(d) HCA systems are not as objective as people might think, as in many instances estimates are used. For example, using an HCA system it is necessary to make subjective judgments in the following areas:

(i) Fixed assets:
   — Net realisable value.
   — Estimated useful lives.
   — Estimated residual values.
   — Recoverable amount (SSAP 12).

(ii) Stocks:
   — Net realisable value.
   — Valuation of obsolete, damaged and slow moving stocks.

(iii) Debtors:
   — Provision for doubtful debts.

The problem of exercising subjective judgment in these areas is common to both HCA and CCA systems.

The additional areas of subjective judgment that arise within CCA can be restricted by using appropriate indices, and if these are used as the source of current cost data (as opposed to directors' valuations) then the results can be relatively objective. There are difficulties associated with the use of indices, for example where there has been significant technological change, but these can be overcome using the concept of a 'modern equivalent asset'.

(e)   HCA cannot be viewed as consistent as accounts are prepared using an unstable unit of measurement, and therefore comparisons over time become invalid. It could be argued that HCA is consistent in that it does charge the same money amounts to the profit and loss account in respect of the consumption of fixed assets; however, the unit in which the charges are measured has changed, and therefore it is consistency in charging the consumption of service potential that really matters. In this respect the current cost convention is superior to the historical cost convention.

5

(a)   The cost of sales adjustment (COSA) allows for the impact of price changes when determining the charge against revenue for stock consumed in the period. It is the difference between the 'value to the business' of stock consumed and the cost of stock charged on a historical cost basis. The resulting charge thus represents the 'value to the business' of stock consumed in earning the revenue of the period.

(b)   (i)   COSA for year ended 31 March 1983 is £559.
      (ii)   Current cost of stock at 31 March 1982 is £5,959.
             Current cost of stock at 31 March 1983 is £5,976.

Workings

Stocks represent two months' production, so the stocks at the end of March are the production of February and March. Materials for this production were purchased one month in advance, i.e. during January and February. So the relevant materials index is the average of the figures for end December and end February.

For 1983 the materials index is ½(301 + 307) = 304
For 1982 the materials index is ½(270 + 274) = 272

It is assumed that labour is paid in the month in which it is employed so the relevant labour index is the average of the figures for end January and end March.

For 1983 the labour index is ½(201 + 204) = 202.5
For 1982 the labour index is ½(186 + 188) = 187

To calculate the cost of sales adjustment for the year ended 31 March 1983, use the formula:

$$C - O - I_a(C/I_a - O/I_0)$$

For materials:

$$2{,}475 - 2{,}435 - 295(2{,}475/304 - 2{,}435/272) = 279 \quad \text{(to nearest whole number)}$$

For labour:

$$1{,}374 - 1{,}388 - 197(1{,}374/202.5 - 1{,}388/187) = 112 \quad \text{(to nearest whole number)}$$

Overhead is 150% of labour cost = 150% × 112 = 168
COSA = 279 + 112 + 168
       = 559

Stock value at 31 March 1982

	£
Materials: £2,435 × 276/272	2,471
Labour: £1,388 × 188/187	1,395
Overhead (150% of labour)	2,093
	5,959

Stock value at 31 March 1983

	£
Materials: £2,475 × 309/304	2,516
Labour: £1,374 × 204/202.5	1,384
Overhead (150% of labour)	2,076
	5,976

Note. The COSA and stock values refer only to the finished stock of pumps.

(c) Stocks of Jackson Pumps plc will comprise raw materials, bought-in electric motors, work in progress and finished goods. With the production time for each pump being one day, it could safely be assumed that for the purposes of stock valuation work in progress would be negligible. Audit work would therefore be concentrated on the three other categories, paying particular attention to high-value stock items.

The audit of the cost of sales adjustment would be performed in the following stages:

(i)   Checking the calculation of the index (or indices) for direct labour cost.
(ii) Checking the age of the stock.
(iii) Checking that the cost of sales adjustment is calculated correctly and that the appropriate indices have been used for raw materials.

To check the calculation of the index for direct labour cost, I would first ask the company about their method of calculation. It is probable that the index for direct labour cost will just be the change in wage rate for the year.

In this case, it is probable that wage rates will have been increased once during the year for all employees which will produce a step change in the index at that date. I would check that the change in the labour index agreed with the change in wage rates. If labour rates did not increase by the same percentage for all employees, it may be appropriate to use a number of indices for direct labour costs. Also, the average index for labour costs for the year, used in the averaging method of calculating the cost of sales adjustment, should be the average of the indices for each month of the year and not the index half-way through the year.

Other factors to consider are:

(i)   Are other wage increases given to employees which result in a higher actual rise in wage costs than is indicated by the annual increase?

(ii) If labour is becoming more efficient, possibly due to more automation, or increasing skills of the employees, it may be appropriate to take this into account when determining the index for labour cost. The accounting policy for determining the index for labour cost should be checked on this point.

The next stage is to calculate the age of major lines of stock. For major lines of raw materials this can be determined from the date of the purchase invoices. For finished stock, purchase invoices can also be used to determine the date for bought-in components, like electric motors. For other components, like machined parts, the quantity and type of materials used will have to be found in order to determine the date of purchase. For finished goods, only the larger-value elements of the finished components would be checked in this way.

For direct labour costs, the date when the stock was manufactured would be found from production records.

From the above investigations the date when the average material cost was incurred and the average labour cost was expended would be determined.

The last stage would be to check the calculation of the cost of sales adjustment. For raw materials it is important to check that an appropriate index has been used for the item and that the date of the index is appropriate for that item of stock. For labour costs the date used should be the average date when that line of stock was manufactured. Once these checks have been made, the calculation of the cost of sales adjustment can be checked for the major lines of stock selected for audit.

Finally, I would check that the cost of sales adjustment looked reasonable. If costs have been increasing by about 10%, the cost of sales adjustment should be about 10% of the average of the opening and closing stock value. Also I would check that the accounting policy for determining the cost of sales adjustment was in accordance with SSAP 16 and consistent with the previous year.

(d) In answering this part of the question it is assumed that monetary working capital is only trade creditors and trade debtors, as is usually the case. Although SSAP 16 says that this adjustment should reflect the finance needed for monetary working capital as a result of changes in input prices of goods and services used and financed by the business, which implies that price changes in the cost of stocks should be used, most companies look at the change in prices for trade creditors and trade debtors when determining this adjustment. This answer considers this latter method.

A weighted average of the indices used for calculating the cost of sales adjustment is likely to be used for calculating the monetary working capital adjustment. I would check that the calculation of this weighted index was reasonable.

In determining whether this index is appropriate for calculating the monetary working capital adjustment, it is necessary to look at trade creditors and trade debtors separately.

Trade creditors comprise mainly the cost of raw materials purchased by the business, so the index which should be used is the index for raw materials. However, the index for stock includes a labour element, and if changes in labour and materials costs were very different, and this had a material effect on the overall index, then it may not be appropriate to use the stock index for creditors. However, in practice, in most manufacturing companies it is likely that the stock index will not produce material errors in calculating the monetary working capital adjustment for creditors.

The appropriate index to use for trade debtors is the index of selling prices. Changes in this index may be very different from changes in the indices for raw material and labour costs. In a recession selling prices may decrease while labour and material costs may be increasing, and if there is a shortage of a finished product, selling prices may increase substantially more rapidly than costs. Therefore, as auditor I would check the increase in selling prices during the year for major sales lines and check whether this is similar to the increase in the stock index. If the difference is significant, then it would be appropriate to calculate an index for selling prices and use it to calculate the monetary working capital adjustment for debtors.

6 Current cost profit and loss account for year to 31 December 1980

	£	£
		6,633,000
Sales		
Historical cost operating profit before interest and taxation		430,460
Current cost adjustments: Depreciation (W1)	55,748	
COSA (W3)	210,515	
MWCA (W4)	50,948	
		317,211
Current cost operating profit		113,249
	carried forward	113,249

278

	£	£
brought forward		113,249
Gearing adjustment (W5)	(105,585)	
Interest paid	8,160	
		97,425
Current cost profit before taxation		210,674
Corporation tax		176,000
Current cost profit attributable to shareholders		34,674
Dividends		78,000
Current cost deficit for year		43,326
Earnings per share		4.4p

Current cost balance sheet as at 31 December 1980

	£	£	£
Fixed (tangible) assets			
Freehold property		300,000	
Plant and machinery (W2)		669,335	969,335
Current assets			
Stocks and work in progress			
(£1,498,730 + £152,400)		1,651,130	
Debtors		973,200	
		2,624,330	
Creditors: amounts falling due			
within one year			
Creditors	792,300		
Taxation	107,000		
Bank overdraft	148,200		
Proposed dividends	48,000		
		1,095,500	
			1,528,830
			2,498,165
Less: Deferred taxation			710,000
			1,788,165
Capital and reserves			
Called-up share capital			800,000
Current cost reserve			353,791
Revaluation reserve			120,000
Profit and loss account (£557,700 − £43,326)			514,374
			1,788,165

Workings

1 Fixed assets/depreciation adjustment

From the information available it is not clear what the historical cost depreciation policy is. For CCA it is necessary to assume that assets are acquired evenly throughout each year.

Year acquired	Index average	£	£	Current cost depreciation (10%) £
1975	962	223,400 × 1970/962	457,482	
1976	1179	190,200 × 1970/1179	317,807	
1977	1354	111,000 × 1970/1354	161,499	
1978	1557	42,000 × 1970/1557	53,141	
1979	1758	85,000 × 1970/1758	95,250	
1980	1970	119,000 × 1970/1970	119,000	
			1,204,178	120,418

Deduct historical cost depreciation   64,670

Current cost depreciation adjustment   55,748

2 For balance sheet at 31 December 1980

		Gross replacement value £	Number of years of depreciation	Net replacement value % Gross replacement value	£
1975	£223,400 × 2000/962	464,449	6	40%	185,780
1976	£190,200 × 2000/1179	322,646	5	50%	161,323
1977	£111,000 × 2000/1354	163,959	4	60%	98,375
1978	£42,000 × 2000/1557	53,950	3	70%	37,765
1979	£85,000 × 2000/1758	96,701	2	80%	77,361
1980	£119,000 × 2000/1970	120,812	1	90%	108,731
		1,218,357			669,335

Deduct historical cost net book
value at 31 December 1980   542,000

Net increase from historical
cost to current cost   127,335

3 **COSA**

It is assumed that indices for stocks can also be used for MWCA.

Stocks and work in progress	1 January 1980 £	31 December 1980 £
Stock	1,025,600	1,286,000
Work in progress	310,000	350,300
Less work in progress specifically allotted to customer (included in MWCA)	(136,000)	(152,400)
	1,199,600	1,483,900

The stocks and unallocated work in progress represent three months' purchases, i.e. purchases in October, November and December. So the relevant indices are the averages of the figures for those three months.

The average for October, November and December 1979 is:

$(136.1 + 137 + 137.2)/3 = 136.7667$ (to 4 decimal places)

The average for October, November and December 1980 is:

$(158.5 + 160.8 + 161.3)/3 = 160.2$

The index at 31 December may be estimated as the average of the mid December and mid January figures.

At 31 December 1979: $(137.2 + 139.7)/2 = 138.45$
At 31 December 1980: $(161.3 + 162.1)/2 = 161.7$

The average for the year 1980 is, therefore: $(138.45 + 161.7)/2 = 150.075$

The cost of sales adjustment is:

$1,483,900 - 1,199,600 - 150.075(1,483,900/160.2 - 1,199,600/136.7667) = 210,515$ (to nearest whole number)

4 **MWCA** at

Work in progress specifically	1 January 1980 £	31 December 1980 £
allocated to customer	136,000	152,400
Debtors	776,400	973,200
Creditors	(591,000)	(792,000)
	321,400	333,300

Using the indices calculated in W3, the MWCA is:

$$333,300 - 321,400 - 150.075(333,300/161.7 - 321,400/138.45)$$
$$= 50,948 \quad \text{(to nearest whole number)}$$

Note. A more realistic MWCA would be calculated by applying indices to each of the constituent parts. However, the question does not provide sufficient information to work out the age of debtors and creditors.

5 Gearing adjustment

The gearing adjustment is:

$$(DA + COSA + MWCA) [ANB/(ANB + \text{average current cost equity})]$$

where DA is the depreciation adjustment and ANB is the average net borrowings.

$$\text{Gearing adjustment} = (£55,748 + £210,515 + £50,948) \times £865,250/£2,599,482$$
$$= £105,585 \quad \text{(to nearest pound)}$$

	1 January 1980 £	31 December 1980 £	Average (4) £
Deferred tax	606,000	710,000	
Taxation	153,000	107,000	
Bank overdraft	6,300	148,200	
Net borrowings	765,300	965,200	865,250
Share capital	800,000	800,000	
Capital reserves	—	120,000	
Revenue reserves	557,700	726,000	
Increases to non-monetary items to current cost at balance sheet date			
Plant and machinery	221,000(1)	127,335(2)	
Stock and work in progress	5,600(1)	14,830(3)	
Proposed dividends	48,000	48,000	
	1,632,300	1,836,165	1,734,232
			2,599,482

Notes

1 From information given in question.
2 From W2.

3   At 31 December 1980

	£
Stocks	1,286,000
Work in progress	350,300
Specifically allocated	(152,400)
	1,483,900

£1,483,900 × 161.7/160.1 − £1,483,900 = £14,830

4   Calculated by adding the figures at 1 January 1980 and 31 December 1980 and dividing by 2.

7

(a)   **Current cost profit and loss account for the year ended 31 March 1984**

	£ thousands	£ thousands
Sales		8,000
Less: Cost of sales		6,200
Gross profit		1,800
Less: Distribution costs	379	
Administration expenses	184	
		563
		1,237
Current cost operating adjustments		
Depreciation	57	
Cost of sales	80	
Monetary working capital	107	
		244
Current cost operating profit		993
Less: Interest payable	75	
Gearing adjustment	(57)	
		18
Current cost profit before taxation		975
Taxation		610
		365
Less: Dividends		
Ordinary interim, paid	100	
Ordinary final, proposed	200	
		300
Retained current cost profit for year		65
Current cost earnings per share		4.3p

(b) Current cost balance sheet as at 31 March 1984

1983 £ thousands	£ thousands		£ thousands	£ thousands
		Fixed assets		
		Tangible assets		
4,381		Gross replacement cost		5,582
876		Accumulated depreciation		1,448
3,505		Net replacement cost		4,134
		Current assets		
	526	Stock	728	
	1,700	Debtors	2,180	
	180	Cash	15	
	2,406		2,923	
		Less: Creditors: amounts falling due within one year		
	985	Trade creditors	1,228	
	150	Dividend payable	200	
	260	Corporation tax	510	
	1,395		1,938	
1,011		Net current assets		985
4,516		Total assets less current liabilities		5,119
		Less: Creditors: amounts falling due after more than one year		
	750	10% debenture stock	750	
		Provision for liabilities and charges		
	150	Deferred taxation	250	
900				1,000
3,616				4,119
		Capital and reserves		
		Called-up share capital		
1,500		Ordinary shares of £1 each		1,500
311		Current cost revaluation reserve		749
1,805		Profit and loss account		1,870
3,616				4,119

284

Current cost revaluation reserve account

1983		£	1983			£
31 Mar	Balance c/d	311	31 Mar	Increase in valuation		
				of: Fixed assets		305
				Stock		6
		311				311
1 Apr	Reversal of increase		1 Apr	Balance b/d		311
	in stock valuation					
	at 31 March	6				
1984			1984			
31 Mar	Gearing: P & L		31 Mar	Increase in valuation		
	account	57		of stock		8
	Prior-year backlog			COSA, P & L		
	depreciation	76		account		80
	Current-year backlog			MWCA, P & L		
	depreciation re			account		107
	assets acquired			Increase in valuation		
	1 Apr 1982	19		of fixed assets		
	31 Dec 1983	–		acquired on		
	Balance c/d	748		1 Apr 1982		380
				31 Dec 1983		20
		906				906
			1984			
			1 Apr	Balance b/d		748

Workings

Ascertain relevant indices to be used.

For plant and machinery

Index at 1 April 1981: (104.5 + 105.5)/2	105
Index at 1 April 1983: (114.5 + 115.5)/2	115
Index at 31 March 1984: (124.7 + 125.3)/2	125
Average for year to 31 March 1984	120
Index at 31 December 1983: (121.8 + 122.2)/2	122
Average for January to March 1984: (122.2 + 123.3 + 124.7)/3	123.4

For COSA and MWCA

Index average for February and March		
1983:	(175.4 + 177.4)/2	176.4
1984:	(200 + 202.4)/2	201.2
1 April 1983:	(177.4 + 179.6)/2	178.5

31 March 1984:   (202.4 + 204.4)/2   203.4
Average for January, February and March:
1983:   (173.3 + 175.4 + 177.4)/3   175.4
1984:   (197.9 + 200 + 202.4)/3   200.1
Average for year to 31 March 1984   190.8

Fixed assets

Historical cost movement

	Cost £ thousands	Depreciation £ thousands	NBV £ thousands
At 1 April 1983 (acquired on			
1 April 1982)	4,000	(800)	3,200
31 December 1983 acquisition	800	—	800
31 March 1984 Depreciation			
charge for year			
Acquisition on 1/4/82:			
£4,000 × 10%	—	(400)	(400)
Acquisition on 31/12/83:			
£800 × 10% × 3/12		(20)	(20)
At 31 March 1984	4,800	(1,220)	3,580

In current cost terms: fixed assets acquired 1 April 1982

	Gross replacement cost £ thousands	£ thousands	Depreciation £ thousands	£ thousands	Net replacement cost £ thousands
At 1 April 1983	4,000 × 115/105	4,381	800 × 115/105	876	3,505
Increase in gross replacement cost		381			
Backlog depreciation					
Prior-year				76 (1)	
Current year				19 (2)	
Depreciation for year			400 × 120/105	457 (3)	
At 31 March 1984	4,000 × 125/105	4,762		1,428	3,334

Notes

1 Historical cost depreciation at 1 April 1983 expressed in current cost terms at 31 March 1984 less current cost at 1 April 1983:
£800,000 × 125/105 − £800,000 × 115/105 = £76,000

2 Current-year backlog depreciation: current-year depreciation in current cost terms at 31 March 1984 less in current cost terms of average for year:
£400,000 × 125/105 = £400,000 × 120/105 = £19,000

3 Can also be calculated by using the 'average depreciable value' (ADV):

Net replacement cost at 1 April 1983 in current cost terms at 1 April 1983, as above

	£ thousands
Net replacement cost at 1 April 1983 in current cost terms at 1 April 1983, as above	3,505
Net replacement cost at 31 March 1984 in current cost terms at 31 March 1984: £3,505,000 × 125/115	3,810
	7,315

Average depreciable value = £7,315,000/2 = £3,657,500
Depreciation for the year is ADV ÷ number of years to be depreciated:
£3,657,500/8 = £457,000   (to nearest thousand pounds)

287

Fixed assets acquired 31 December 1983

	Gross replacement cost		Depreciation		Net replacement cost
	£ thousands	£ thousands	£ thousands	£ thousands	£ thousands
At 31 December 1983	800			–	800
Increase in gross replacement cost		20			
Backlog depreciation					
Prior year				–	
Current year				0.26 (1)	
Depreciation for year			$20 \times 123.4/122$	20.23	
At 31 March 1984	$800 \times 125/122$	820		20	800

Note

1 Current-year depreciation in current cost terms at 31 March 1984 less in current cost terms of average:

$£20,000 \times 125/122 - £20,000 \times 123.4/122 = £262$ (to nearest pound)

Summary

	Acquired 1 April 1982	Acquired 31 December 1983	
	£ thousands	£ thousands	£ thousands
For depreciation adjustment			
Historical cost depreciation	400	20	420
Current cost depreciation	457	20	477
Depreciation adjustment	57	–	57
For balance sheet at 31 March 1984			
Gross replacement cost	4,762	820	5,582
Accumulated depreciation	1,428	20	1,448
Net replacement cost	3,334	200	3,534

To calculate the COSA and MWCA, use the formula:

$$C - O - I_a(C/I_a - O/I_0)$$

COSA = £720,000 − £520,000 − 190.95(£720,000/201.2 − £520,000/176.4)
     = £80,000   (to nearest thousand)

Stock for current cost balance sheet:

At 31 March 1983: £520,000 × 178.5/176.4 = £526.000   (to nearest thousand)
At 31 March 1984: £720,000 × 203.4/201.2 = £728.000   (to nearest thousand)

MWCA = £952,000 − £715,000 − 190.95(£952,000/200.1 − £715,000/175.37)
     = £107,000   (to nearest thousand)

Gearing adjustment

Shareholders' equity in current cost terms

	31 March 1984	31 March 1983
	£ thousands	£ thousands
Per historical cost balance sheet		
Share capital	1,500	1,500
Profit and loss	2,057	1,805
Dividends payable	200	150
Add: Increase (to current cost) in non-monetary items		
Fixed assets		
Acquired 1 April 1982:		
£3,505,000 − £3,200,000	–	305
£3,333,000 − £2,800,000	533	–
Acquired 31 December 1983:		
£800,000 − £780,000	20	–
Stock: 31 March 1983: £526,000 − £520,000	–	6
31 March 1984: £728,000 − £720,000	8	–
	4,318	3,766

Average current cost shareholders' funds: £4,318,000 + £3,766,000)/2 = £4,042,000

Net borrowings	31 March 1984 £ thousands	31 March 1983 £ thousands
10% debenture stock	750	750
Deferred taxation	250	150
Corporation tax	510	260
	1,510	1,160
Less: Cash	15	180
	1,495	980

Average net borrowings: (£1,495,000 + £980,000) = £1,237,500

The gearing adjustment is:

$$(DA + COSA + MWCA)[ANB/(ANB + \text{average current cost shareholders' funds})]$$

where DA is the depreciation adjustment and ANB is the average net borrowings.

Gearing adjustment = (£57,000 + £80,000 + £107,000)[£1,237,500/(£1,237,500 + £4,042,000)] = £57,000   (to nearest thousand)

8

Current cost balance sheet as at 31 December 1981

1980 £ thousands	£ thousands		£ thousands	£ thousands
		Fixed assets		
		Tangible assets		
	360	Land (1)	400	
	875	Buildings (2)	1,200	
	1,374	Vehicles and equipment (3)	1,577	
2,609				3,177
		Investments		
		Other investments, other than		
450		loans, at market value		500
3,059				3,677
		Current assets		
	429	Stocks (4)	661	
	475	Debtors	700	
	4	Bank and cash balances	295	
3,059	908	carried forward	1,656	3,677

1980 £ thousands	£ thousands		£ thousands	£ thousands
3,059	908	brought forward	1,656	3,677
	——	Less: Creditors: amounts falling due within one year	——	
	350	Bank overdraft	–	
	250	Creditors	350	
	100	Corporation tax	116	
	21	ACT payable	32	
	50	Dividend payable	75	
	771		573	
137	——	Net current assets	——	1,083
3,196		Total assets less current liabilities		4,760
		Less: Creditors: amounts falling due after more than one year		
–		15% debentures	1,000	
		Provision for liabilities and charges		
	150	Deferred taxation	216	
150	——		——	1,216
3,046				3,544
		Capital and reserves		
		Share capital: authorised, issued and fully paid		
1,000		Ordinary (£1 shares)		1,000
		10% cumulative preference		
250		(£1 shares)		250
1,250				1,250
300		Share premium		300
745		Revaluation reserve (5)		1,485
751		Profit and loss account (6)		509
3,046				3,544

Workings (all figures in £ thousands)

Asset valuation

(1) **Land**

	Current cost	
	1981	1980
Per professional valuation	400	360

291

			Index	Current cost 1981	1980

(2) **Buildings Historical**

Cost 31 December 1980	1,000	1,250/1,000			1,250
Accumulated depreciation	(300)	1,250/1,000			(375)
Net	700	1,250/1,000			875
Cost 31 December 1981	1,150	per valuation		1,600	
Accumulated depreciation	(273)	see below		(400)	
	877			1,200	

Depreciation of buildings

At 1 January 1981 (as at 31 December 1980, above)	375
Less: Accumulated depreciation to 31 December 1980 on buildings demolished	102
	273

Taking from current cost at 1 January 1981 and 31 December 1981

$$\text{Index} = \frac{\text{valuation at 31 December 1981 less additions during year}}{\text{valuation at 31 December 1980 less buildings demolished}}$$

$$= \frac{1,600 - 275}{1,250 - 120} = \frac{1,325}{1,130} \qquad \frac{1,325}{1,130} \times 273 = \qquad 320$$

Add: Depreciation for year on assets held at both end 1980 and end 1981

Historical cost at 31 December 1980	1,000
Less: Demolished during 1981	100
	900

$$\text{Index} = \frac{\text{valuation at 31 December 1981 less additions during year}}{\text{historical cost at date of acquisition}}$$

$$= \frac{1,600 - 275}{900} \text{ or } \frac{1,325}{900}$$

Historical cost depreciation is 900 × 5% × 1,325/900 =   66.25

Add: Depreciation for year on assets acquired during
the year ended 31December 1981
Current cost value at 31 December 1981: 275
   Depreciation at 5%   13.75

                                             400.00

(3) Vehicles and equipment at 31 December 1980

Acquired during		Historical cost		Current cost Index		
1978	Cost	400		150/100	600	
	Accumulated depreciation	(300)		150/100	(450)	
	NBV	——	100	——		150
1979	Cost	600		150/115	782	
	Accumulated depreciation	(300)		150/115	(391)	
	NBV	——	300	——		391
1980	Cost	1,000		150/135	1,111	
	Accumulated depreciation	(250)		150/135	(278)	
	NBV	——	750	——		833

Per balance sheet at 31 December 1980				
Cost	2,000		2,493	
Accumulated depreciation	(850)		(1,119)	
NBV	——	1,150	——	1,374

Reconciliation of historical cost from 31 December 1980 to 31 December 1981

As at 31 December 1980		
Cost	2,000	
Accumulated depreciation	(850)	
NBV	——	1,150
Additions in year: Cost		700
Disposals in year (all acquired in 1978)		
Cost	(400)	
Accumulated depreciation	300	
NBV	——	(100)
Depreciation charge for year (25% p.a.) re acquisitions		
in 1978	Nil	
in 1979	(100)	
	(50)	
in 1980	(250)	
in 1981	(175)	
Per P & L account	——	(575)
		1,175

Per balance sheet at 31 December 1981		
Cost	2,300	
Accumulated depreciation	(1,125)	
NBV	——	1,175

Vehicles and equipment at 31 December 1981

Acquired during		Historical cost		Current cost Index		
1979	Cost	400		200/115	696	
	Accumulated depreciation	(300)		200/115	(522)	
	NBV	——	100	——		174
	Considered obsolescent					
	Cost	200		see note	250	
	Accumulated depreciation	(150)		below	(187)	
	NBV	——	50	——		63
	carried forward		150			237

Acquired during		Historical cost		Current cost Index		
	brought forward		150			237
1980	Cost	1,000		200/135	1,481	
	Accumulated depreciation	(500)		200/135	(741)	
	NBV		500			740
1981	Cost	700		200/175	800	
	Accumulated depreciation	(175)		200/175	(200)	
	NBV		525			600
Per balance sheet at 31 December 1980						
	Cost	2,300			3,228	
	Accumulated depreciation	(1,125)			(1,650)	
	NBV		1,175			1,577

Note: asset acquired during 1979 considered obsolete by end 1981

This equipment purchased, at a cost of £200,000, was deemed to be obsolescent *by* 31 December 1981 and was to be replaced by modern equipment *during 1982*; the directors having contracted for this from the supplier. However, it should be noted that a normal full year's depreciation (£50,000) has been charged in the 1981 financial statements, and that it is shown in the balance sheet at (cost less accumulated depreciation) £50,000. Bearing in mind the prudence concept and the need to write off immediately any permanent diminution in value of an asset it can therefore be reasonably assumed that:

(a)   It is the directors' intention to scrap this equipment during 1982, when the new equipment is installed, and that any book (historical cost) profit or loss will be reflected in the 1982 financial statements.

(b)   At 31 December 1981 the net book value of the equipment is less than its realisable value otherwise a further provision would have been needed to take into account any permanent diminution of value.

(c)   The equipment is still in use.

Based on these assumptions it could be argued that one could calculate the net current replacement cost using the relevant indices (200/115), which, if based on the assumption above that it is not less than the recoverable amount (SSAP 16, paragraphs 42 and 43), would give:

Gross replacement cost	348
Accumulated depreciation	261
Net replacement cost	87

However, going on the information provided by the examiner it is apparent that he is expecting it to be valued on the basis of the modern equivalent asset.

The modern equivalent asset would be used, as in this case, when it is the intention to replace the asset and would be calculated as below:

Current cost of modern asset: £350,000.
Output of existing asset: 100%.
Output of modern asset: 140%.
Operating costs per unit and asset lives: no information so assumed to be identical.

Current cost of existing service potential (output):

$$£350,000 \times 100/140 = £250,000$$

This is the gross replacement cost.

Depreciation based on £250,000 from the date of acquisition (1979) at 25% p.a. on gross replacement cost

At 31 December 1980 no adjustment as appropriate indices used and there are no technological changes to adjust for.

At 31 December 1981

Depreciation (current cost) charge for year: 250 × 25%	62.5
Accumulated depreciation (current cost)	
Three years to 31 December 1981: 3 × 250 × 25%	187.5

(4) **Stocks**

	1981	1980
Historical cost × $\dfrac{\text{Index at 31 December}}{\text{Index at 30 November}}$	650 × 125/123 = 661	425 × 100/99 = 429

(5) Revaluation reserve in current cost balance sheet at 31 December 1980 comprises:

	£
Historical cost revaluation reserve	232,000
Increase in net replacement value of fixed assets (3,059 − 2,550)	509,000
Increase in value of stocks (429 − 425)	4,000
	745,000

For the purpose of answering the question there has been no transfer made between the P & L account and the current cost revaluation reserve for the current cost operating adjustment, (COSA, MWCA and gearing) for the period up to 31 December 1980 as there is not sufficient information.

Similarly the figures at 31 December 1981 for the revaluation reserve of P & L account will not reflect those adjustments prior to 31 December 1980.

(6) **Retained earnings**

At 31 December 1980, per historical cost balance sheet		751
Retained historical cost earnings for year		75
		826
Current cost operating adjustments		
Depreciation	(208)	
COSA/MWCA	(177)	
Gearing	68	
		(317)
Current cost retained earnings (P & L account) at 31 December 1981		509

15   Stock Exchange requirements and the City Code

INTRODUCTION

The City Code was first issued in 1968 as a code of conduct for take-overs and mergers. The Code was considered necessary because past governments in the UK have been reluctant to introduce legislation governing the conduct of mergers and take-overs.

Question 1 deals in depth with the reasons for instituting the City Code.

Question 2 looks at the secrecy required by rule 7 in respect of take-over bids.

Question 3 looks at the rules of the City Code applicable to partial bids. Mandatory bid rules follow the partial bid rules and question 4 deals with them.

Question 5 identifies some ways in which mergers could occur and the reasons for them.

Finally, question 6 deals with the fiscal considerations of mergers.

QUESTIONS

1 Past governments in the UK have been reluctant to introduce legislation to deal with the conduct of mergers and take-overs. Rules have therefore been drawn up by representatives of the major financial bodies operating within the City of London, to form the City Code on Mergers and Take-overs. The first rules were issued by the working party in 1968 and these rules are revised from time to time.

You are required to offer detailed reasons for instituting the City Code.

15 marks

2 Rule 7 of the City Code emphasises the importance of secrecy in respect of take-over bids.

You are required:

(a) To detail the procedure laid down by the City Code where company A intends to put forward a take-over bid for company B. *10 marks*

(b) To detail the important disclosure requirements laid down by the Licensed Dealers (Conduct of Business) Rules 1960 and the City Code in connection with a take-over bid. *10 marks*

Total 20 marks

3 Concerning partial bids, the rules of the City Code are exclusively relied on.

You are required to state the provisions contained in the Code which have been made in order to prevent gaining control of a company 'on the cheap'.

20 marks

4

(a) Mandatory bid rules follow the rules relating to partial bids. Mandatory bid rules may be applied where some of company B's shares have been acquired by company A or there has been an increased holding of B's shares by purchase and not necessarily by bid. You are required to exemplify three cases where there is a duty to make a mandatory bid for all the equity share capital of company B. *10 marks*

(b) Section 209 of the Companies Act 1948 may be invoked, by a person who has made a bid, to acquire compulsorily the shares of a small minority who have not accepted the bid.

You are required to state the conditions under which section 209 may be invoked. *10 marks*

Total 20 marks

5 A merger may be defined as the blending of two or more companies, the shareholders of each blending company becoming substantially the shareholders of the blended undertakings.

298

(a)   You are required to identify three ways in which a merger could occur.

6 marks

(b)   List the benefits that may arise from a merger.   *8 marks*

(c)   List the disadvantages that may arise as a result of amalgamating.   *6 marks*

Total 20 marks

6   You are required to discuss the ways in which relief from stamp duty may be obtained in a merger.

25 marks

ANSWERS

1   The City Code on Take-overs and Mergers was instituted because there is no legal control with regard to:

(a)   The offer document which is not a prospectus within the meaning of section 38 of the Companies Act 1948, because it concerns the purchase of shares already in issue. In contrast, shares are unissued until the bid is accepted in a prospectus situation.

(b)   Achieving control of a company by partial bids. It is not necessary to own 50% of the voting shares of a company in order to control it.

(c)   It has been difficult and sometimes still is difficult to prevent insider dealing particularly where directors' interests are concerned. Information on how the company is performing will generally be first available to people close to the company. They would therefore be in a position to deal in the company's shares before anyone else in the market has had a chance to revalue them in the light of the fresh information. The Companies Act 1980, part 5, has, however, made this kind of dealing a criminal offence.

(d)   Misleading profit forecasts could influence potential investors, who otherwise would not invest in those securities.

(e)   Directors' tactics: for example, it would now be an offence for the directors of the company to be acquired to issue additional shares to a company or persons who would not accept the bid.

2   The general rule is that secrecy must be maintained during negotiations.

(a)   (i)   The offer by A should first be put to the board of B or its advisers.

     (ii)   The shareholders of B must then be informed by B's board but the Code states that this obligation lies equally with the offeror too.

     (iii)   If A's bid is not firm, then B's directors must publish a 'talks announcement' as soon as possible.

     (iv)   Joint statements are desirable whenever possible and persons with knowledge of the discussions are forbidden from dealing in B's shares until a bid or the breaking off of a bid is announced.

(b)   The offer document must contain:

     (i)   The latest quotes of the shares of A and B plus fluctuations over the last six months.

     (ii)   A statement that the offer is open for at least 21 days together with the number of shareholders of B who must accept before the offer becomes unconditional.

     (iii)   A statement concerning the shares already held by A in B (including nominees); shares held in B by directors of A and persons acting in concert with them, e.g., pension fund trustees.

     (iv)   A statement concerning any compensation to B's directors for loss of office; details of B's directors' service contracts where they have more than 12 months to run.

(v)	Details of the consideration A is offering and a date when B's shareholders will receive that consideration.
(vi)	Any changes in the financial position of A and B since the last accounts.
(vii)	Any of the matter specified in the fourth schedule to the Companies Act 1948 which the Stock Exchange wishes to be included. Also there is a provision that the offer document must be drafted with the same skill and care as a prospectus.
(viii)	The bid terms must be received by the board of B three days before its dispatch to the shareholders of B. Further, the recommendations of B's directors must also be accompanied by a disclosure of their shareholdings in A and B and whether they intend to accept the offer.

3

(a) The Panel's consent is required for any partial offer.

(b) In the case of an offer which would result in the offeror (A in this question) holding shares carrying over 50% but less than 100% of the voting rights of the offeree company (in this question B), consent will not normally be granted if an offer for the whole of the equity share capital of B has already been announced or if A, or persons acting in concert with it, have acquired selectively, or in significant numbers, shares in B during 12 months preceding the application for consent. This requirement is to prevent 'warehousing' the shares of B before the take-over bid is made. This practice is particularly pernicious where A or others have acquired shares in B through nominees. Where this is so the share register of B will contain shareholders who are 'tame' in the sense that they will accept A's offer in any case which may make the partial bid more easily successful, and yet the other shareholders in the class are not aware of the strength of A's bargaining position.

If permission is granted the offer must be conditional upon approval of the offer by shareholders in respect of over 50% of the voting rights not held by A or persons acting in concert with it.

(c) In the case of an offer which would result in the offeror holding shares carrying from 30% to 50% (both inclusive) of the voting rights of the company, it used to be provided that the consent of the Panel would only be granted in exceptional circumstances and in any event not unless the board of B recommends the offer. In the latest edition of the Code these restrictions have been removed.

Now such an offer is allowed if it receives the approval of shareholders in respect of 50% of the voting rights not held by A or persons acting in concert with A. And even this requirement may be waived if over 50% of the total voting rights are held by one shareholder. (The reason for this is that the controlling position of such a shareholder would not be prejudiced by such an offer, however unwelcome, since only a minority holding could be gained by it.)

(d) In the case of an offer which would result in the offeror holding shares carrying less than 30% of the voting rights of a company, consent will normally be granted.

(e)   Partial offers must be made to all shareholders of the class.

(f)   Where a company has more than one class of equity share capital a comparable offer must be made for each class, but A is under no obligation to bid for the non-equity shares, i.e., preference shares, of B as well.

Thus a partial bid, even if approved, ends up by being a bid for all of the equity share capital of the company.

(g)   Where there is a partial offer A and persons acting in concert with it may not purchase shares in B during the offer period, nor if the partial offer is successful may they purchase such shares during a period of 12 months after the end of the offer period unless the Panel consents.

(h)   If more than one class of equity capital is involved, separate offers must be made for each class. A should state if it intends to resort to compulsory acquisition under Companies Act 1948, s. 209, and that the section will be used only in respect of each class separately.

4

(a)   Under the rules of the Code the following situations could result in a mandatory bid.

   (i)   On 1 January A has no shares in B. In five transactions thereafter A or persons acting in concert with it acquire shares carrying 30% or more of the voting rights of B.

   (ii)   On 1 January A has no shares in B. In one transaction thereafter A or persons acting in concert with it acquire shares carrying 30% or more of the voting rights of B.

   (iii)   On 1 January A, or A and persons acting in concert with it, hold not less than 30% but not more than 50% of the voting rights of B. During the 12 months following A and/or persons acting in concert with it acquire additional shares increasing the percentage of their voting rights by more than 2%.

In cases (i), (ii) and (iii) the duty to make a mandatory bid for all the equity share capital of B arises.

The offer to be made must, in respect of each class of share capital involved, be in cash or be accompanied by a cash alternative at not less than the highest price paid by A and persons acting in concert for shares of that class within the preceding 12 months.

Immediately upon an acquisition of shares which gives rise to an obligation to make an offer, A must make an announcement of the offer. The announcement should include confirmation by a financial adviser or other appropriate independent party, e.g., a merchant bank, that resources are available to the offeror sufficient to satisfy full acceptance of the offer.

Except with the consent of the Panel, no nominee of A or persons acting in concert shall be appointed to the board of B, nor shall A and persons acting in concert transfer or exercise the votes attaching to any shares held in B until the offer document has been posted.

(b) The Companies Act 1948, s. 209, can be used by a person, who has made a bid, to acquire compulsorily the shares of a small minority who have not accepted his offer. The provisions of the section are as follows:

(i) Where A starts with not more than 10% of B or no holdings in B at all, but 90% of B's shareholders accept A's offer within four months then A may, within two months after the end of the four-month period, serve a notice on dissentients that he intends to acquire their shares. The dissentients have one month from the date on which the notice was given to appeal to the court. If there is no appeal or the court does not order otherwise, A acquires the shares.

(ii) Where A starts with more than 10% of B, s. 209 applies only if three-quarters in number and 90% in value of B's other shareholders accept within four months of the offer.

The court will seldom interfere if the offer is fair but will not allow the section to be used for improper purposes such as the expulsion of a minority (*Re Bugle Press Ltd,* 1960).

Under The Companies Act 1948, s. 209, where A has acquired 90% of B but does not intend to buy out the dissentients then A must notify the dissentients of its acquisition of 90% of B's shares. The dissentients then have three months to request A to buy them out and on receipt of such a request A must do so.

5

(a) (i) Holding company method: either a new limited company is formed (non-trading) or one of the existing companies is designated the holding company.
(ii) Complete amalgamation or absorption: amalgamation of companies to form a new company comprising the combined assets of both.
(iii) Pooling arrangements: pooling of activities only, for example, two or three companies set up a common research establishment. Note that this type of arrangement could, if warranted, be prevented under the Fair Trading Act 1973.

(b) Possible benefits of a merger:

(i) The closing down of redundant capacity in a depressed trade climate.
(ii) More intensive use being made of existing manufacturing assets; economy in capital expenditure.
(iii) Economy in the use of current assets, for example, reductions in stock levels may be possible.
(iv) Ease of access to capital markets; resilience to set-backs.

(v)   Saving in overhead expenditure.
(vi) Research and development expenditure may be rationalised.
(vii) Diversification of industry may be effected.

(c)   Possible disadvantages arising as a result of mergers:
   (i)   Personal touch may be eliminated.
   (ii) Loss of trade name.
   (iii) Inconvenience and expense; stamp duties, professional fees, etc.
   (iv) Monopoly power may have disastrous consequences for free competition.
   (v)   Personality problems may occur.

6 Two common methods of amalgamation are covered in section 55 of the Finance Act 1927: the issue of shares of one company as consideration for:

(a)   Acquisition of the assets of another company.
(b)   Acquisition of not less than 90% of the shares of another company.

Where there is a legal transfer of ownership of assets but the conveyance is technical in nature and the property in substance remains that of the selling company, that is, the assets remain *in situ*, then relief from stamp duty is available. Further, where the transferee company is incorporated or increases its capital with the object of acquiring the whole or part of an undertaking, or not less than 90% of the issued share capital of the 'existing company' then:

(a)   *Ad valorem* duty under the heading 'conveyance on sale' is not to be charged on any instrument made for the purpose of, or in connection with, the transfer of the undertaking or shares or on any instrument made for the purposes of, or in connection with the assignment to the transferee company of any debts of the existing company.

(b)   Where a company issues unissued shares which have been authorised, a claim for exemption from conveyance on sale duty does not apply.

(c)   Furthermore, for a claim for exemption from conveyance on sale duty to be allowed:

   (i)   The instrument must be adjudicated.
   (ii) Where the transferee company is a limited company under the Companies Acts, the instrument must be:

      (1)   Executed within 12 months from the registration of the transferee company or the date of the resolution for the increase of its capital; or
      (2)   Made in pursuance of an agreement which has been filed, or particulars of which have been filed, with the Registrar of Companies within such period of 12 months.

   (iii) Any debts taken over as part of the consideration must, except in the case of debts due to banks or trade creditors, have been incurred at least two years before the proper time for making a claim for exemption.

In addition, capital duty is not payable (Finance Act 1973, sch. 19, para. 10).

It should therefore be noted that mergers and take-overs involve incidental expenses such as stamp duty and professional fees.

Stamp duty is charged on the transfer of assets or shares from one ownership to another. The duty on conveyance or transfer on sale is at the rate of £2 per cent of any property, that is, *ad valorem* stamp duty.

Stamp duty is also charged on the authorised share capital of a newly formed company which is limited. Stamp duty in connection with shares of a newly formed company is known as capital duty. Capital duty is at the rate of 50p per £100.

Professional fees take the form of valuation fees for properties or other assets, accountancy and legal fees for professional advice.

For stamp duty purposes, broadly speaking, a reconstruction is defined as the taking over of an old company by a new company and an amalgamation/merger is the blending of two existing companies.

16   Users and objectives of accounts

INTRODUCTION

The Corporate Report was issued by the Accounting Standards Committee in 1975 and was followed by the United Kingdom Government Green Paper in 1977 entitled "The Future of Company Reports". Although all the recommendations in these two documents have not as yet been incorporated into statutory or accounting standard requirements they have resulted in a number of changes being made in information provided in the annual reports of companies. They have also led to much discussion about who are the users of corporate reports and what are their information needs. As a consequence these documents and subsequent developments play an important part in the evolution of corporate reporting. The examinations of all the professional bodies contain questions involving knowledge of The Corporate Report and the objectives of accounts in general. It is therefore not sufficient for a student simply to have a sound technical knowledge of accounting. A student must be aware of current issues and debates within the professsion which have affected or will affect the way in which financial reporting is carried out. The five questions which appear in this chapter have all been taken from recent examination papers of professional accounting bodies.

QUESTIONS

1 'The fundamental objective of corporate reports is to communicate economic measurements of and information about the resources and performance of the reporting entity useful to those having reasonable rights to such information' *(The Corporate Report)*.

Analyse the above quotation and discuss each part in relation to financial reporting.

20 marks

2 What purpose is the balance sheet of a limited company really intended to serve? What main factors or influences determine the form and content of company balance sheets generally? To what extent are company balance sheets effective in serving what you regard as their functions?

16 marks

3

(a) Who were considered to be the potential users of financial reports in *The Corporate Report?* *8 marks*

(b) What do you consider to be their information needs? *8 marks*

(c) How would you expect a consideration of user needs to influence financial reporting? *9 marks*

Total 25 marks

4 Certain accounting theorists have made suggestions for the amplification of published financial statements, in a manner calculated to increase their interest and usefulness to, among other persons, a company's employees. Such changes are also recommended by the Accounting Standards Committee in *The Corporate Report* (1975) and again by the UK Government in their Green Paper, *The Future of Company Reports* (1977).

You are required:

(a) To outline (but not to illustrate) the functions and formats of TWO additional statements, not at present required in the UK or the Republic of Ireland by law or by any Accounting Standard, which would be helpful to a company's employees as distinct from its shareholders. *10 marks*

(b) To appraise the usefulness of the said statements for their ostensible purposes. *6 marks*

Total 16 marks

5 There has been a considerable debate over recent years about whether greater disclosure is required in published company reports, as a result of which such reports tend to give far more information than was the case a few years ago. Discuss some of the arguments for and against greater disclosure in company reports quoting examples of additional information which is being given, either because it is legally required, recommended by the professional bodies or the Stock Exchange or simply because it is becoming accepted practice.

12 marks

ANSWERS

1 The best way in which to discuss a quotation such as this is to break it down into the key phrases which are as follows:

(a) 'Communicate'. The quotation states that corporate reports must communicate, which means that the information must not only be sent to a user of the report but must be understood by that user. Communication without understanding on behalf of the recipient is meaningless. In many cases there is considerable doubt about whether the recipients of corporate reports understand the information, which raises the question of whether the information should be sent in another form, perhaps considerably simplified.

(b) 'Economic measurements of and information about the resources and performance of the reporting entity'. The information which is traditionally received is a profit and loss account, balance sheet and sources and applications of funds statement, all of which are audited. Other non-audited information is the directors' report, chairman's statement and other statistical data. Often all information is in terms of historical costs but developments are taking place in the area of adjusting accounts for the effects of inflation. However, there is much debate about whether other useful information should be given, e.g., forecasts, social and environmental aspects. This also raises the question of whether such information should or can be audited.

(c) 'Useful to those having reasonable rights'. The emphasis here is on the fact that the information must be useful and must be given to persons who have a right to expect it. This will mean that decisions will have to be reached about who are the users of corporate reports and what are their requirements. Much research has been and is being conducted in this area at the present time. Only when users are clearly identified can their needs be established. There is no doubt that users encompass more than just the owners of the enterprise, i.e., the shareholders. Creditors and tax authorities are certainly other parties who have an interest, and the list could be more extensive than this. As the list extends there is the problem of measuring the costs of providing the information against the benefits to be expected.

2 Company balance sheets are part of the annual report of a company and are intended to provide information for decision-making by a variety of users, including present and prospective shareholders, and creditors, employees, government agencies, tax authorities etc. Traditionally they were regarded as being mainly for shareholder use, the emphasis being on the stewardship function but it is now recognised that the purpose of accounts is not for stewardship purposes only but as an aid to decision-making. It is also recognised that it is not simply a case of satisfying shareholders' interests but there is a responsibility to a much wider audience (*The Corporate Report* and subsequent discussions have emphasised this point).

The form and content of company balance sheets are governed or influenced by statutory requirements (i.e., the Companies Acts), Statements of Standard Accounting Practice and Stock Exchange requirements (for listed companies only). Where there are no Statements of Standard Accounting Practice governing any matters, accounting principles which are generally accepted would influence the form and content of the accounts. Leading companies also influence developments in the area of content and presentation of accounts generally.

Although there has been an increase in the amount of information provided to try to meet the needs of different users and there has been some improvement in the usefulness of the information provided, as a result of the efforts of the professional bodies, problems still remain. Because user needs are different it is rather difficult to provide all the information which each requires in one statement. The balance sheet still tends to be of more use regarding the stewardship function rather than providing information which would be useful for decision-making. One main area of difficulty has arisen by adherence to the historic cost basis, often resulting in a misleading view of a company's position because some asset values are based on out-of-date costs. Even attempts at various forms of accounting for inflation have not always been met with unanimous enthusiasm, as a result of which some companies do adjust historical accounts in respect of inflation and others do not. Even amongst those who do there are wide divergences in practice. One further point which should be mentioned is that one of the greatest aids to decision-making is information about the future, an area where most companies would be most reluctant to commit themselves.

3

(a)   *The Corporate Report* considered the following groups to be the potential users of financial reports:

> equity investor group
> loan creditor group
> employee group
> analyst adviser group
> business contact group
> government
> public

Examples of persons from these groups may be given.

(b)   The needs of users of financial reports will vary depending upon which group they belong to. The general needs may be summarised as follows:

(i)   Equity investor: information necessary for decisions about buying and selling shares, e.g., evaluation of performance, comparison with other entities.
(ii)   Loan creditors: long term, stability of the entity; short term, liquidity.
(iii)   Employees: the security and prospects of employment.
(iv)   Analyst adviser: similar to that of the equity investor group, but may require more sophisticated information.
(v)   Business contact: customers, the continuance of supply of goods; competitors, ability to make comparisons.
(vi)   Government: information to assess the effects of government policy.
(vii)   Public: the need to assess the impact of entity on the community.

It is advisable to discuss in more detail the general points summarised above in respect of some (but not all) of the user groups, e.g.:

(i)   Equity investors will need to be able to estimate the future prospects of the entity, including its capacity to pay dividends, and to predict future levels of investment. They should also be able to estimate the value of their present and prospective interest in the entity. An assessment of liquidity is important, including the present and future working capital requirements and ability to raise finance.

(c)   The following are the main matters to be discussed.

The main objective of financial statements may be considered to be the provision of information which meets user needs. Accounting is thus providing a service. The needs of users should be ascertained and the processes by which they take decisions. Accounting should provide the information for these decision models. Accountants may seek to educate users where the decision models are defective. The needs of users thus influence financial reporting.

It may be argued that the needs of the different user groups coincide and that a general-purpose financial statment will meet all needs. Alternatively, these needs may not coincide, in which case separate reports will be needed for each group.

Financial statements may not be read or understood by most potential users. Perhaps financial statements should therefore be simplified. However, the needs of most users could be met indirectly by meeting the needs of the analyst adviser group and this group may require more sophisticated reports.

4

(a)   Two additional statements, not required by law or by any accounting standard, which would be helpful to a company's employees as distinct from shareholders are:

(i)   A value added statement
(ii)   An employment report

The value added statement is a simple and effective way of putting profit into proper perspective *vis-à-vis* the whole enterprise as a collective effort by capital, management and employees. The statement shows value added as the wealth the reporting entity has been able to create by its own and its employees' efforts. It also shows how the value added has been used to pay those who contributed to its creation. It may in time be preferred to the profit and loss account as a means of expressing the results of an enterprise. The statement provides a useful measure to help gauge performance and activity and the value added figure can be a pointer to the net output of the firm and can be used as a performance measure when related to other key figures (e.g., capital employed). The statement should show turnover less bought-in materials and services which represent value added and the application of the latter, i.e., to employees, dividends and interest payments, payments to the government for taxation and the amount retained for reinvestment.

The employment report is a report primarily concerned with information about time worked by employees and the numbers employed. It will contain amongst other things information about average numbers employed for the financial year and actual numbers on the first and last day, reasons for changes in numbers in broad terms, age distribution and sex of employees, functions of employees, changes in operations during the year (i.e., plant and acquisitions and disposals), employment costs and fringe benefits, pension and training arrangements, safety and health information, etc. The report is more of a statistical than an accounting document and has no set format.

(b)   The value added statement is generally considered to be employee oriented and to be easily understood by employees. There is evidence that the meaning and significance of profits are widely misunderstood. The statement shows employees as participators in the business, and not just costs in earning profit for the shareholders. It clearly shows how the value added has been apportioned between those who contributed towards it.

The employment report will make available information of use not only in judging efficiency and productivity but also significant information concerning the workforce of the reporting entity, its personnel policies and industrial relations record. It can help to form a judgment on the extent to which the company is a responsible and conscientious employer, aware of its social and economic obligations as a provider of livelihood to a large number of people. Comparisons with other comparable companies will be useful to union officials to assess the employer's standing in the industry.

5   Some of the arguments which have been put in favour of greater disclosure are:

(a)   It helps to maximise economic welfare, since the more information people have the more likely they are to make the best decisions regarding the allocation of resources within the economy.

(b)   It is generally recognised that there are many different users of corporate reports, other than shareholders, who are traditionally assumed to be the main users. These other users may want more or different information than has been provided in the past.

(c)   It is an aid to motivation of management who will wish to be seen that they have performed well in the additional information provided.

(d)   The more information that can be provided about the current value of an organisation's resources, the less likely it is to be involved in a take-over situation which may not be favourable for the company's investors. Once the latter know the true value of the assets they are more likely to make correct decisions about their use.

Some arguments against greater disclosure are:

(a)   More disclosure provides more information to competitors which could perhaps be of some disadvantage to the company.

(b)   Often so much information can be given in corporate reports that there is a danger of confusion. Perhaps simplified reports would have more impact.

(c)　The provision of more information entails greater costs, which must be measured against the benefits obtained.

(d)　There is a considerable amount of subjectivity involved in certain areas which are being suggested for additional disclosure, e.g., forecasts and budgets. It could be argued that it is not advisable to give information on matters which may be extremely difficult to predict.

There are several examples of additional information which is now being given including:

(a)　Legally required. The Companies Acts have added to the amount of information to be disclosed, e.g., cost of sales, selling and distribution, etc. (Companies Act 1981).

(b)　Professional bodies. New SSAPs appear fairly often, usually adding to disclosure requirements, e.g., SSAP 18 requires much more information about contingent liabilities and also deals with the question of contingent assets.

(c)　The Stock Exchange. Requirements here apply to listed companies and information which has to be given includes, amongst other things, information concerning interim results.

(d)　Other matters. Although there is no requirement as yet to produce the information a number of companies are including a value added statement as part of their corporate report.

17 Accounting Standards Committee and other regulatory influences

INTRODUCTION

With the implementation of EEC directives into statute law in the UK the Accounting Standards Committee (ASC) has found it necessary to set up a number of working parties to look into the compatibility of currently issued SSAPs and company law.

SSAPs may be interpreted as dogmatic or firm recommendations which are expected to be complied with where necessary in accounting practice.

It is the intention of the ASC to limit the number of SSAPs to those areas which are considered to be of fundamental importance.

Guidance is to be given to those areas not considered to be of fundamental importance, by the issue of SORPs (statement of recommended practice) and franked SORPs (which apply to specific industries).

Four questions have been set in this chapter to cover the role and development of the ASC. The implications of International Accounting Standards and EEC directives are also considered within the framework of the questions.

QUESTIONS

1 The need to conform to two sets of accounting standards, international and UK-Irish, may create problems for accountants.

You are required:

(a) To set out the objectives of the International Accounting Standards Committee in preparing International Accounting Standards, and the obligations of the members in support of those objectives.   *6 marks*

(b) To explain the difficulties that arise from the existence of the two sets of standards.   *3 marks*

(c) To explain what has been done to reconcile the demands of the two sets of standards.   *6 marks*
                                                                   Total 15 marks

2 The report, *Setting Accounting Standards* (Accounting Standards Committee, 1981) affirmed that accounting standards are necessary and will continue to be necessary in order to complement the statutory regulations.

State, with reasons, whether or not you agree with this statement.
                                                                        20 marks

3 The Accounting Standards Committee published the report of one of its working parties, *Review of the Standard Setting Process*. When introducing the report and, in particular, the SORP (Statement of Recommended Practice) Ian Hay Davison, the Chairman of the ASC, was quoted as saying: 'We have taken off our jackboots. We are not at all sure it's sensible to be so draconian. The compliance climate has changed.'

You are required:

(a) To outline the proposed standard-setting procedure set out in the report.
                                                                        5 marks

(b) To define:

      (i)   Statement of Intent.
      (ii) Statement of Recommended Practice.   *7 marks*

(c) To explain what you think Ian Hay Davison meant by the above quotation.
                                                                        3 marks
                                                                   Total 15 marks

4 Commentators frequently express or imply the view that a major objective in setting accounting standards is to combat practices calculated to make the profit and loss account present an unduly favourable picture of the year's profit or loss, without omitting any items from the accounts or materially misstating any relevant amounts.

316

You are required (in relation to individual companies, not groups):

(a) To identify two practices of the kind referred to above. *4 marks*

(b) To summarise the action taken by the Accounting Standards Committee to restrain each of the practices that you have chosen in (a). *12 marks*
Total 16 marks

ANSWERS

1

(a) The objectives of the International Accounting Standards Committee (IASC) are contained within the 'Preface to International Accounting Standards' (revised 1971) and are:

> to formulate and publish in the public interest, standards to be observed in the presentation of audited financial statements and to promote their worldwide acceptance and observance.

The obligations of the members (including the UK and Republic of Ireland), in agreeing to support the above objectives, are:

(i) To support the standards
(ii) To use their best endeavours:

    (1) To ensure that published financial statements comply with these standards, or disclose the extent of non-compliance, and to persuade governments, securities market authorities, and the industrial and business community that the statements should comply with the standards.

    (2) To ensure that auditors satisfy themselves that financial statements comply with the standards or disclose the fact of non-compliance, and that in the event of non-disclosure reference to non-compliance is made in the audit report.

    (3) To ensure that, as soon as practicable, appropriate action is taken in respect of auditors whose reports do not comply with (2).

(iii) To seek to secure general acceptance and observance of the standards internationally.

(b) Difficulties that arise from the existence of the two sets of Standards are:

(i) Legal problems. The Accounting Standards Committee (ASC) takes into consideration the laws and regulations of the UK and Republic of Ireland together with any impending EEC directives relating to the harmonisation of company law within the EEC. The IASC has to accommodate the laws of all its members.

(ii) Conflict(s) between standard-setting bodies. With the member countries' standard-setting bodies being independent from the IASC and also having different membership it is quite possible that they could reach different decisions relating to the same topic area: this is particularly possible when a member country has issued its own standard prior to the IASC.

(c) The reconciliation of the demands of the two sets of accounting standards has been effected as follows:

(i) With the IASC's objective 'to harmonise as far as possible the diverse accounting standards and accounting policies at present in use in different countries'.

(ii)   When formulating standards the IASC concentrates on the essentials and tries to avoid making the standards so complex that they cannot be applied effectively by all the member countries. Revision of an IAS could/should lead to a greater degree of harmonisation.

(iii) Standards issued by the IASC do not override local regulations governing the issue of financial statements in a member country. If an IAS conforms with local regulations, then the financial statements which comply with these will automatically comply with that IAS. When an IAS differs from, or conflicts with, local regulations, then it is the duty of member countries to ensure that either the financial statements, or the auditor's report thereon, indicate in which respect the IAS has not been observed.

(iv)   The councils of the six accountancy bodies that form the Consultative Committee of Accounting Bodies (CCAB) support the activities of the IASC in promoting and observing the IASC's objectives – see (a). They seek to incorporate the provisions of the IAS within the body of UK-Irish SSAPs in so far as the provisions are not included within the law. IASs (not already covered by legal requirements or SSAPs) come into effect when their provisions have been incorporated into SSAPs issued by the councils of the six UK and Irish bodies; they do not override UK or Irish law and SSAPs will automatically ensure compliance with IASs unless the SSAP states otherwise. In that case a suitable addendum is made to the IAS as issued in the UK and Ireland, and non-observance must be noted in the financial statements or the auditor's reports – see (iii).

2   The *Statement of Intent on Accounting Standards in the 1970s* (ICAEW 1970) gave the following reasons for the establishment of the Accounting Standards Committee (ASC) and Statements of Standard Accounting Practice (SSAPs):

(a)   To encourage uniformity of practice by narrowing the areas of difference and variety in accounting practice.

(b)   To ensure disclosure of accounting bases adopted.

(c)   To ensure disclosure of departures from established definitive accounting bases.

(d)   To give wider exposure for major proposals on accounting standards by involving interested bodies in the discussion of exposure drafts before they become a SSAP.

(e)   To promote a continuing programme for encouraging improved accounting standards in both legal and regulatory measures.

At the time legal requirements on financial reporting placed hardly any emphasis on accounting methods; however, new Companies Acts have been issued in 1976, 1980 and 1981 and in the latter there has been a definition of basic accounting principles and accounting valuation rules to be used in the preparation of statutory accounts. Further, there are requirements within the 1981 Act which require disclosure of information previously required by SSAPs.

The basic accounting principles, which closely follow those laid out in SSAP 2, are:

(a)   The company is presumed to be carrying on business as a going concern.

(b)   Accounting policies must be applied consistently from one financial year to the next.

(c)   Items must be determined on a prudent basis and in particular:

      (i)   Only profits which are realised at the balance sheet date may be included in the profit and loss account.

      (ii)   All liabilities and losses which have arisen or are likely to arise in respect of the financial year or a previous financial year must be taken into account, even if they only become apparent between the balance sheet date and the date on which the directors sign the balance sheet (post balance sheet events).

(d)   All income and charges relating to the financial year must be taken into account, regardless of the date of receipt or payment (accruals basis).

(e)   When determining the aggregate amount of any item, each individual asset or liability falling under that item must be separately defined.

The accounting rules laid down are 'historical cost accounting' and 'alternative accounting rules' the latter opening the statutory door for current cost accounts to be submitted to the Companies Register as the published accounts of the company.

To the extent that these basic principles and rules have been incorporated into statute it would seem that the development of standards could have two main purposes:

(a)   To become the vehicle from which future changes/improvements to statute law are made; dealing with matters of major and fundamental importance affecting the generality of companies.

(b)   To provide a framework of best accounting practice for those topic areas which, although important to various groups, cannot be applied to the generality of companies.

In the *Review of the Standard-Setting Process* (ASC June 1983) there is a stated intention to follow the above purposes. Standards for which compliance is mandatory will be few in number and will cover those major and fundamental areas. The newly proposed Statement of Recommended Practice (SORP) would seem to be following the second of the above purposes. The SORP will not be mandatory and it is suggested that it will be the area which will complement statute law for those areas where the Companies Act(s) refer to best/current accounting practice.

The question of whether or not accounting standardisation can exist without a conceptual framework has led to the ASC being criticised frequently for its failure to develop an agreed conceptual framework on which a logical series of pronouncements (SSAPs and SORPs) could be based. This would inevitably mean a requirement to define the meaning of 'profit', the purpose of the balance sheet and the implications

320

of capital maintenance. There has to date been little agreement amongst academics as to the form of such a framework.

In conclusion, and following the latest published intentions of the ASC on standard setting, it can be said that SSAPs are, and will continue to be, necessary but not as a complement to statute, more as a basis for future law-making. The ASC would seem to intend complementing statute by issuing SORPs.

3

(a)   Outline of standard-setting procedure:

    (i)   Identification of topic area.
    (ii)   Research study commissioned and carried out.
    (iii)   Working party formed.
    (iv)   Initial (working party's) feedback to ASC.
    (v)   Technical drafting and consultation.
    (vi)   Consideration of draft by ASC.
    (vii) Publication of exposure.
    (viii) The exposure period.
    (ix)   Summary of comments and decision on future progress.
    (x)   Redrafting and further consultative meetings by working party.
    (xi)   Consideration of draft standard by ASC.
    (xii) Draft standard sent to CCAB councils.
    (xiii) Consideration and approval of draft standard by six (CCAB) councils.
    (xiv) Standard issued by six (CCAB) councils.

(b)   (i)   A Statement of Intent is a public statement issued by the ASC setting out a brief summary of how the ASC intends to deal with a particular accounting matter. It will not be as detailed as an exposure draft, and it will be issued with the intention of focusing attention on the main issues relating to a particular topic and on the accounting policies which are proposed.

       (ii)   A Statement of Recommended Practice (SORP) is a statement issued by the ASC covering a topic area which is of sufficient importance to require an authoritative pronouncement but does not meet all of the criteria to justify the preparation and issue of an accounting standard. It is intended that a SORP will be a 'stand-alone' document, i.e., it will not relate to a standard. SORPs will not be mandatory but will be of such quality and status as to be widely respected, and compliance will be encouraged.

            As standards (SSAPs) will only relate to matters of major and fundamental importance affecting the generality of companies, it follows that SORPs will generally deal with:

           (1)   Matters which, whilst being of widespread application, are not of fundamental importance; or
           (2)   Matters which are of limited application (e.g., relating to a specific industry).

(c)   Although a good deal of latitude in complying with SSAPs is allowed because of the subjectivity involved, it can be seen that a move away from 'dictatorial' standards is more realistic.

In order for standards to be complied with they must gain wide acceptance from interested user groups. SSAP 16 is a good example of a standard not having wide acceptance nor willing compliance but having a very active lobby proposing radical change. Therefore it seems more reasonable to have:

(i)   Mandatory standards covering those areas of major/fundamental importance, non-compliance requiring disclosure/qualification; and

(ii)   Non-mandatory SORPs.

4

(a)   The question refers to two 'practices calculated to make the profit and loss account present an unduly favourable picture of the year's profit or loss'. Three such practices are:

(i)   The amortisation over a number of years of expenditure which may be more properly written off in the year when it was incurred (spent); e.g., large promotional expenditure which 'earns'/generates sales over a number of accounting periods.

(ii)   The inconsistent treatment of items within the profit and loss account purely because of their (material) size(s). This would apply to large credits of an extra-ordinary nature being treated as ordinary items; large credits of an exceptional nature not being disclosed: conversely the treatment of exceptional payments as extraordinary.

(iii)   Reserve accounting as such has been prohibited within UK financial reporting. However, company law permits the following to be charged directly against specified reserves:
— Preliminary expenses.
— Expenses (including discount) on any issue of shares or debentures.
— Premium on redemption or purchase of the company's own shares or debentures.

(b)   The Accounting Standards Committee (ASC) has issued, as Statements of Standard Accounting Practice (SSAP), a number of pronouncements aimed at combating the practices identified in (a) above. At the date of going to print they had also issued two Discussion Papers of relevance: 'Review of SSAP 6, Extraordinary items and prior-year adjustments' and 'Review of SSAP 12, Accounting for depreciation'.

(i)   **Questionable use of income smoothing devices**

The Companies Act 1981, schedule 1 requires full disclosure of all transfers to and from reserves, and thus outlaws the cruder forms of income smoothing by abuse of reserve accounting — see (ii) and (iii) below. The danger today lies in proper and consistent application of the 'fundamental accounting concept' of the accruals basis of accounting (the revenue-cost matching principle). Thus, where expenditure ought properly to be written off in the year when it is incurred, it might instead be written off over two or more years. If an asset (especially of an intangible nature) ought properly to be amortised over a short period of years, it might instead be amortised over a longer period. The object of such practices may be to minimise fluctuations in reported profits, or to avoid showing a loss in a given year, thus (it is hoped) improving the stock market rating of the company's equity shares. On the other hand, similar results might be obtained by upward revaluation of assets as at the year-end (where it is reasonable to suppose that appreciation in money values occurs over time), and the writing-off of the appreciation to the credit of profit and loss account, in lieu of taking credit for the full appreciation when the asset is disposed of.

Neither the law nor accounting standards give clear guidance in the general case of income smoothing. The Companies Act 1981 has an overriding requirement that the accounts must give a true and fair view, and this must preclude the wilful overstatement of assets in the balance sheet which is the inevitable result of policies such as those described above. SSAP 12, 'Accounting for depreciation', lays down rules for proper depreciation of physical fixed assets (other than freehold land), and for write-down of such assets if it is clear that their economic value has fallen through accelerated obsolescence or other external cause. Consistent depreciation formulae must be used, and excessively long asset lives must not be assumed. SSAP 13, 'Accounting for research and development', requires all research expenditure to be written off in the year when it is incurred, with normal depreciation of fixed assets used for research purposes. It also requires all development expenditure to be similarly expensed, unless a case can be made for capitalising it, subject to stringent criteria designed to guarantee eventual recovery of the expenditure out of revenue or cost savings from the project. Amortisation of development expenditure, so capitalised, must commence with commercial production of a product or use of a process, and must be related either to sales or to the period over which sale will take place or the efficiency of production be improved. Even so there is considerable scope for discretionary amortisation, possibly over a recovery period which has been generously estimated, to say the least. The Companies Act 1981 requires that when development expenditure has been capitalised then the financial statements have to include a note of the period of the amortisation and the directors' reasons for choosing that length of time. Further, the Act provides that development costs which are shown as an asset in the financial statements are to be regarded as a realised loss for the purposes of establishing the profits available for distribution, unless there are special circumstances which justify the directors in treating the costs otherwise. In such a case a note must be appended to the company's financial statements stating that development costs are not to be treated as a realised loss and explaining the circumstances which justify this treatement. The Act does not describe the 'special circumstances' which might justify the treatment of development costs as other than a realised loss; however, the Act does refer to the application of generally accepted accounting principles, and, in this instance, the proper application of SSAP 13 (as described above) would provide those circumstances.

There is little in the SSAPs directly to restrain other forms of income smoothing, such as the carrying forward of the cost of an advertising campaign, asserted to increase sales of the following, rather than the current year — even though no identifiable asset is created. An accountant or auditor seeking to resist such practices can appeal only to general principles of accounting and to the legal requirement for a true and fair view. Indeed, SSAP 9, 'Stocks and work in progress', actually requires the inclusion in work in progress (on a conservative basis) of profit earned to date on a long-term contract, and hence its crediting to profit and loss account as the contract proceeds. Again, SSAP 4, 'The accounting treatment of government grants' (1974), requires government grants, received in aid of capital expenditure, to be amortised to revenue *pari passu* with the depreciation of assets bought with the grants; the 'flow-through' method, of taking credit for the whole grant in the year of receipt, is barred. Otherwise accounting standards offer little specific guidance on income smoothing.

(ii)   **Manipulation of extraordinary items**

SSAP 6, 'Extraordinary items and prior-year adjustments', argues against the carrying to reserves of extraordinary items, and for their inclusion, as separate items, in the profit and loss account. Extraordinary items are defined as 'those items which derive from events or transactions outside the ordinary activities of the business and which are both material and expected not to recur frequently or regularly'. They do not include 'items which though exceptional on account of size and incidence. . ., derive from the ordinary activities of the business', or prior-year items merely as such. Examples of extraordinary items are profits or losses arising from the following: discontinuance of a significant part of the business, the sale of a long-term investment, the writing-off of intangibles (including goodwill) because of unusual events or developments, and the expropriation of assets. Items which, though abnormal in size and incidence, do not rank as extraordinary, since they derive from the ordinary activities of the business, include abnormal charges for bad debts, write-offs of inventories, development expenditure, or losses on long-term contracts, and most adjustments of prior-year tax provisions. SSAP 6, part 3 (the Standard proper), states that the profit and loss account should show a profit or loss after extraordinary items, reflecting all profits and losses recognised in the accounts of the year other than prior-year adjustment and unrealised surpluses on revaluation of fixed assets, which should be credited direct to reserves. Items of an abnormal size and incidence, which are derived from the ordinary activities of the business, should be included in arriving at the profit for the year before taxation and extraordinary items, and their nature and size disclosed. The discussion paper 'A review of SSAP 6' re-emphasises and clarifies those items which require specific disclosure due to the nature of their circumstances. In particular, it highlights the recent trend of companies separately disclosing the costs incurred from the discontinuance of operations. There has also been some discussion about the appropriate treatment for the results of such businesses relating to periods prior to the decision to terminate.

In the USA, APB Opinion No. 30, 'Reporting the results of operations', requires companies to show the results for the year of discontinued operations, together with any gain or loss on the disposal of these operations, as a separate element of the income statement after post-tax income from continuing operations but before extraordinary items. This treatment isolates the results of continuing operations, thus emphasising the company's future expectations rather than its performance for the year.

Although there are no similar requirements in the UK, SSAP 14, 'Group accounts', includes the following requirement in paragraph 30: 'In the case of material additions to or disposals from the group, the consolidated financial statements should contain sufficient information about the results of the subsidiaries acquired or sold to enable shareholders to appreciate the effect on the consolidated results.' This refers only to the situation where the termination of an activity is effected by the disposal of a subsidiary but it should ensure that, in those limited circumstances, there will be sufficient information available for the users of the financial statements to be able to assess the company's future expected performance, based on its continuing operations.

The analysis of results between those relating to continuing businesses and those arising from discontinued operations would provide useful information to the reader of financial statements.

Extraordinary items (less attributable taxation) should be shown separately in the profit and loss account for the year, after the results derived from ordinary activities, and their nature and size disclosed. (The Companies Act 1981, schedule 1, now requires more detail — separate statements of extraordinary income, extraordinary charges, extraordinary profit or loss, tax on extraordinary profit or loss — as well as the net figure after tax.)

(iii) **Questionable use, or avoidance, of reserve accounting**

The Companies Acts permit certain charges to be debited direct to reserves; e.g., the 1948 Act, s. 56, permits the preliminary expenses of a company, or the expenses of, or commission or discount on any issue of shares or debentures, to be written off against share premium account. A premium payable on redemption or purchase of the company's shares or debentures may be debited direct to share premium account. The articles of association of many property and investment holding companies also require them to credit all profits on sale of properties or investment to capital reserve. SSAP 6, 'Extraordinary items and prior-year adjustments', recommends that all such items should pass through the profit and loss account for the year, and be transferred thence to the appropriate reserve accounts.

SSAP 6 also deals with another aspect of reserve accounting — the treatment of prior-year adjustments. These are defined as 'those material adjustments applicable to prior years arising from changes in accounting policies and from the correction of fundamental errors'. They exclude the normal recurring corrections and adjustments of accounting estimates made in prior years (e.g., the annual adjustment of the previous year's corporation tax charge in the light of the assessment subsequently agreed with the Inland Revenue); such adjustments should be passed through the profit and loss account.

In accordance with the 'fundamental accounting concept' (SSAP 2), or 'accounting principle' (Companies Act 1981), of consistency in accounting policies from year to year, a change in accounting policies should not be made unless it can be justified as giving a fairer presentation of the results and financial position of the business, e.g., in accordance with a new Statement of Standard Accounting Practice which introduces a new accounting basis or expresses a preference for one not at present used by the company. There must be a choice between two or more accounting bases; the adaptation of an existing policy to new circumstances or events is not a change in accounting policy. Where there is such a change, the cumulative adjustments applicable to prior years have no bearing on the current year's results and should therefore not pass through the profit and loss account, but be accounted for by restating prior years, with adjustment of the opening balance of retained profits and, where practicable, of the previous year's results in the corresponding figures.

Similar treatment should be applied to corrections of fundamental errors in previous years' accounts, of such significance as to destroy the true and fair view and hence the validity of those accounts, and such as would have led to their withdrawal had the errors been recognised at the time. Such corrections should not be included in the current year's profit and loss account, but should be incorporated as adjustments to the opening balance of retained profits.

SSAP 6, part 3 requires prior-year adjustments (as defined above) to be accounted for by restating prior years, with the result that the opening balance of retained profits will be adjusted accordingly. The effect of the change should be disclosed where practicable by showing separately in the restatement of the previous year the amounts involved. Items that represent the normal recurring corrections and adjustments of accounting estimates made in prior years should be included in the profit and loss account for the year and, if material, their nature and size should be disclosed. A statement of retained profits/reserves, showing any prior-year adjustments, should immediately follow the profit and loss account for the year.

18 Transfer pricing

INTRODUCTION

Problems on transfer pricing occasionally rear their heads in financial accounting and other areas of professional examinations. The growth in mergers and the progressive use of decentralisation as a means of controlling large organisations draws attention to the importance of pricing goods which are transferred from one division to another.

While the transfer price is only an internal bookkeeping exercise and would not affect the overall profitability of a company directly, divisional managers will be rightly concerned with the transfer pricing policy where divisions are judged on their separate profit performances.

There are many bases for transfer pricing. For example, one might use cost including an attributable share of the overheads. Others are: market price (if available), marginal cost, average variable cost, full cost (actual or standard with or without a charge for reasonable profit), or a negotiated price method may be used.

The questions in this chapter, whilst not exhaustive give an idea of how some bases of transfer pricing are used.

QUESTIONS

1 The managing director of your company, Mr Carr, is in an anxious state when he calls you to his office. The company operates decentralised divisions for the various stages of manufacture of a variety of industrial machinery.

As you are the chief accountant, he mentions the continuous problems he has been experiencing in respect of the decentralised operations. Specifically, he raises the following questions:

(a) Why are intra-company transfer prices necessary?   *2 marks*

(b) What are the two most common ways in which intra-company transfers may be priced?   *2 marks*

(c) What is the most important drawback of transfer pricing based on cost?
                                                                         3 marks

(d) Dual objectives are involved and transfer pricing policies must endeavour to satisfy these objectives. What are these objectives?   *3 marks*
                                                           Total 10 marks

2 The managing director of Harris Ltd, Mr Harris, has asked your advice on the following matters concerning transfer pricing in the divisions of his company.

(a) Where reliable market prices cannot be established for the purposes of transfer pricing, what impact has this condition on divisional performance measurement?

(b) Can you give a common symptom of the conflict between the dual objectives of divisional performance and overall company performance where transfer pricing is employed?

(c) If an optimum economic decision is required in a given situation, what is a general rule for transfer pricing?

(d) What is meant by 'outlay cost' in the context of transfer pricing?

(e) Market price is often used as a basis for transfer pricing. Why is its use considered a special case rather than a panacea?

(f) What three problems regarding systems design are also applicable to transfer pricing?

(g) The nature of transfer pricing forces its use to be confined to profit centres. Do you agree?

(h) When does imperfect competition exist?
                                                                        15 marks

3 A. Wood Ltd is a company which operates four factories. Each factory makes components which are incorporated into the products sold by one or more of the other factories. To encourage a competitive environment, the directors have decided that each factory should become a separate profit centre. This will necessitate the use of transfer prices for the inter-factory components.

You are required:

(a) To describe three different methods of establishing the transfer prices.

9 marks

(b) To state which method you would recommend for A. Wood Ltd, giving reasons for your choice.

6 marks

(c) To prepare, for the method chosen, a policy statement outlining how the pricing system would be operated among the different factories.   *5 marks*

Total 20 marks

4 A manufacturing company, Hassel Ltd, has a separate division that produces standard machine casings. For the past four years, about 70% of the output has been sold to another division within the company while the remainder has been sold outside the group. The summarised operating results for the last reference period were as follows:

	Inter-divisional	External
Turnover 10,000 × £35*	£350,000	5,000 × £50 = £250,000
	£	£
Variable costs @ £25/unit	250,000	125,000
Fixed costs	75,000	37,500
Total costs	325,000	162,500
Gross margin	25,000	87,500

*The price of £35 is arrived at by deducting marketing and administration expenses applicable to outside business from the outside selling price.

The buying division has a chance to get a firm contract with an outside supplier at £32.50 per case for the following year. The selling division says that it cannot sell at £32.50 since no profit could be earned at this price. The selling division would be left with 10,000 cases if the buying division bought externally.

You are required to discuss the problem.

20 marks

ANSWERS

1

(a) Where intra-company transfers of goods and services occur, some method of transfer pricing is necessary in order that the profitability of individual divisions may be assessed.

(b) The two most common ways for pricing intra-company transfers are based on some version of market price or some version of cost.

(c) Cost-based transfer pricing tends to ensure that the division utilising this method and transferring services or goods will recuperate its cost. It will seem that there is no incentive to control costs in the transferor division.

(d) One objective of transfer pricing is to measure the profitability of divisions separately. The other dual objective of transfer pricing is that its operation and measurement should also meet the overall objectives of the firm.

2

(a) If market prices cannot be established for products at their transfer stage, this may cause the whole process of measuring divisional performance to be rendered futile.

(b) A common symptom is the desire of one division within a company to buy from outside the company because the selling division's price is not competitive. This will result in under-recovery of fixed overhead costs to the detriment of the overall company profitability.

(c) In order to make optimum economic decisions, a transfer price should be based on the *additional* outlay cost incurred to the point of transfer and the opportunity costs for the firm as a whole, where opportunity costs are defined as the maximum contribution forgone by the firm as a whole if the goods are transferred internally.

(d) Outlay costs represent the expenses to be incurred in the production and transfer of goods or services.

(e) In many circumstances, intermediate market prices simply do not exist. Furthermore, if they do exist, the markets are imperfect and pricing will not be accurate.

(f) The three problems may be identified as:

  (i) Goal congruence; that is, problems of conflicting goals of the division with those of the organisational whole.
  (ii) Performance evaluation; that is, it is difficult to arrive objectively at a 'fair' price for transfer purposes.
  (iii) Imperfect competition; this also influences a 'fair' transfer price.

(g)   The problem is the apportionment of overhead costs to divisions which are not the direct cause of the cost.

(h)   Imperfect competition occurs when one seller or buyer acting alone can exert an influence on the market price.

3

(a)   An answer could have dealt with any three of the following alternative methods of transfer pricing:
   (i)   Market price. The price would be that at which an outside competitor would be prepared to supply. Provided the supplier factory is able to produce the components at a variable cost which is lower than the competitive price, it is in the company's interest that it should be given the order.
   (ii)   Negotiated price. Where competitive prices are not available, prices could be negotiated between the factories concerned. These would be regarded as commercially based and would be in lieu of market prices. Not being linked with some firm base they could be unrealistic.
   (iii) Manufactured cost. This would be the cost at which completed work is transferred to finished stock, being exclusive of marketing and general administration costs. Such a basis would be beneficial to the buyer factory as the price would usually be less than market price.
   (iv)   Full cost. It is almost certain that the supplying factory will incur some marketing and administration expense in connection with inter-factory transfers, but whether or not it is on the same scale as for external sales may be arguable. Compared with buying on the open market, such a basis would favour the buyer factory though to a lesser extent than method (iii).
   (v)   Cost-plus. The price would include not only 'full cost' but an added profit margin. This is a fair basis for the supplying factory but, unless exceptions are made, it could result in the buying factory paying more than a fair market price.

   Where cost is an element in arriving at a price, such cost may be actual or standard. Standards are preferable as unpredictable month-by-month fluctuations are avoided and there is also a fairer sharing of the inefficiency factor. No factory operates to perfection and the buyer should be prepared to pay a reasonable amount towards the difficulties and lapses from perfection inherent in manufacture, but the buying factory should not be charged with additional cost arising from exceptional carelessness or lack of control. Standard costs provide an excellent basis as they are usually based on good attainable performance and include only reasonable allowances for lapses from perfection.

(b)   It is suggested that the market price method should be chosen as it offers the following advantages:

   (i)   It offers a fair reward to the supplying factory as well as an incentive to produce efficiently.
   (ii)   It leaves the buying factory in the same position as it would have been had the associated factory not existed.

(iii) It cannot lead to controversy about the efficiency or inefficiency of the manufacturing unit.

(iv) Executive time is not devoted to the bargaining process.

(c) Recommended procedure for operating transfer pricing.

(i) Inter-factory sales will be effected at market price.

(ii) No factory will be obliged to accept an order from an associated factory at market price if the former is not equipped to manufacture at a cost which, at least, allows a reasonable contribution towards its fixed costs, or if the acceptance of such an order would result in more profitable work being displaced.

(iii) Where a factory is prepared to supply components at market price, the buyer factory will be obliged to buy from it unless it can be established that there are reasons to doubt that quality or delivery will be satisfactory.

(iv) Cases where difficulties arise concerning inter-factory pricing will be referred to the chief accountant who will give a ruling based on the overriding company interest.

4   If the selling division does not sell at £32.50 per case to the buying division, the consequences will be:

	£	£
Sales, 5,000 cases @ £50 =		250,000
Variable costs	125,000	
Fixed costs	37,500	
Plus: Unrecovered	75,000	
Total costs		237,500
Gross margin		12,500

If the selling division meets the external price of £32.50, the results would be as follows:

Inter-divisional

	£	£
Sales: 10,000 cases at £32.50		325,000
Variable costs	250,000	
Fixed costs	75,000	
Total costs		325,000
Gross margin		Nil

External

	£	£
Sales: 5,000 cases at £50		250,000
Variable costs	125,000	
Fixed costs	37,500	
Total costs		162,500
Gross margin		87,500

Thus selling division gains £75,000 by quoting £32.50 per case to buying division.

Change in net income from the company point of view if the buying division buys the cases from outside at £32.50 per case:

	£
Outside purchase costs: 10,000 × £32.50	325,000
Loss of contribution by selling division = £325,000 − £250,000	(75,000)
Net cost if cases bought externally	250,000
Existing inter-divisional variable costs	250,000

Thus overall company income would not be affected at £32.50 per case. However, if the price were to fall below £32.50, this would result in an overall loss to the company.

Index

References in roman type are to questions and those in *italics* are to answers.

Accounting policies 122–3, *127–8*,
  158–60, *186–7*
  fundamental concepts 122, *125–6*
    departures from 122, *126*
Accounting standards
  degree of compliance 316, *322*
  national and international
    difficulties of compliance with two
      sets 316, *318*
    reconciling demands of 316,
      318–19
    necessity 316, *319–21*
    purpose 122, *126–7*
    standard-setting procedure 316, *321*
Acquisitions
  accounting policies 122–3, *128*
  calculation of number of shares to be
    issued 190–1, *198*
  financial effects on shareholders
    109–10, *115–16*
  secrecy provisions of City Code 298,
    300–1
  see also City Code on Mergers and
    Take-overs
Act *see* Corporation tax, advance
Adjusted selling price, as method of stock
  valuation 58, *65*
Advance corporation tax *see* Corporation
  tax, advance
Amalgamations 192–3, *201–3*
  advantages and disadvantages 298–9,
    303–4
  cash payments for shares 194–5, *206*
  ledger accounts, closing entries 194–5,
    207–8
  methods 298–9, *303*
  see also City Code on Mergers and
    Take-overs
Assets
  deprival value *273–4*
  fixed
    depreciation 83, *88–90*
    revaluation 83, *87–8*
    schedule in published accounts
      83–4, *90–1*
    value in directors' report 83, *88*
  information required for valuation
    256, *271*
  net relevant cash flow pattern 85,
    95–6
  revaluation accounts 261–3, *285*
  valuation, effect of rapid technological
    change on 256, *271*
  value to business 256, 257, *270–1*,
    273–4
  see also Depreciation

Balance sheets
  compliance with Companies Acts
    1948–1981 150–2, 156–60,
      161–71, 178–81, 182–7
  current cost 258–63, *278–90*
    adjusted from historical cost 264–8,
      290–6
  following acquisition 195–7, *213*
  following amalgamation 194–5,
    206–7
  following capital reconstruction
    216–17, 224–6, 228, *244–5*
  following capital reduction 222–4,
    240–3
  following share issue for acquisition
    190–1, *198–200*
  government grants 121, *124*
  on transfer of business to limited
    company 191–2, *201*
  purpose and functions 308, *309–10*
  redemption of shares 133, *138–9*
  redraft for capital reduction scheme
    221–2, *237–8*
  showing corporation tax 3–7, *10–12*,
    14, 16, 19–20
  see also Post balance sheet events
Base stock method of valuation 58, *66*

Capital
  entity and proprietary concepts of
    capital 248, *251*
  maintenance, comparison of accounting
    methods 248, *251–2*
  monetary working capital adjustment
    257–8, *278*
  relationship with income 248, *250–1*
Capital reconstruction 222–4, *238–9*
  balance sheet 216–17, *228*
  formation of new company 217–19,
    230–2
  with creditors' voluntary liquidation
    217–19, *229–32*
Capital reduction schemes 219–20,
    221–4, *232–5, 235–7, 238–9*
  calculation of minimum profit
    required 224–6, *243–4*
  effect on forecast future earnings
    222–4, *240–3*
  formalities required 224–6, *243*
  purpose 216, *227*
City Code on Mergers and Take-overs
  mandatory bid rules 298, *302–3*
  on partial offers 298, *301–2*
  reasons for instituting 298, *300*
  secrecy provisions 298, *300–1*
Contingencies, accounting methods
    121–2, *125*

Contracts
    and work in progress valuation   60–1,
       71–2
    long-term, in balance sheet   63, 76
    loss-making   63–4, 79
Corporate reports
    additional statements suggested   308,
       311–12
    degree of disclosure   308, 312–13
    information needs fulfilled   308,
       310–11
    objectives   308, 309
    potential users   308, 310
Corporation tax   3, 4–5, 5–7, 8–9,
       12–13, 14, 18
    advance 3, 4–5, 5–7, 8–9, 12, 14,
       17
       unrelieved, debit balances   32
    in ledger accounts   7, 20–2
    mainstream   3, 8–9
    underprovision   43, 48–9
    see also Deferred taxation
Cost of sales adjustments   257–8, 275–6
    auditing   257–8, 276–7
Costs
    allocation of joint costs   62, 75–76
Current cost accounting   258–63, 278–90
    balance sheet, adjusted from historical
       cost balance sheet   264–8, 290–6
    consistency   257, 275
    objectivity   257, 274–5
    related to market prices   257, 273
    underlying concept   256, 272
    voluntary disclosures to shareholders
       256, 272–3
Current cost operating adjustments   256,
    269
Current cost reserve   256, 270
Current purchasing power basis   248,
    251–2

Debenture interest payable   5–7, 19
Deferral method of accounting for timing
    differences   25, 26–7, 30–1, 34
Deferred taxation   4–5, 12, 15, 25–6,
    31–2
    accounting policy   122–3, 128
    charges to profit and loss account
       27–8, 35–7
    disclosure in accounts   28–9, 38–40
    postponement of provision   25, 30
Depreciation   43, 49
    accounting policy   122–3, 127
    adjustments   83–4, 91
    deferred taxation, charges to profit and
       loss account   27–8, 35–7
    definition   83, 86
    factors in assessing and allocation to
       accounting periods   83, 86
    fixed assets   83–4, 90–2
    freehold land and buildings   83, 84–5,
       86–7, 92–4

Depreciation – continued
    historical cost, in period of inflation
       83, 89–90
    net relevant cash flow pattern   85,
       95–6
    of fixed assets   83, 88–90
    providing asset replacement fund   83,
       89
    under historical and current cost
       accounting methods   257, 273
    wasting assets   83, 86–7
    see also Assets
Directors' reports   158–60, 187–8
Distribution costs, included in cost of sales
    61–2, 74
Dividends received, taxation entries   5–7,
    17

Earnings per share
    adjustment of previous years for
       comparison purposes   108–9,
       113–15
    basic   108–9, 111, 113, 117–18
    compared with previous years   111,
       117–18
    definition   107, 112
    effect of acquisitions   109–10, 116–17
    fully diluted   197–9, 111, 113,
       117–18
    disclosure in published accounts
       111, 117
    'net' and 'nil' basis   107, 112
Exceptional items   43, 44–5, 48, 51
Extraordinary items   43, 44–7, 48, 52,
    53–4
    manipulation in statements   324–5

First in, first out (FIFO) method of stock
    valuation   58–9, 66–7
Freehold land and buildings, depreciation
    83, 84–5, 86–7, 92–4

Gearing adjustment   256, 270
Goodwill
    accounting policy   122–3, 128
    on acquisition   43, 48
    written off   43, 49
Government grants
    accounting methods   121, 124
    accounting policies   122–3, 128

Hire purchase arrangements, in stock
    valuation   60–1, 72
Historical cost accounting   248, 251–2

Income
    accounting and economic,
       comparison   248, 250, 252–3
    computation of investment   248–9,
       254
    measurement
       comparison of methods   248,
       251–2

Income – *continued*
 importance to corporate entity
  248, *250*
 related to capital measurement
  248, *250–1*
 questionable use of smoothing devices
  316–17, *322–4*
 transactions basis 248, *250*
Income tax, Schedule F 3, 4, *9, 15, 18*
International Accounting Standards,
 objectives 316, *318*

Last in, first out (LIFO) method of stock
 valuation 58–9, *66–7*
Last in, last out method of stock valuation
 58, *66*
Liability method of accounting for timing
 differences 25, 26–7, *30–1, 33–4*
Liquidation
 accounts 195–7, *208–10*
 journal entries 192–3, *201–2*
 prior to reconstruction 217–19,
  229–32
 sundry shareholders accounts 195–7,
  208–10
Losses
 borne by shareholders 216, *227*
 foreseeable 63–4, *78–9*
 see also Capital reduction schemes

MCT *see* Corporation tax: mainstream
Manufacturing accounts 154–5, *171–3*
Mergers *see* Amalgamations

Net borrowings 256, *270*
Net realisable value method 248, *251–2*
 definition 58, *65*
Notes to accounts 152–3, 154–5, 156–8,
 158–60, *162–4, 168–71, 174–6,*
 179–80, 183–6

Obsolescence, definition 83, *86*
Operating statements, showing taxation
 4–7, *15, 19–20, 22*
 corporation tax 3–4, *10–12, 13*
 deferred taxation 25–6, *33*
Overhead costs
 apportionment 59, *68–70*
 in calculating selling price 59, *68–70*
 inclusion in cost 58, *65*
 recovery base 63–4, *77*

Post balance sheet events 121, *124–5*
Prices, related to production costs 59,
 68–70
Prior year adjustments 43, 44–7, *48,*
 50, 51–2, 53–4
Profit
 adjusted figures 60, *71*
 attributable 63–4, *78*
 distributable, provisions of Companies
  Act 1980 137, *147–8*

Profit – *continued*
 effect of pricing policy adopted 59,
  68–70
Profit and loss account 44, 45, *49, 51–2,*
 154–5, *171–7*
 before and after incorporation 193–4,
  204–6
 compliance with Companies Act
  1948–1981 150–3, 156–60,
  161–71, 178–81, 182–7
 current cost 258–63, *278–90*
 effect of accounting standard treatment
  316–17, *322–6*
 government grants 121, *124*
Property
 investment in, valuation and depreciation
  provision 85, *95*
 see also Freehold land and buildings

Raw material stock valuation 58–9,
 60–1, *66, 72*
Realisation account 217–19, *229*
Reconstruction accounts 216–17, *227–8*
Replacement cost method 248, *251–2*
 as basis of valuation 58, *65*
Research and development 98, *100*
 accounting policy 122–3, *127*
 acquisition of special knowledge 98,
  101
 carrying forward to future periods
  98–9, *101–2*
 expenditure on specified projects 98,
  101
 in balance sheet and profit and loss
  account 98–9, *102–3*
 pure and applied research 98–9,
  101–2
 related to patent 98, *101*
Reserve accounting, questionable use of
 325–6
Reserves, statement of 44, *49–50*
Revaluation of assets 44–5, *51,* 261–3,
 285
Royalties receivable, taxation entries 5–7,
 19

Shares
 allotment on amalgamation 192–3,
  202–3
  cash payments 194–5, *206*
 issue to fund redemption of preference
  shares 133, *139*
 purchase by company 136, *144–5*
 purchase or redemption by private
  limited companies 136, *145*
 redemption 133, *138–9*
  at par and at premium, comparison
   137, *146–7*
  premium payable 134–5, *140–4*
  using distributable profits 133–4,
   139

337

Shares − *continued*
 sundry members accounts 217−19,
  229
 see also Capital reduction schemes
Stamp duty, methods of obtaining relief
  299, *304−5*
Statements of Intent 316, *321*
Statements of Recommended Practice
  (SORP) 316, *321*
Stock valuation 58−9, 63−4, *66*, 76−7
 accounting policy 122−3, *128*
 adjustments 60, *71*
 alternative methods 58, *65−6*
  comparison 58−9, *66−7*
 auditor's review of system 61−2,
  73−4
 in balance sheet 63, *76*
 statement of accounting policy 58, *66*

Take-overs *see* Acquisitions
Taxation
 timing differences 25, *30*
 see also Corporation tax; Deferred
  taxation; Income tax
Timing differences 25, *30*
 'deferral' and 'liability' methods 25,
  30−1

principal bases for tax computations
  28−9, *37−8*
Trading accounts 154−5, *171−3*
 before and after incorporation 193−4,
  204−6
Transfer of business to limited company
 balance sheet 191−2, *201*
 journal entries 191−2, *200*
Transfer pricing
 characteristics and problems of 328,
  330−1
 comparison of internal and external
  purchasing 329, *332−3*
 function 328, *330*
 methods 328, 329, *330, 331−2*
 objectives 328, *330*
Turnover, accounting policy 122−3, *127*

Wasting assets, depreciation 83, *86−7*
Work in progress 63−4, *76−7*
 accounting policy 122−3, *128*
 alternative methods of valuation 58,
  65−6
 calculating attributable profit 60−1,
  71−2
 in balance sheet 63, *76*
 treatment of anticipated losses 60−1,
  72−3